Between Two Absolutes

Between Two Absolutes

Public Opinion
and the Politics of Abortion

Elizabeth Adell Cook,
Ted G. Jelen,
and Clyde Wilcox

Westview Press
BOULDER • SAN FRANCISCO • OXFORD

All rights reserved. No part of this publication may be reproduced or transmitted in any form or by any means, electronic or mechanical, including photocopy, recording, or any information storage and retrieval system, without permission in writing from the publisher.

Copyright © 1992 by Westview Press, Inc.

Published in 1992 in the United States of America by Westview Press, Inc., 5500 Central Avenue, Boulder, Colorado 80301-2877, and in the United Kingdom by Westview Press, 36 Lonsdale Road, Summertown, Oxford OX2 7EW

Cook, Elizabeth Adell.
    Between two absolutes : public opinion and the politics of abortion / by Elizabeth Adell Cook, Ted G. Jelen, Clyde Wilcox.
        p. cm.
    Includes bibliographical references and index.
    ISBN 0-8133-8286-6 (cloth) — ISBN 0-8133-8287-4 (pbk.)
    1. Abortion—United States—Public opinion.   2. Abortion—Political aspects—United States.   3. Pro-life movement—United States.   4. Pro-choice movement—United States.   5. Abortion—Religious aspects.   6. Public opinion—United States.   I. Jelen, Ted G.   II. Wilcox, William Clyde.   III. Title.
    HQ767.5.U5C66   1992
    363.4'6'0973—dc20   92-25268
                                                                                        CIP

Printed and bound in the United States of America

The paper used in this publication meets the requirements
of the American National Standard for Permanence of Paper
for Printed Library Materials Z39.48-1984.

10   9   8   7   6   5   4   3   2   1

For Christopher, Elaine, and Robert

Contents

Tables and Figures

Tables

Figures

Preface

This book is an examination of the shape and direction of public attitudes toward abortion. Our motivation in writing this book is based on our belief that, in the last analysis, the abortion controversy will be settled in the court of public opinion. As we write this, the United States Supreme Court has recently upheld certain restrictions on access to legal abortion in the case of *Webster v. Missouri Reproductive Services* and is considering permitting states to regulate abortion further in the pending case of *Casey v. Planned Parenthood*. The direction that the Court is taking on this issue is quite clear. State governments will be allowed increasing discretion in regulating abortion and may (in the event of an outright reversal of *Roe v. Wade*) be allowed to prohibit the practice entirely. Thus, control of access to abortion is being removed from the federal courts and put into the hands of elected officials such as members of Congress, governors, and state legislators. If one assumes that elected officials are, in some sense, responsive to public opinion, it matters a great deal what ordinary citizens think and believe about the practice of abortion.

We will consider the distinctions made by members of the mass public toward legal abortion and will look closely at the types of people likely to favor or oppose abortion. In addition, considerable attention will be paid to other factors that influence people's abortion attitudes, the role of religion in shaping the abortion debate, and the likely consequences of abortion attitudes for electoral politics in the United States. Although we regard public attitudes toward abortion as interesting in their own right, we will also be concerned with the consequences of abortion politics for American politics generally.

This book is *not* a treatise on the moral or ethical issues raised by the abortion issue. We have no special insight into questions such as "Is the fetus a person?" "Does legal abortion encourage immoral sexual behavior?" or "Is the abortion right necessary for full female equality?" We will, however, investigate the empirical connections between these beliefs and abortion attitudes. We will consider (for example) the question of whether people who hold traditional conceptions of gender roles are less supportive of legal abortion than people with more "feminist" orientations but will not consider directly the merits of any of the claims made by protagonists in the abortion debate. Similarly, this book is *not* a work of legal scholarship. We will not evaluate claims about the constitutional basis for an abortion right or the more general right to privacy. Interested readers are referred to our bibliography, which lists a number of excellent works on these and related topics.

Finally, this book is not a work of advocacy. Although we each have our own opinions on the abortion issue, we hope that they do not intrude on this book. We have attempted to present both sides to every point and to interpret the data dispassionately. We will use the terms "pro-life" and "pro-choice" at various points in this volume, although we do not intend these terms to indicate an endorsement of a particular position. Both sides of the abortion debate seem to suspect that the other has the more powerful symbol (life or choice). Moreover, at demonstrations in Washington, D.C., activists on both sides routinely chant that the other side is misnamed. The pro-life forces chant, "Pro-choice, your name's a lie: babies don't choose to die!" while the pro-choice groups shout, "Right to life, your name's a lie, you don't care if women die." Our use of these terms merely indicates our adoption of the name each group has chosen for itself.

The issue of legalized abortion has general implications for the conduct of American politics. Our focus here is limited to public attitudes on abortion, but we hope that our discussion will illuminate these larger issues as well.

Chapter 1 presents a brief overview of the abortion debate in the American context. In Chapter 2, we describe the survey data on which this book is based and perform some preliminary demographic analyses. Chapter 3 contains an analysis of some of the reasons people have for favoring or opposing legal abortion, and Chapter 4 contains an investigation of the role of religion in shaping abortion attitudes. Chapter 5 consists of an attempt to describe the characteristics of pro-life and pro-choice citizens as well as to characterize people with more nuanced or qualified abortion attitudes. The effects of the abortion issue on election outcomes is examined in Chapter 6. Finally, in Chapter 7 we venture some cautious predictions about the future of the debate over legalized abortion and attempt to project the style of abortion politics after a reversal or modification of *Roe v. Wade.*

Elizabeth Adell Cook
Ted G. Jelen
Clyde Wilcox

Acknowledgments

A number of people made valuable contributions to this book. Thanks are due to Jennifer Albertson, Ashley Andrus, Mary Bendyna, Mary Cook Garcia, and several anonymous reviewers for helpful comments on earlier drafts of this work. Lara Hewitt, April Morgan, John O'Donnell, and Eric Pages spent long hours in the library searching for reference materials. Carolyn Jeskey helped with the Bibliography, and Roland Gunn constructed the index. Amy Eisenberg, Cindy Hirschfeld, and the Westview staff were enormously helpful in preparing the manuscript. Finally, Seema Shah, Eileen Clark, Jeanne Norris, and Gregory Peck provided invaluable assistance in converting a rather messy manuscript into camera-ready copy.

E.A.C.
T.G.J.
C.W.

1

Abortion and American Politics

In 1991, the residents of Wichita, Kansas, experienced the emotional fervor of the abortion debate firsthand. Members of Operation Rescue, a pro-life group that blockades the entrances of clinics performing abortions, came to Wichita in large numbers. They sat in front of a clinic that performed third-trimester abortions, refusing to let patients pass. Members of pro-choice organizations also came to Wichita to help usher women seeking abortions into the clinics. Federal Judge Patrick Kelly issued an order forbidding the blockades, but they continued.

The city police were needed to maintain order, to escort patients into the clinics, and to arrest the Operation Rescue members and cart them off to jail. Upon release, the pro-life demonstrators again sat in front of the abortion clinic. The Reverend Marion (Pat) Robertson came to encourage the demonstrators, and newly elected pro-life Governor Joan Finney also spoke to the crowds. Traffic slowed on the town's major east-west thoroughfare as drivers watched the action. The city's residents had their normal routines disrupted, and the municipal budget had to absorb the extra costs of police working overtime and additional jail meals. In all, two thousand people were arrested in Wichita over the course of forty-six days.

In January 1992, on the nineteenth anniversary of the historic *Roe v. Wade* decision, more than seventy thousand anti-abortion activists marched in Washington, D.C. Some of these pro-life activists also blockaded entrances to clinics that provide abortion. The Washington Area Clinic Defense Task Force formed human chains to help clinic patients past the chanting demonstrators. Operation Rescue did not announce in advance which clinics it intended to target, so radio dispatchers helped Task Force personnel find the clinics that were being blockaded. As one patient was being escorted into a clinic, a woman from the crowd cried "Don't kill your baby, don't kill your baby." The escorts began to chant "Woman's right to choose." The demonstrators responded by singing the Lord's Prayer and by reciting the Hail Mary. Eventually hundreds of pro-life demonstrators were arrested for violating a 1989 federal court order that prohibited attempts to conspire to blockade clinics. Demonstrators were fined fifty dollars and released.[1]

The abortion issue arouses a level of intensity among activists that is seldom seen in American politics. Over the past thirty years, few other political issues have inspired widespread marches, civil disobedience, and even occasional violence. The intensity of the pro-choice activists dates from recent U.S. Supreme Court decisions that limit the reach of the *Roe* decision. The intensity of the pro-life demonstrators dates from *Roe* itself.

In 1973, the U.S. Supreme Court invalidated virtually every state law designed to restrict women's access to legal abortion. In the cases of *Roe v. Wade* and *Doe v. Bolton*,[2] the Court, by a 7 to 2 margin, held that women have a constitutionally protected right to legal abortion. This right to abortion was found to be a specific instance of a more general "right to privacy." The right to privacy, in turn, was found to have a constitutional basis in the "penumbra" of rights around the First, Third, Fourth, Fifth, and Ninth Amendments.[3] In other words, even though the Constitution makes no *explicit* mention of a right to privacy, the Court held that such a right is implied by the intentions of the framers in posing the Bill of Rights.

In the *Roe* decision, the Court divided pregnancies into thirds, or *trimesters*. The Court ruled that during the first trimester, states cannot legally restrict abortion. During the second trimester, states can only impose regulations necessary to preserve a woman's health. Only in the third trimester, when the fetus is generally *viable* (that is, capable of surviving outside the womb), can states impose regulations for the purpose of preserving fetal life.[4]

For a number of years after *Roe*, the Supreme Court consistently struck down attempts by state legislatures to restrict access to legal abortion. A few examples illustrate the extent to which the Supreme Court was intent on preserving abortion rights. In the case of *Planned Parenthood of Missouri v. Danforth*,[5] the Court overturned a measure that would have allowed the prospective father a veto over a woman's abortion decision. Similarly, in *Akron v. Akron Center for Reproductive Health*, the Court held that a law requiring parental consent for the abortions of minors must contain alternative processes by which minors can legally terminate pregnancy.[6] One such process might involve a private hearing before a judge to determine the suitability of the abortion decision. Finally, in *Thornburgh v. American College of Obstetricians and Gynecologists*, the Court struck down a variety of provisions designed to discourage women from having abortions. The provisions would have exposed women who sought abortions to mandatory, detailed descriptions of fetal development, descriptions of the risks and possible psychological traumas involved in abortion, and reminders about the availability of support from the father or from social service agencies.[7] With the important exception of allowing Congress to restrict Medicaid funding for abortion,[8] for sixteen years the Court took the position that, with very few exceptions, governments could not seek to restrict access to abortion.

This string of rulings in support of legal abortion was interrupted in 1989 by the case in Missouri of *Webster v. Reproductive Health Services.*[9] This change in course was not altogether unexpected, for several of the justices from the original *Roe* majority had retired and been replaced by more conservative jurists. In *Webster*, the Court ruled, by a 5 to 4 margin, that some state-imposed restrictions on abortion are constitutionally permissible. The Court did not strike down a preamble to the Missouri law that declared that human life begins at the moment of conception. It also approved provisions restricting the performance of abortions in public hospitals even if a woman pays her own bill, and requiring physicians to perform a number of tests of fetal viability before performing an abortion.[10] The legal importance of the *Webster* decision goes beyond the actual provisions of the decision. The Court did not overrule *Roe v. Wade*, despite an impassioned plea by Justice Anton Scalia for it to do so, but *Webster* seems to invite state legislatures to write restrictive abortion laws, which will then be subject to judicial review. In other words, the ultimate importance of *Webster* will be the effect of this decision on state legislatures. In 1989 and 1990, a number of state legislatures imposed restrictions on legal abortion, and in some cases these restrictions went far beyond those sanctioned in *Webster*. The abortion issue has thus been returned to the legislative agenda. State legislatures have become battlegrounds for the abortion issue, and this has influenced a number of state legislative elections. Because governors can propose or veto abortion restrictions, abortion has become a factor in gubernatorial elections as well.

This book is about public attitudes toward abortion. Abortion has been a strongly contested political issue, at least since *Roe*, occasioning the mobilization of previously indifferent citizens into political activity and often producing acts of civil disobedience or lawbreaking. Abortion is a highly emotional, symbolic issue, capable of generating strong feelings and rhetoric. With the return of the abortion issue to the legislative arena, public attitudes about abortion assume an even greater importance. National and state legislatures are elected bodies, whose power is derived from public support. Thus, a fundamental premise of this book is that it matters a great deal what ordinary citizens think and feel about abortion. In a democracy, public opinion is regarded as the ultimate authority, and a system cannot be regarded as democratic if the wishes of ordinary people are not taken into account. The future of the abortion issue may, in large part, be decided in the court of public opinion.

Two diverse elements in the American political culture lead to strong reactions by individuals to the abortion issue. First is the American commitment to Lockean individualism, which provides that the freedom to do as one pleases is an important value.[11] The philosopher Brian Barry has described an Anglo-American commitment to the "harm principle," in which people are to be permitted to do as they please as long as they do not harm anyone else.[12] Thus, individual autonomy is a central value of the American political culture.

However, a second element of the American political culture is a tradition of private and civil religion, with most people adhering to a somewhat vague "Judeo-Christian" tradition.[13] The religious sensibilities of the American people are an important part of societal proscriptions of such extramarital sexual practices as adultery, homosexuality, or sexual activity among teenagers. In these cases the religious values may take precedence over the American commitment to individual liberties.

As we shall see, the abortion issue involves, at least in part, a debate about "proper" sexual behavior. Historically, some have always regarded abortion as a means by which women could avoid the consequences of sex outside of marriage. The data on which this book is based suggest that abortion is part of a large constellation of attitudes relating to sexual morality, the appropriate roles of women in society, and the centrality of childrearing in family life. Many Americans still hold fairly traditional attitudes toward these subjects. However, the commitment to individual autonomy implies that private sexual behavior is not usually a fit subject for government regulation. The high value we place on individual freedom means that many Americans must often tolerate the practice by others of sexual behavior of which they disapprove.[14]

The abortion issue derives some of its power from the fact that it constitutes an area within which the two strands of the American political culture collide. Unlike the more "private" behaviors of adultery or contraception, abortion is regarded by some as a fit subject for government regulation because of the claim that the fetus is a person, bearing a "right to life." In answer to the question, "Who is being hurt?" by an abortion, the answer is often "the unborn." This is not to say that a respect for human life is the *only* reason people oppose legal abortion. Indeed, the chapters that follow will show that the desire to save human life is only one of several rationales for those opposed to legal abortion. Yet, regardless of the motivations that individuals have in opposing abortion, to assert the "human" status of the embryo is an important rhetorical position because the claim of embryonic "personhood" is necessary to make abortion seem an "other regarding" behavior. The possibility that harm may be done to another "person" through abortion is an important means by which abortion becomes a *political* and not a *private* issue.

Abortion: A Concise and Contested History

Most treatments of abortion devote some attention to the historical dimensions of the issue. Advocates of both pro-life and pro-choice policies often argue that abortion has been viewed in a consistent manner throughout history but that many recent changes constitute a sharp departure from the past. Thus, pro-life advocates have argued that the Supreme Court has unearthed novel constitutional rights in the *Roe* decision. Critics of *Roe* have often noted that terms such as "abortion," "trimester," or even "privacy" cannot be found in their copies of the Constitution. They argue that the discovery of abortion rights in the Constitution constitutes the rawest form of judicial legislation.[15] These pro-life spokespersons suggest that the *Roe* decision imposed legal abortion on unwilling state governments and citizens in violation of the historical traditions of these states. Implicit in such accounts is the notion that abortion had always been viewed as something close to murder prior to the *Roe* decision,[16] and, thus, the legalization of abortion is a radical break with a consistent tradition in Western civilization.[17]

Conversely, pro-choice advocates often point out that the criminalization of abortion is a relatively recent phenomenon and that legislation designed to limit or prohibit abortion was passed with a variety of motives in mind. Indeed, several accounts of the rash of anti-abortion laws passed during the nineteenth century stress that considerations of embryonic life competed with many other values as a source of "pro-life" motivation.[18] Thus, many historical treatments of abortion written by authors sympathetic to an abortion right emphasize the relatively common practice of abortion and argue that nineteenth-century criminalization is the atypical historical period.

By contrast, our reading of the history of abortion is that, whatever previous practices have been, the past is not a particularly useful guide to the abortion debate. Although both sides of the controversy have been able to use the historical record for rhetorical purposes, the issue of abortion has always been highly controversial, and both sides have lacked a common frame of reference throughout history. In this section, we review some of the more important issues raised in accounts of the history of abortion.

First, it seems clear that abortion is not a new practice. Some women have always sought to control their own fertility and have used abortion as one means of exercising such control. Some accounts of early abortion practices in the United States have emphasized the use of abortifacient drugs (drugs used to induce abortions), including natural herbs and poisons[19] as well as medical treatments for "menstrual blockages."[20] At various times in early American history, abortion services were advertised rather blatantly if somewhat euphemistically. For example, in the 1840s, abortifacient drugs were marketed as "French lunar pills," "female pills," or "French renovating pills." The latter were marketed as "a blessing to mothers," but carried the caution that pregnant women should not use them because "they invariably produce a miscarriage." Advertisements for abortion products and services were regarded by many as unacceptable, especially when such messages appeared in "family" newspapers.[21] Thus, the practice of abortion has existed and has been condoned by some and condemned by others for most of American history.

Second, as Kristin Luker points out, "the moral status of the embryo has always been controversial."[22] For example, although Plato and Aristotle were both familiar with the practice of abortion and approved it in some instances,[23] the Pythagoreans regarded the embryo as a person from the moment of conception.[24] Early Canon Law, associated with the Roman Catholic Church, fixed the period of "ensoulment" or "animation" at forty or eighty days after conception, depending on the sex of the embryo.[25] Indeed, the Catholic position that the embryo is "human" from the moment of conception was not directly enunciated until 1951, when Pius XII argued that the right to life from God in the maternal breast is "immediate",[26] although such doctrine had been implicit in Church law some years prior to Pius XII's teaching.

Anglo-American common law, the accumulated weight of judicial decisions in English and American history, had recognized that abortion was not to be considered a criminal act if such abortion was performed prior to quickening--the point at which the mother first becomes aware of fetal movement.[27] As quickening typically occurs around the fifth month of pregnancy, common law provided considerable latitude for early abortions. Moreover, because the mother was the only reliable witness to the "fact" of quickening, abortions were often available until quite late in a pregnancy as a practical matter.[28] Thus, although the belief that personhood is conferred on the embryo immediately upon conception has a very long pedigree, such beliefs have always been contested. The human status of the embryo has always been problematic, and many people and institutions, including at various points in its history the Catholic Church, have sought to make distinctions based on the embryo's age.

Third, the regulation of abortion has always been a mixed-motive game, with a variety of values at stake. During his 1988 presidential campaign, Marion (Pat) Robertson claimed that legalized abortion is bad economics because the prospective earnings of the unborn would be necessary to continue to finance the Social Security system.[29] Although Robertson's idea is certainly a novel contribution to the theory of public finance, it does represent a rather extreme instance of the tendency of the abortion issue to embody a diverse set of value judgments.

Although embryonic life is *one* important value in the abortion debate, it is not the *only* value at stake. For example, Luker notes a number of differences between the pro-life and pro-choice activists she interviewed in their attitudes toward gender role specialization and female sexuality. Pro-choice activists are much more likely to allow alternative sexual relationships to traditional marital monogamy and to regard men and women as essentially similar than are pro-life activists.[30] Condemnation of abortion as a means by which "morally loose" women can avoid the consequences of their "immoral behavior" is a frequent theme in the history of the abortion debate, and as we shall show in later chapters is an important predictor of contemporary abortion attitudes as well. Many political cultures have viewed the control of female sexuality as a problematic issue,[31] and the threat of illegitimacy has been one means by which the potential costs of extramarital sexual behavior have been increased.[32] Restricting access to abortion is thus one means by which communities can enforce their sexual norms by raising the costs attached to their violation.

Aside from the sexual and gender role implications of the abortion controversy, other values are often at stake as well. Rosalind Petchesky argues that abortion restrictions have historically been a response to concerns over differential rates of fertility. She notes that, in the mid-nineteenth century, upper-class "Yankee" women were considerably less fertile than their poorer, immigrant counterparts. Eugenics, the "science" of improving humanity through hereditary means, may have been an important consideration in early abortion regulation by preventing upper-class women from having abortions and therefore encouraging childbearing among the "better" classes.[33]

Similarly, some early anti-abortion laws were apparently motivated at least in part by a desire to preserve the health of women who might seek to abort. James Mohr notes that the first statutes designed to limit abortions had as one of their purposes the control of certain toxic poisons, which were commonly in use as abortifacients.[34] Other measures took note of the frequency with which the surgery associated with some abortions resulted in damage to the uterine wall or produced other, occasionally fatal, health hazards to the prospective mother.[35] Some anti-abortion rationales are thus timebound and depend to some extent on the state of medical technology at the time of their enactment.

Finally, Kristin Luker also notes the tendency of the abortion debate to be connected to the "vested interests" of the various participants.[36] In Luker's account, the different interests of employed women and housewives provide much of the energy for the current activist-level debate on the abortion issue. Housewives may fear that the status of motherhood is devalued, along with their own status, to the extent that legal abortion makes motherhood an option that some women may forgo. If motherhood, instead of being a biological and social destiny, is regarded as one of several alternatives available to women, then women whose identity is centrally involved in the roles of wife and mother may seem less "worthy" or valuable than women with other resources to offer. Legal abortion thus threatens women engaged in "traditional" homemaker tasks with a significant loss of status. For similar reasons, women employed outside the home also seek to enhance the value of their careers and outside activities by asserting as much control over their fertility as possible. Without such control, the status that employed women may achieve in their careers is always contingent in some way on their continued ability to avoid or defer motherhood.

The vested interests of other parties to the abortion issue have also had an impact on the debate. Several analysts have commented on the extent to which abortion regulation in the United States in the nineteenth century has been connected to the desire of physicians for professional status.[37] The strict licensing requirements, rigorous educational training, high prestige, and long apprenticeship with which we associate the medical profession are relatively new. As recently as the previous century, physicians had to compete with a great many unlicensed practitioners for prestige and patients. One way the medical profession distinguished itself was to take a firm position against abortion. A public stand against legal abortion enhanced the status of medical doctors in at least two ways. First, it allowed physicians to display their biological expertise in public explanations of why the embryo should be regarded as human, thus demonstrating their sophistication in physiology. Second, an effective prohibition on legal abortion would have limited public access to "less qualified" competitors such as druggists and midwives.[38]

Thus, it is difficult to draw firm conclusions from the history of the abortion debate. Although the issue of embryonic life has been central to the debate throughout much of recorded history, there does not seem to have existed a consensus on the personhood of the embryo at any point. Moreover, the abortion controversy has also involved a good many other issues that are only tangentially related to matters of embryonic life and death.

The Abortion Issue: The Search for an Analogue

A different kind of historical perspective may provide some insight as to the possible impact an ongoing debate on abortion may have for the practice of politics in the United States. A series of comparisons between the contemporary debate about abortion and other political issues may illuminate the possible implications of the abortion issue. To what extent does the abortion issue resemble other major issues in American politics, and to what extent might the abortion controversy affect the general direction of American political discourse?

Abortion Politics as Normal Politics

A useful starting point in a general discussion of abortion politics may be to consider the possibility that abortion may not be an unusual issue at all. In American politics, the vast majority of controversial issues are ultimately settled in some manner.[39] The American political system is designed to operate by compromise, and most issues are ultimately negotiated between contending sides. Once some issues are settled, a consensus often arises in support of the policy. For example, although the opponents of Social Security argued bitterly and denounced the system as "impractical," "socialistic," and "Bolshevist," there is overwhelming support for Social Security today. Presidents and members of Congress routinely exempt Social Security from general promises to cut or balance the federal budget, and candidates who support cuts in Social Security benefits run the strong risk of early retirement. As one observer noted, "Social Security is the third [electrified] rail of American politics: touch it and you're dead."[40]

Perhaps more typical than the consensus surrounding Social Security is the tacit agreement to conduct political debate within relatively narrow boundaries. For example, there seems to be general agreement that the federal government should spend money on both national defense and education, but the details of these programs are negotiated in Congress every year. Obviously, a frequent source of political conflict is the level of funding a specific program might receive, but debate takes place at least as often over substantive details of policy. Should we fund "high-tech" weapons, or should more effort go into the training and retention of ground troops? Should education policy assign a high priority to basic academic research, or should elementary education receive a larger share of educational funding? Issues such as these are never "settled" in any final sense, but conflict over such matters has largely been routinized and managed. People can and do debate such matters, but there is a clear sense that the discussion is ongoing, and no participant really expects a total or final victory.

Initially, abortion would seem a poor candidate for settlement through what might be termed "normal politics." Abortion, after all, is a highly emotional issue that exists at the intersection of a number of more basic concerns. Amy Fried terms the abortion issue a "condensational symbol," which means that the abortion issue "stands for" a number of basic concerns of the American people, including the sanctity of human life, standards of appropriate sexual behavior, the importance and status assigned to childrearing, and appropriate gender roles.[41] Activist-level debate about the abortion issue seems concerned with such ultimate values that compromise is difficult to envision.

However, there does exist some evidence suggesting that the absolutes with which pro-choice and pro-life activists debate the issue of abortion may not be shared by a majority of the American people. If we understand the concept of a "right" to mean a prerogative that can only be abridged under the most extreme circumstances, a majority of Americans do not support either an unlimited "right to life" or an unlimited "right to choose." Rather, a majority of Americans appears to believe that the status of the embryo and the prerogatives of the mother must be weighed and balanced in some fashion.

A preliminary look at public opinion data suggests that few people regard the embryo as a full-fledged person, bearing rights and liberties that others are bound to respect. Very few people take a consistently pro-life position, which would involve a prohibition on all abortions, with the possible exception of those required to save the life or preserve the health of the prospective mother.[42] Instead, most people are willing to make fairly precise and subtle distinctions.[43] Although right-to-life activists argue that abortion is murder, for most Americans the embryo seems to occupy what Kent Greenawalt has termed a "borderline status."[44] That is, although the *potential* life of the embryo is deserving of some respect (a decision to abort a pregnancy would seem to have a greater moral importance than, say, cosmetic surgery), the embryo does not seem to most people to be entitled to the full range of protections the legal system affords humans. Most Americans believe that the potential life of the embryo has some moral value, but they also feel that the embryo has no fundamental right to life that the legal system is bound to respect.

Conversely, public opinion surveys have shown that most Americans are quite intolerant of abortions that seem casual or capricious. Many people believe that the decision to abort is often made too hastily or without adequate consideration of the moral implications. A large majority of the public supports waiting periods and prohibitions on abortion for gender selection. Even though many people believe that a woman's privacy interests should be given great weight,[45] there seems to exist broad public sentiment that the reasons for desiring abortion do matter and that some reasons for undergoing an abortion are impermissible.

In her insightful book *Decoding Abortion Rhetoric*, Michelle Condit shows that treatments of the popular media reflect the conflict between the values of embryonic life and personal autonomy. Using content analysis of movies, television programs, and other mass media, Condit reports that characters contemplating abortion are typically portrayed in sympathetic lights if they evince concern for the potential life they carry, the interests of their male partners, and the opinions of other relevant persons. Casual or repeat aborters are not accorded the same respect and are usually treated with derision and contempt.[46]

In a more systematic analysis of public opinion, Everett Carl Ladd shows that privacy and embryonic life are both highly valued by the

American public. When the question of whether abortion is "the same thing as murder" is raised, the American people are about equally divided on the issue. Abortion is also strongly disapproved as a "primary means of birth control," and a majority of the American people believe abortion is too easy to obtain. Many feel that abortion should be prohibited or made more difficult to obtain. However, large majorities of the American people favor legal abortion in cases in which the mother's health is in danger, in cases of rape or incest, or when there is the strong possibility of fetal defect. Thus, while the American public has many reservations about abortion, there is a willingness to approve abortions for "serious" reasons. The values of embryonic life and personal choice both seem to be given great weight in public attitudes about abortion. Further, Ladd argues that the fact that these two interests are highly valued does not indicate ambivalence on the part of the American public but rather reflects a compromise between two deeply held principles.[47]

Interpreting public opinion surveys is a difficult and tricky business, in part because many members of the mass public (whose involvement in politics is intermittent or casual) are unconstrained by considerations of logic or consistency.[48] Nevertheless, some of the evidence in recent studies suggests that both life and choice considerations matter to substantial numbers of American citizens. Because both values are desired, neither is accorded the status of a fundamental right by the general public. This is not to say that the trade-off many Americans feel between the values of life and choice is morally correct, or even internally consistent. However, it does suggest that there might be a basis for compromise on the abortion issue. The abortion issue might be settled in some manner not completely satisfactory to either pro-life or pro-choice activists but perhaps acceptable to a substantial proportion of the American people.

If analyses of the American political culture suggest that a compromise on the abortion issue is possible, why has such an accommodation not been reached? One possible answer is that the Supreme Court, through its decision in *Roe v. Wade*, bypassed the normal legislative process, and legitimated a relatively extreme position on the issue.[49] Several analysts have suggested that, during the 1960s and early 1970s, state legislatures were moving in the direction of abortion law *reform*, which typically involved making the procedural requirements for abortion less burdensome while retaining state jurisdiction over the issue, before the Supreme Court mandated abortion law *repeal*.[50]

For example, in 1959, the American Law Institute (ALI) published a model abortion law, which recommended that abortion be permitted in cases in which there existed "substantial risk that mother or child will suffer grave and irremediable impairment of physical or mental health" or in cases of "forcible rape." An abortion based on the rape rationale would require the certification of two physicians. Between 1967 and 1972, several states adopted ALI-type "reform" laws, but only New York's could be regarded as the *repeal* of state jurisdiction over abortion.[51]

Some analysts have suggested that although the *Roe* decision might represent an adequate practical solution to the abortion issue, the decision should have been made by democratically elected legislatures and not by unelected federal judges.[52] It is important to note that the *Roe* decision is itself a compromise in that an absolute right to abortion is not asserted; *Roe* provides guidelines about *when* abortion can be regulated by state governments but not *why* such regulation may be permissible. *Roe* suggests that women have a nearly absolute right to a first-trimester abortion, regardless of their reasons for desiring to terminate their pregnancies. This decision does not give much weight to the publicly held value of embryonic life. As a result, there is some evidence that the *Roe* decision had a moderate polarizing effect on public opinion.[53]

If the trend begun by the *Webster* decision continues and state legislatures are granted greater discretion in formulating abortion policy, perhaps a stable resolution of the abortion issue is possible. Such a resolution might involve moderate restrictions on the timing and reasons for legal abortions. For example, state legislatures might be free to restrict abortions for "frivolous" reasons such as sex selection or to impose brief waiting periods. As a practical matter, such regulations would have little effect on the incidence of abortion. However, if the abortion issue is primarily symbolic, the impact of state regulation on actual abortions may be beside the point. Perhaps there is substantial public support for restriction of "nonserious" abortion because people feel that the law does not balance their concerns for fetal life or their anti-promiscuity values with their support for their values of individual choice.

It is important to point out that our description of possible compromises of the abortion issue does not suggest our endorsement or approval of such approaches. Claims by both sides of the abortion controversy that a majority of the public supports their position are incorrect, however, and the opinions of ordinary citizens are much more "centrist" than activist-level discourse might suggest. Thus, abortion can be conceived as an example of normal politics, but one in which the apparent public compromise was ruled unacceptable by the Supreme Court.

Abortion Politics as Dysfunctional Politics

Another approach to the abortion issue suggests that, in the absence of a satisfactory resolution of the dispute, continued debate over the abortion issue is somehow dysfunctional for the performance of democratic politics. There are some types of issues where compromise is difficult, and therefore democratic governments do not handle them very well. Continued debate over intensely emotional, "non negotiable" issues may reduce respect for the government or for democratic norms generally. Democratic government seems to require an attitude of "civility," in which a commitment to the rules of political engagement supersedes a desire for particular policy outcomes. If large numbers of people come to regard government policy-making process as generally biased against their preferences or values, such democratic civility may be threatened.

Advocates of legalized abortion often explicitly compare criminalized abortion and the Prohibition Amendment in the 1920s.[54] In both cases, government sought to regulate private behavior in accordance with a particular, controversial set of moral intuitions. Prohibition, it is argued, resulted in a large and rapid increase in criminal activity as well as a generalized disrespect for the law. The lesson of Prohibition is thought to be that government should not seek to "legislate morality" or to seek to enforce laws that do not enjoy the support of the community. Such laws and such actions are seen to result in disrespect for law and the political process in general.

Pro-choice advocates also suggest that efforts to enforce measures recriminalizing abortion are likely to be futile or result in the abridgement of other fundamental freedoms. In a very powerful magazine advertisement, Planned Parenthood shows a woman answering her front door. Outside are two plainclothes policemen, inquiring about her "miscarriage."[55] Implied in this message is that other freedoms besides "freedom of choice" are at stake in the abortion debate. In this instance, Fourth Amendment protections against unreasonable search and seizure are depicted as threatened by zealous enforcement laws regulating abortion. More generally, such rhetoric is designed to place a controversial right to abortion in a more general context of personal freedoms that Americans take for granted. Any weakening of the privacy right, which provides the basis for abortion rights, might lead to a "slippery slope" on which all such freedoms are jeopardized.[56]

Advocates of restrictions on abortion also make use of historical analogies. For example, a powerful, frequently used rhetorical device is to compare the legalization of abortion with the Nazi Holocaust.[57] This analogy is intended to draw attention to the claim that abortion is murder and that the taking of human life is not less morally reprehensible because the practice is common. A somewhat richer analogy is occasionally drawn between the abortion issue and the issue of slavery. In particular, *Roe v. Wade* is sometimes compared by pro-life advocates to the infamous 1857 case of *Dred Scott v. Sanford*,[58] in which the Supreme Court declared that blacks had no rights that the government is bound to respect. In both cases, it is argued, the Court has arbitrarily declared a group of "people" (slaves in the *Dred Scott* case and human embryos in *Roe*) to be "nonpersons," or, at least, "noncitizens," and legitimized the brutal, inhuman treatment of those so categorized. It might also be argued that, in both cases, the Court went well beyond the compromised solutions proposed by legislative bodies. The effect of *Dred Scott* was to invalidate the carefully crafted Missouri Compromise; *Roe* invalidated the efforts of state legislatures to reform their abortion laws without surrendering state jurisdiction over abortion.

Whatever the force of such historical analogies, they are unlikely to seem plausible to someone not already committed to the legal restriction of abortion. Comparisons between abortion and genocide or slavery may not persuade the uncommitted, but they do galvanize the converted. A feature that the Holocaust and slavery issues have in common is that, ultimately, "normal" political discourse was not sufficient to decide the issue. Both controversies were resolved through general warfare, involving extensive recourse to physical violence. The battles over Prohibition involved a similar, if less pervasive, breakdown of the political system. From the standpoint of the pro-life movement, the point of comparisons between these two issues and the contemporary abortion controversy is that such analogies may serve to motivate and justify political acts outside the bounds of democratic "civility." That is, "normal" democratic politics involves such values as respect for opposing viewpoints, a willingness to compromise differences, and the ability to tolerate unfavorable outcomes while continuing to work for the policies one prefers.

In contrast to these "civil" values, a small, but highly visible minority of pro-life activists has resorted to picketing, a legal but disruptive tactic, preventing people from entering abortion clinics, and vandalizing buildings in which abortions are performed. Although such activities fall outside the bounds of normally acceptable political discourse, they may be viewed in a different light if the moral issue involved in abortion is in any way comparable to slavery or genocide. If abortion is, in fact, murder, destroying property, the most extreme tactic used by the pro-life movement, may seem to be a morally appropriate strategy. Because most Americans would regard human life as having a higher value than property, the prevention of murder by destroying property may be a praiseworthy, if illegal, means of preventing the taking of innocent life. For some, the abortion controversy poses a clear conflict between morality and legality, which may be resolved in favor of the former.

Operation Rescue, which uses civil disobedience to hamper the operations of clinics that perform abortions, has been compared in a similar vein to both desegregation efforts in the South and efforts to resist desegregation. Pro-life proponents see Operation Rescue workers as similar to citizens who disobeyed laws discriminating against African Americans. Pro-choice activists see the same behaviors as similar to anti-desegregation protestors who tried to prevent black children from entering formerly white schools. Thus, civil disobedience may be seen as noble or ignoble depending on the morality of the laws being broken.

Such calculations are likely to be quite disturbing to those who place a high value on democratic civility and stability. A public discussion of the possible necessity of occasionally violent lawbreaking suggests that "normal" methods of conflict resolution such as elections or litigation may have broken down and that a few pro-life activists are close to withdrawing legitimacy from the the norms of democracy. Democratic politics may only be possible if people are willing to accept, however temporarily, unfavorable outcomes, and if citizens attach a high priority to "playing within the rules." If particular policies on the abortion issue become more important to some activists than the procedures by which political decisions are made, "democracy" as Americans understand the term may not be possible.

Even if the passions generated by the abortion debate do not result in widespread extralegal political activity and are confined to ordinary political participation, abortion politics may still result in the distortion of democratic politics. Abortion is a classic instance of a subject that is thought to generate "single-issue voting."[59] Although a detailed analysis of the effects of the abortion issue must await our discussion in Chapter 6, it seems important to note that elections hold an important place in most theories of democracy. Although there are always problems in interpreting election results, elections are a central means by which public preferences may be translated into public policy. If a politically significant number of people cast votes purely on the basis of candidates' stands on the abortion issue, their preferences on other issues may be distorted or underrepresented. For example, many analysts believe that the abortion issue was an important determinant of the outcome of the 1989 gubernatorial election in Virginia between Douglas Wilder and Marshall Coleman.[60] Concerning this election, Laurence Tribe poses an important question: "What about the Republican women in the suburbs of Virginia who believed they had to vote for Douglas Wilder in order to preserve their reproductive freedom, who, on most other grounds, would have preferred Marshall Coleman as their governor?"[61]

Like many other states, Virginia is, at this writing, confronting a number of difficult and costly problems in the areas of taxation, transportation, race relations, and public education. To the extent that the 1989 gubernatorial election was decided by the abortion issue, the ability of the public to hold the governor accountable on these other issues was limited. Similarly, Richard Nixon notes with some exasperation the effects of the abortion issue on a recent Senate race: "In 1980, the Republican nominee for Senate in Colorado, Mary Estill Buchanan, lost in a very close election. I was surprised when a Republican friend told me he had not voted for her. I asked why. He replied, 'She was wrong on abortion.' As a result we got six more years of Gary Hart, who was wrong on everything."[62]

The general point here is that elections, with all their imperfections, are nevertheless an important means by which ordinary citizens can attempt to control the behavior of public officials. Most acts of governance have very little to do with the abortion controversy, and excessive concentration on this or any other single issue may distort and limit that control. Moreover, such distortion can occur even if a relatively small number of citizens are "single-issue" voters. Given that some contested elections in American politics are settled by fewer than ten percentage points, a rather small number of votes can occasionally be decisive. If such voters are highly visible through polls, demonstrations, or news media accounts, their effectiveness may be magnified, through the strategic calculations of candidates. Put simply, if Governor Wilder believes that he owes his office to his pro-choice position, that belief may be more important to his conduct of the governorship than the actual facts of the matter.

Thus, some analysts would argue that the abortion issue is perhaps detrimental to the practice of traditional democratic politics. Democracy is often thought to require a respect for opposing viewpoints and a commitment to abide by legal procedures. If even a small minority of the American people regard the abortion issue as superseding this commitment to democratic civility, the practice of democratic politics may be distorted or threatened.

Abortion Politics as Empowerment Politics

Thus far, we have considered the possibility that abortion may be an issue like any other, with no special characteristics. We have also reviewed arguments suggesting that abortion may be an issue which cannot be handled within the normal confines of democratic competition. A third possibility remains to be considered. The abortion issue may, in fact, enhance democracy by empowering certain persons whose interests had previously been underrepresented. Formerly apolitical people, perhaps especially women, may be mobilized in some fashion by the controversy over reproductive freedom.

The most obvious case in which abortion politics might lead to empowerment is that access to legal abortion might give women a greater freedom over other aspects of their lives. Some women have always sought to control their own fertility because childrearing imposes strong limits on the other activities in which women might engage. The time and energy devoted to pregnancy, postnatal convalescence, and childrearing are often thought to be incompatible with the demands of full-time employment. Although, in principle, there is no reason that some of these tasks cannot be shared with a woman's husband (assuming she is married), women disproportionately bear the costs of pregnancy. Unlike nearly every other industrialized country, the United States has no national parental-leave policy to allow women and men paid leave for a period surrounding birth, so pregnancy may endanger a woman's job. In addition, research has shown that after the mother returns to the labor force, two-career couples divide housework quite unevenly, with women performing far more than half of chores.

Thus, some companies unofficially (and illegally) reduce the responsibilities, rewards, and opportunities for women whose energy is, or will be, divided between employment and child-care duties.[63] Some might regard this as an improvement over an outright refusal to hire women of childbearing age, but the "mommy track" reserved for women clearly represents a denial of equal opportunity in the workplace.

An example of fertility-based gender discrimination might make this point less abstractly. A young married woman of our acquaintance was the top salesperson on a small sales force. At one point in her employment with this company, she was denied a windfall benefit of increased client opportunities that was granted to all of her male coworkers. When she inquired about the apparent inequity, she was informed that, as a married woman, she was considered a "temporary employee," who would eventually quit to have a baby. Aside from the questionable judgment of the supervisor in admitting discrimination, the denial of the benefit clearly reflected a belief that the woman's status as an employee was somehow qualified by her biological and social status as a fertile female.

The discretion over the timing or the fact of childbearing which abortion provides is regarded by some as essential for full female equality.[64] Women will likely always be subject to discrimination based on their fertility until it can be established that childbearing is a controllable aspect of women's lives. The slavery analogy is used by pro-choice advocates in this regard. As Kristin Luker puts it, "motherhood, so long as it is involuntary, is potentially always a low-status, unrewarding role to which women can be banished at any time."[65] Others argue, with a rhetorical flourish, that this sort of involuntary motherhood has much in common with slavery. Legal abortion provides women a means by which fertility can be controlled, and childrearing can be planned and coordinated with other roles women may desire.

It is often argued that contraception could potentially provide women with fertility control, without some of the moral implications of abortion. Effective *prevention* of pregnancy, it is claimed, should eliminate or reduce drastically the need for legal abortions. From the standpoint of female fertility control, however, such arguments are problematic. First, contraception requires resources, such as money and sophistication, which are not available to all women. The pill and intrauterine device (IUD) are rather expensive, pose health risks for some women, and require regular medical monitoring.[66] Moreover, effective contraception often requires detailed knowledge about such phenomena as menstrual cycles that is often lacking in very young or economically deprived women. For example, Zelnik, Kantner, and Ford report the following reasons that some teenage girls fail to use contraception: "It's the wrong time of the month," "I'm too young," "I don't have sex often enough," "[I] just can't [get pregnant]."[67] It thus seems likely that the women who can least afford to become pregnant are also least likely to have the resources and skills necessary to use contraception effectively.

Yet, approximately half of women who seek abortions had been using some form of contraception when they became pregnant.[68] Even if a woman faithfully and conscientiously uses a highly effective method of contraception, she still runs the risk of an unintended pregnancy. No method of birth control is completely infallible, and accidents do happen. Moreover, very small risks taken repeatedly over time eventually become very large. A contraceptive method that is "almost completely reliable" will ultimately become very unreliable as the "almosts" accumulate.

A little arithmetic might clarify this last point. Let us make the conservative assumption that a young woman becomes sexually active at age eighteen, and remains fertile until age forty. Such a woman would be fertile for twenty-two years. Assuming that our hypothetical woman was sexually active during the entire period of her fertility, that she used a contraceptive method that was 99 percent effective per year, and that the probability of contraceptive failure was equal in each year, then the probability that she would effectively prevent pregnancy throughout the entire period of her fertility would be $.99^{22}$, or about 80 percent. In other words, the chance that she would become pregnant at some point during her fertility would be about 20 percent even if a highly reliable contraceptive method was used conscientiously. No contraceptive method except sterilization is this effective in practice, however. A woman who conscientiously uses a contraceptive method that is 95 percent effective for 22 years has a 68 percent chance of becoming pregnant by accident at some point during her sexually active years, assuming an equal probability of pregnancy in each year. Indeed, at least one study has shown that women who have been sterilized have between a 2 percent and a 4 percent chance of getting pregnant if they are sexually active for only ten years.[69]

Thus, without legalized abortion, the ability of women to control their own fertility is limited by the reliability of their contraceptive method or their unwillingness to forgo sexual intercourse. Of course, a desire to prevent illicit sexual relations has always been an element of efforts to regulate or criminalize abortion. However, the fact that no contraceptive method is 100 percent effective is a limitation on the sexuality of *married* women as well. Legal abortion thus provides what no contraceptive method can: an absolute means of controlling whether and when a woman bears a child. Abortion rights might be compared to the women's suffrage movement of the early twentieth century, in that both the right to vote and the right to terminate a pregnancy intentionally enhance female claims to full equality with men.

Perhaps paradoxically, the abortion controversy may also have empowered pro-life women. In her classic study, *Abortion and the Politics of Motherhood*, Kristin Luker notes that many pro-life activists in California were recruited from the ranks of formerly apolitical housewives. These women did not involve themselves in politics until they experienced the shock of learning that not everyone viewed the abortion issue as they did. Luker reports that the belief that a human embryo is, in fact, a human being and that abortion is therefore murder, was simply part of the "common sense" background assumptions these women held. The realization that contrary beliefs not only existed, but were gaining social and legal acceptance as well, galvanized pro-life activists into intensive political participation.[70]

As the abortion controversy has continued, pro-life organizations, many of which have an explicitly religious base, have used preexisting religious and social networks to recruit new members. For many women, pro-life organizations provide an opportunity for political involvement that is sanctioned by their church and family. The longevity of the abortion controversy has led to the creation of relatively permanent local right-to-life structures, which, like other civic organizations, are constantly seeking new members. In some cases, new members may not actively seek out pro-life organizations; rather, their friends and acquaintances bring them along to meetings.

The general point here is that the abortion issue has created an incentive to engage in active political participation for many previously apolitical citizens. In this way, the abortion issue may have served as a source of citizenship renewal. As we write this, it is too early to tell what the implications of the *Webster* decision are likely to be. However, if abortion is returned to the arena of state legislatures in any substantial way, the remobilization of pro-choice advocates may also increase political participation.[71]

Conclusions

It is thus a matter of some importance what ordinary people think about the abortion issue. As *Roe v. Wade* is substantially limited in the post-*Webster* era, the abortion issue is likely to return to the more obviously "political" arenas of legislatures and elections. In such settings, public opinion has a vital role to play.

The balance of this book is devoted to an examination of public attitudes toward the abortion issue. We begin this inquiry in Chapter 2, with a look at the social and demographic basis of public opinion on the abortion issue.

Notes

1. Details for this account are taken from Christine Spolar and Karlyn Barker, "386 Arrested in D.C. Clinic Blockades," *The Washington Post,* January 22, 1992, p. D1. See also Tom Morganthau, "Target: Wichita," *Newsweek,* August 19, 1991, pp. 18-20.

2. 410 U.S. 113 (1973); 410 U.S. 179 (1973).

3. *Griswold v. Connecticut,* 382 U.S. 527 (1965). See also *Loving v. Virginia,* 388 U.S. (1967); and *Eisenstadt v. Baird,* 405 U.S. 438 (1972).

4. Laurence H. Tribe, *Abortion: The Clash of Absolutes.* (New York: Norton, 1989), pp. 11-16.

5. *Planned Parenthood v. Danforth,* 428 U.S. 52 (1976).

6. *City of Akron v. Akron Center for Reproductive Health, Inc.,* 462 U.S. 416 (1973).

7. *Thornburgh v. American College of Obstetricians and Gynecologists,* 476 U.S. 747 (1986).

8. *Maher v. Roe,* 432 U.S. 464 (1977); *Harris v. McRae,* 448 U.S. 297 (1980).

9. *Webster v. Reproductive Health Services,* 492 U.S. 490 (1989).

10. *Webster;* see also Tribe, *Abortion,* pp. 21-26. The Court did not rule on the preamble of the Missouri bill.

11. See, for example, Louis Hartz, *The Liberal Tradition in America* (New York: Harcourt, Brace and World, 1955); and Donald J. Devine, *The Political Culture of the United States* (Boston: Little, Brown, 1972).

12. Brian Barry, "How Not to Defend Liberal Institutions." *British Journal of Political Science* 20 (1990) pp.1-14. See also John Stuart Mill, *On Liberty* (New York: Bobbs-Merrill, 1956).

13. See, for example, Kenneth D. Wald, *Religion and Politics in the United States* (New York: St Martin's, 1991).

14. John Kenneth White, *The New Politics of Old Values* (Hanover, N. H.: University Press of New England, 1988), pp. 24, 110-111.

15. See Robert H. Bork, *The Tempting of America: The Political Seduction of the Law* (New York: Simon and Schuster, 1990).

16. Kristin Luker, *Abortion and the Politics of Motherhood* (Berkeley: University of California Press, 1984), p. 11.

17. See John T. Noonan, Jr., "An Almost Absolute Value in History," in John T. Noonan, Jr., ed., *The Morality of Abortion: Legal and Historical Perspectives* (Cambridge: Harvard University Press, 1970) pp. 1-59.

18. See, for example, Luker, *Abortion and the Politics of Motherhood*, pp. 3-39; James C. Mohr, *Abortion in America: The Origins of National Policy, 1800-1900* (New York: Oxford University Press, 1978); Tribe, *Abortion*, pp. 27-51.

19. Mohr, *Abortion in America*, p. 43.

20. Luker, *Abortion and the Politics of Motherhood*, p. 19.

21. Mohr, *Abortion in America*, pp. 53-54.

22. Luker, *Abortion and the Politics of Motherhood*, p. 3. Following Luker, we will refer to the potential life of the unborn as an "embryo" throughout its development, despite the fact that the term embryo technically applies only to the first eight weeks of pregnancy. We do this because the term "embryo," unlike "fetus" or "baby," has not become a symbol for either side of the abortion controversy. Thus, we sacrifice a certain degree of scientific precision for the sake of political neutrality.

23. Noonan, "An Almost Absolute Value in History," p. 5.

24. Luker, *Abortion and the Politics of Motherhood*, p. 4.

25. Luker, *Abortion and the Politics of Motherhood*, pp. 12-13; Noonan, "An Almost Absolute Value in History," pp. 34-35; John Connery, *Abortion: The Development of the Roman Catholic Perspective* (Chicago: Loyola University Press, 1977), pp. 112-124.

26. Noonan, "An Almost Absolute Value In History," p. 45.

27. Luker, *Abortion and the Politics of Motherhood*, pp. 14-16; Mohr, *Abortion in America*, pp. 3-6. 121; Rosalind Pollack Petchesky, *Abortion and Woman's Choice* (Boston: Northeastern University Press, 1990), pp. 30, 53.

28. Mohr, *Abortion in America*, p. 3.

29. Roger Simon, *Road Show: In America, Anyone Can Become President, It's One of the Risks We Take* (New York: Farrar Strauss Giroux, 1990), p. 140, 145-146.

30. Luker, *Abortion and the Politics of Motherhood*.

31. Bruno Bettelheim, *The Uses of Enchantment* (New York: Knopf, 1976); Carol Gilligan, *In a Different Voice* (Cambridge: Harvard University Press, 1982).

32. Ted G. Jelen, "Respect for Life, Sexual Morality, and Opposition to Abortion," *Review of Religious Research* 25 (1984) pp. 220-231; and "Changes in the Attitudinal Correlates of Opposition to Abortion," *Journal for the Scientific Study of Religion* 27 (1988), pp. 211-228.

33. Petchesky, *Abortion and Woman's Choice*, pp. 25-66.

34. Mohr, *Abortion in America*, pp. 21-23.

35. Mohr, *Abortion in America*, pp. 27-29.

36. Luker, *Abortion and the Politics of Motherhood*, p. 7.

37. Luker, *Abortion and the Politics of Motherhood*, pp. 27-39; Mohr, *Abortion in America*; Petchesky, *Abortion and Woman's Choice*, pp. 78-84; Marian Faux, *Roe v. Wade* (New York: Macmillan, 1988).

38. See Luker, *Abortion and the Politics of Motherhood*, pp. 27-39; and Petchesky, *Abortion and Woman's Right*, pp. 78-84.

39. Robert Dahl, *A Preface to Democratic Theory* (Chicago: University of Chicago Press, 1956), pp. 92-97.

40. *Newsweek* (May 24, 1982), pp. 24-26.

41. Amy Fried, "Abortion Politics as Symbolic Politics: An Investigation into Belief Systems," *Social Science Quarterly* 69 (1988), pp. 137-154; Luker, *Abortion and the Politics of Motherhood*; Pamela Johnston Conover and Virginia Gray, *Feminism and the New Right: Conflict Over the American Family* (New York: Praeger, 1983).

42. Jacqueline Scott and Howard Schuman, "Attitudes Strength and Social Action in the Abortion Dispute." *American Sociological Review* 53 (1988):785-793.

43. Everett Carl Ladd, "Abortion: The Nation Responds." *The Ladd Report #8*. (New York: W.W. Norton, 1990).

44. Kent Greenawalt, *Religious Convictions and Political Choice* (New York: Oxford University Press, 1988).

45. See Ladd, "Abortion: The Nation Responds," and Tribe, *Abortion: The Clash of Absolutes*, pp. 235-236.

46. Celeste Michelle Condit, *Decoding Abortion Rhetoric* (Urbana: University of Illinois Press, 1989).

47. See Ladd, "Abortion: The Nation Responds." See also Philip E. Converse and Gregory Markus, "'Plus ca Change...' The New CPS Election Study Panel," *American Political Science Review* 73 (1979), pp. 32-49.

48. The literature on the lack of sophistication of the mass public is huge. For a seminal source, see Philip E. Converse, "The Nature of Belief Systems in Mass Publics," in David Apter, ed., *Ideology and Discontent* (New York: The Free Press, 1964), pp. 206-261. For an excellent review and summary of this literature, see Herbert Asher, *Presidential Elections and American Politics* (Belmont, Calif.: Brooks-Cole, 1991).

49. For a general account of this process, see David Adamany, "The Supreme Court's Role in Critical Elections," in Bruce A. Campbell and Richard J. Trilling, eds., *Realignment in American Politics: Toward a Theory* (Austin: University of Texas Press, 1980), pp. 229-259.

50. See Faux, *Roe v. Wade*, pp. 102-123; Luker, *Abortion and the Politics of Motherhood*, pp. 66-125.

51. Tatalovich and Daynes, *The Politics of Abortion: A Study of Community Conflict in Public Policymaking* (New York: Praeger, 1981), pp. 61-81.

52. See, for example, Lawrence M. Friedman, "The Conflict Over Constitutional Legitimacy," in Gilbert Y. Steiner, ed., *The Abortion Dispute and the American System* (Washington, D.C.: Brookings), pp. 13-29.

53. Charles Y. Franklin and Liane Kosaki, "Republican Schoolmaster: The U.S. Supreme Court, Public Opinion, and Abortion," *American Political Science Review* 83 (1989), pp. 751-771.

54. Luker, *Abortion and the Politics of Motherhood*, p. 74.

55. *Ms*, June 1989, p. 67.

56. The analogy of a "slippery slope" is most frequently used in the area of Constitutional law relating to free expression. The metaphor is meant to suggest that once "a little regulation" is admitted in a particular area, there is no means by which unreasonable or oppressive restrictions can be avoided.

57. See Condit, *Decoding Abortion Rhetoric*.

58. *Dred Scott v. Sanford* 19 Howard 393 (1857).

59. John E. Jackson and Maris A. Vinovskis, "Public Opinion, Elections, and the 'Single-Issue' Issue," in Gilbert Y. Steiner, ed., *The Abortion Dispute and the American System* (Washington, D.C.:Brookings, 1983), pp. 64-81.

60. Debra L. Dodson and Lauren D. Burnbauer, with Katherine Kleeman, *Election 1989: The Abortion Issue in New Jersey and Virginia* (New Brunswick: Eagleton Institute of Politics, 1990).

61. Tribe, *Abortion: The Clash of Absolutes*, p. 195.

62. Richard M. Nixon, *In the Arena* (New York: Simon and Schuster, 1990), p. 288.

63. See "The Mommy Track," *Business Week*, March 20, 1989, pp. 126-134; "Is the Mommy Track a Blessing--Or a Betrayal?" *Business Week*, May 15, 1989, pp. 98-99; and "Advocating a 'Mommy Track,'" *Newsweek*, March 13, 1989, p. 45.

64. Luker, *Abortion and the Politics of Motherhood*, pp. 117-118, 175-186.

65. Luker, *Abortion and the Politics of Motherhood*, p. 176.

66. Many pro-life activists oppose the IUD and several types of birth-control pills on the grounds that they prevent the implantation of fertilized ovum, which they believe constitute human life.

67. Melvin Zelnik, John F. Kantner, and Kathleen Ford, *Sex and Pregnancy in Adolescence* (Beverly Hills, Calif.: Sage Publications, 1981). See also Frank Furstenberg, Richard Lincoln, and Jane Meuken, eds., *Teenage Sexuality, Pregnancy, and Childbearing* (Philadelphia: University of Pennsylvania Press, 1981); and James Trussell and Barbara Vaughn, "Aggregate and Lifetime Contraceptive Failure in the United States," *Family Planning Perspectives* 21 (1989), pp. 224-226.

68. C. F. Westoff, "Contraceptive Paths Toward Reduction of Unintended Pregnancy and Abortion," *Family Planning Perspectives* 20 (1988), p. 4. Although half of abortion patients had been contracepting when they became pregnant, this does not mean that they had been using their preferred method correctly or consistently.

69. There are no real long-term studies of contraceptive failure, so it is unclear how these calculations fit actual data. It may be, however, that annual risks of pregnancy decline over time, as women and their partners become less fertile. If this is true, these estimates may overstate the odds of accidental pregnancy. Even with these assumptions, however, the risk of accidental pregnancy is large. John Ross, "Contraception: Short-term vs. Long-term Failure Rates," *Family Planning Perspectives* 21 (1989), pp. 275-277, shows that the actual risk of failure for regular pill users over ten years is between 27 percent and 47 percent, with the best single estimate 38 percent. Those who regularly contracept with condoms face an approximately 68 percent chance of an unplanned pregnancy over 10 years.

70. See Luker, *Abortion and the Politics of Motherhood*, pp. 128-133. For a contrary view of abortion activists, see Robert J. Spitzer, *The Right to Life Movement and Third Party Politics in America* (Westport, Conn.: Greenwood, 1987).

71. Tribe, *Abortion: The Clash of Absolutes*, pp. 117-180.

2

The Social Bases
of Abortion Attitudes

Most of this book will offer explanations for differences in abortion attitudes in the mass public. In this chapter, we describe social group differences in abortion attitudes. How do members of various social groups differ in their attitudes toward abortion? Do young people have different attitudes than their parents and grandparents? Do men think differently than do women? Do blacks and whites have different attitudes? Do the rich and poor think differently, or southerners and those who live in the northeast? What are the group bases of abortion attitudes?

Social characteristics are often useful predictors of attitudes. Why might members of various social groups hold different political attitudes? First, members of social groups have different objective interests. Impoverished Americans are more likely to favor spending on social programs, at least in part because they are more likely to benefit from them. Wealthy Americans are more likely to favor cuts in the capital gains tax rate because such an action would decrease their tax bill, but it would have little direct effect on the tax payments of the working poor. Parents of small children favor more spending for schools because their children will benefit, whereas retired Americans are less supportive of spending on education because they will not benefit directly.

Of course, self-interest is not the only explanation for social group differences. Various social groups have different life experiences and may be socialized into different roles in society. Affluent blacks may be more supportive of government spending on social programs than affluent whites because they encounter friends and relatives who benefit from these programs. Men may be less willing than women to support programs for the disadvantaged because they are less likely to be encouraged to show sympathy toward others. Those with a college education have experienced an entirely different type of socialization than those who did not finish high school. This socialization can lead those with college degrees to be more tolerant of those with whom they disagree and to be more supportive of gender and racial equality.

Of course, many social group (or demographic) differences in attitudes are attributable to other factors. For example, southerners are more likely to hold orthodox religious beliefs, and older citizens are more likely to approve of distinct and unequal sex roles. When we find that southerners are less supportive of legal abortion than northerners, therefore, this may be due to greater religiosity among southerners. In the next two chapters we will focus on the attitudinal and religious basis of these group differences. Similarly, when we find that the oldest citizens are less supportive of legal abortion than those who grew up during or after the 1960s, this may be due to the traditional views of the oldest Americans on the role of women in families. In this chapter, we will first present an overview of abortion attitudes in America, then discuss social group differences in support for and opposition to legal abortion.

Attitudes Toward Legal Abortion: Methods of Analysis

In almost every year since 1972, the National Opinion Research Center (NORC) at the University of Chicago has conducted a national survey of social and political attitudes. This General Social Survey (GSS)[1] has included a battery of six questions measuring support for legal abortion. These items ask respondents whether they believe that it should be possible for a pregnant woman to obtain a legal abortion:

--if there is a strong chance of serious defect in the baby
--if she is married and does not want more children
--if the woman's own health is seriously endangered by the pregnancy

--if the family has a very low income and cannot afford any more children

--if she became pregnant as a result of rape

--if she is not married and does not want to marry the man

These six items can be used to measure attitudes toward legal abortion. By counting the number of circumstances under which each respondent supports legal abortion, we have created a scale that runs from 0 (when the respondent approves of abortion under no circumstances) to 6 (when he or she approves of abortion in all six circumstances).

Because these questions have been asked for eighteen years, we were able to examine changes in attitudes toward abortion. Throughout this book, we generally concentrate our analysis on recent attitudes (the GSS surveys from 1987 through 1991). When attitudes or relationships have changed over time, however, we report and try to explain those changes. These GSS data constitute the core of our analysis, but we use other survey data when they are needed to more fully describe abortion attitudes.

Statistical analysis reveals that the public sees these six questions as measuring two related but distinct attitudes: support for abortion in circumstances of physical trauma (where the mother's health is in danger, where the fetus is seriously defective, or where the pregnancy results from rape) and support for abortion in social, more "elective" circumstances (poverty, when an unmarried woman does not want to marry the father, or when a married couple wants no more children). In this book we refer to these sets of circumstances as *traumatic abortion* and *elective abortion*.[2]

Because each set of circumstances contains three separate questions, the scales we have created to measure these attitudes range from 0 (when the respondent supports abortion in none of the circumstances) to 3 (when the respondent favors abortion in all three circumstances). For most purposes, we simply report relationships involving the combined abortion scale. We use the traumatic/elective distinction when the pattern of relationships differs for the two components of abortion attitudes.

The distinction between traumatic and elective circumstances is an important one to public attitudes, but most abortions in the United States are done for elective reasons. A very recent survey of abortion

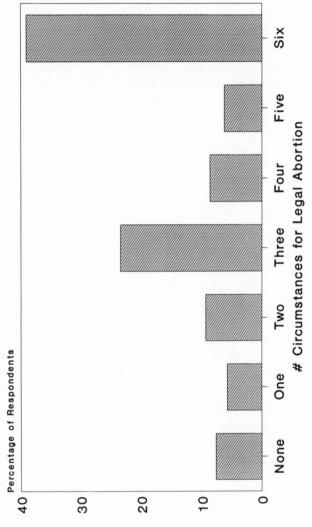

Figure 2.1
Respondents Favoring Abortion in
Zero to Six Circumstances

Source: Compiled from the General Social
Survey, 1987-1991

patients revealed that only seven percent listed one of the three traumatic reasons as their primary reason for getting an abortion. Most abortion patients indicated financial problems, the desire to avoid raising a child outside of marriage, or their belief that they were not yet mature enough to raise a child as their primary reason for obtaining an abortion.[3]

In this book, we divide Americans into three groups: pro-life respondents who oppose abortion in all six circumstances, pro-choice citizens who favor legal abortion in each circumstance, and situationalists who think abortion should be legal in some but not all circumstances. We make more precise distinctions among the situationalists in Chapter 5.

Abortion Attitudes: An Overview

There is a general societal consensus that abortion should be legal in each of the traumatic circumstances. Seventy-six percent of those surveyed from 1987 through 1991 supported abortion under all three circumstances in our trauma scale--mother's health, fetal defect, and rape, with only 7 percent opposing abortion in all three circumstances. In contrast, the public is deeply divided on abortion in elective circumstances. Nearly half (47 percent) of all respondents between 1987 and 1991 opposed abortion in all three social circumstances (poverty, unmarried woman, or a couple who wants no more children), while more than a third (37 percent) support legal abortion under all three conditions.

In all of the surveys between 1972 and 1991, more Americans have favored unlimited access to abortion than have favored banning abortions under all circumstances. In the period 1987 to 1991, only 8 percent of respondents opposed abortion in all six circumstances, but 39 percent favored abortion in all six instances. Figure 2.1 shows the distribution of attitudes on support for legal abortion, and Figure 2.2 shows attitudes on traumatic and elective abortion. Although Figure 2.1 shows that few Americans favor an outright ban on abortion, Figure 2.2 shows that Americans are deeply divided on allowing abortion for social reasons.

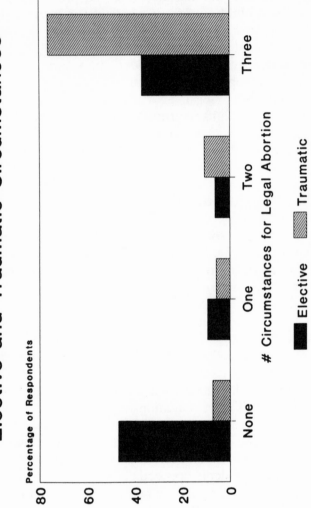

Figure 2.2
Respondents Favoring Abortion in
Elective and Traumatic Circumstances

Percentage of Respondents

None   One   Two   Three

Circumstances for Legal Abortion

■ Elective   ▨ Traumatic

Source: Compiled from the General Social
Survey 1987-1991

Activists on both sides of the abortion debate frequently assert that the majority of Americans support their position. Pro-choice activists point out (correctly) that the public does not want a ban on abortion. Pro-life activists note (also correctly) that the public disapproves of abortion on demand. In fact, the majority of Americans hold positions that do not fall neatly in either camp--they support legal abortions in some but not all circumstances.

The narrow majority of Americans in every survey favored limited legal access to abortion. Between 1987 and 1991, 53 percent favored some limitations on access to abortion without an outright ban. A majority of those who favored limited access to abortion favored allowing it in all three of the traumatic circumstances, but in none of the three elective circumstances. Thus, neither the pro-life nor pro-choice movement has the support of an absolute majority of Americans.[4]

Figure 2.3 shows public attitudes toward legal abortion since 1972. The lines are remarkably flat, suggesting that abortion attitudes are generally stable in the aggregate.[5] For eighteen years, the "average" position on abortion has hovered near allowing abortion in four of the six possible circumstances, allowing abortions in between two and three traumatic circumstances, approving of abortion in between one and two elective circumstances.

Figure 2.4 shows support for legal abortion since 1972 plotted on a narrower range that emphasizes the small changes in attitudes over time. A closer look reveals that support increased in 1973 after the *Roe v. Wade* decision and remained relatively high until the early 1980s, when support declined. This decline was greatest in support for elective abortion. After 1989, support for legal abortion increased again to levels that nearly matched those of the 1970s.

It may be that the decline in support for legal abortion in the early 1980s was influenced by the strong pro-life position of President Ronald Reagan. During this period, the percentage of those taking a pro-life position did not increase nor did the percentage of pro-choice citizens markedly decrease; instead those Americans who supported abortion in some but not all circumstances reduced the number of circumstances under which they favored legal abortion.

38

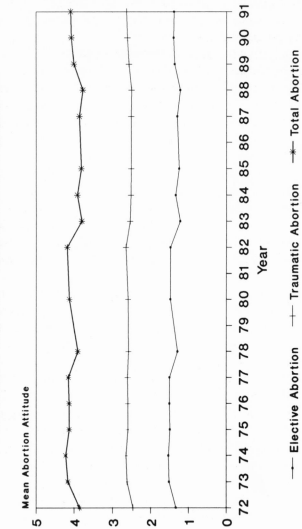

Figure 2.3
Mean Level of Support for Legal
Abortion under Various Conditions

Mean Abortion Attitude

Year

72 73 74 75 76 77 78 79 80 81 82 83 84 85 86 87 88 89 90 91

Elective Abortion   Traumatic Abortion   Total Abortion

Source: Compiled from the General Social
Survey 1972-1991

An explanation for the recent increase in support is less obvious. Data from *CBS News/New York Times* public opinion polls from 1985 through 1989 reveal that support began to gradually build in mid-1987 but jumped sharply between July 1988 and January 1989. This change occurred *before* the *Webster* decision, so that decision could not have led to attitude change.

Some analysts have argued that public support for legal abortion increased in *anticipation* of a Supreme Court ruling of greater limits on legal abortion.[6] We think this unlikely. It is true that with each new conservative Court nomination (especially Judge Robert Bork), the uncertain future of *Roe* was prominently discussed in the media. Yet the public did not pay close attention to the policy implications of Supreme Court confirmation debates.

If the increased support for legal abortion in 1989 was due to the anticipation that *Webster* would return the abortion issue to state legislatures, attitude change should be larger among those who would be most likely to have heard of the pending case. In fact, attitude change was slightly lower among the best educated respondents and among those who regularly read a newspaper. Moreover, data from a national opinion poll by *CBS News/New York Times* in autumn 1989 revealed that more than 70 percent of the public were not aware of the *Webster* decision soon after the opinion was handed down. We interpret these data to suggest that the public did not increase its support for legal abortion in anticipation of future Court decisions that would restrict *Roe*, but there is insufficient survey data to test this hypothesis fully. It is possible, however, that the increasing support for legal abortion since 1989 is in part a response to continued media attention to the changing membership of the U.S. Supreme Court and to the likely overruling of *Roe*, and to visible organized activity by pro-choice groups. If *Roe* is overturned soon, this would suggest further increases in the numbers of pro-choice citizens.

We have seen that the public is generally supportive of legal abortion for circumstances that involve physical trauma, but deeply divided over circumstances that are more social in origin. In 1990, ABC News surveyed the general public to determine their willingness to personally undergo an abortion under a series of different circumstances. The questionnaire listed seven distinct circumstances, ranging from a painful disease that would cause the child's death by

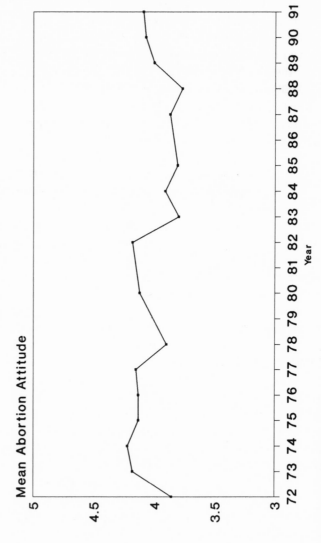

Figure 2.4
Mean Support for Legal Abortion:
A Closer Look

Mean Abortion Attitude

Year

Source:Compiled from the General
Social Survey 1972-1991

age 4 (63 percent said they would abort) to abortion for sex selection (3 percent indicated that they would abort). In all, 70 percent of the public indicated their willingness to abort under at least one circumstance, and 30 percent indicated willingness to abort in three or more different situations.

Of course, these questions were hypothetical. Faced with a concrete decision, probably many of those who indicated a willingness to abort would hesitate, and many who indicated that they would not abort would seriously consider the alternative. What these data do show is that most Americans not only want to keep abortion legal under situations of physical trauma, but also would consider personally aborting under difficult circumstances.

State Differences in Abortion Attitudes

If the Supreme Court overturns *Roe*, abortion regulation will return to state governments. By mid-1991, two states and one territory (Louisiana, Utah, and Guam) had passed stringent restrictions on abortion, and other states had passed legislation calling for parental notification or consent and/or waiting periods. Some states did not limit access to abortion. Although Governor Robert Martinez of Florida called a special session of the legislature to limit abortion, the legislature refused to comply. Moreover, the state of Maryland (which is heavily Roman Catholic) recently legislated a guarantee of abortion rights, and in late 1991 the Republican governor of Massachusetts, William Weld, introduced a similar legislative package.

If abortion is to be decided at the state level, interstate differences in abortion attitudes become important. The 1989 *CBS News/New York Times* national survey discussed above was administered along with separate surveys in Florida, California, Illinois, Pennsylvania, Texas, and Ohio. Figure 2.5 shows the percentage of respondents in each state who took consistently pro-choice or pro-life positions. There are important state differences, with more than 45 percent of residents of California and Florida consistently supporting legal abortion but only 35 percent of those in Ohio.

In Table 2.1 we show the percentage of respondents in each state who favor legal abortion under each circumstance. It is interesting that in all six states (and in the national survey), the public generally

42

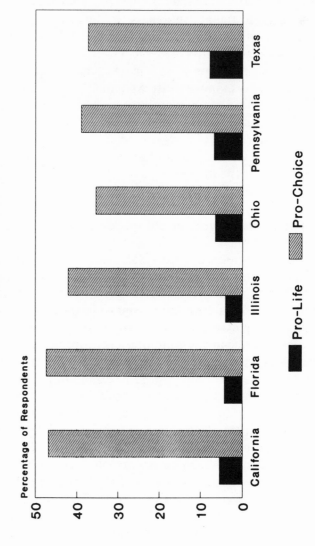

Figure 2.5
Pro-Life and Pro-Choice Respondents
in Selected States

Source: Compiled from the 1989 CBS News/
New York Times Surveys

TABLE 2.1 Respondents Supporting Legal Abortion in
Various Circumstances, 1989, by State (in percent)

	CA	FL	IL	OH	PA	TX
Mother's health	94	94	94	92	92	92
Rape	86	88	86	86	85	84
Fetal defect	79	79	75	73	75	72
Poverty	60	60	57	49	52	47
High school student	56	56	52	46	50	46
Interrupt career	46	47	42	37	37	35

Source: CBS News/New York Times survey, 1989.

orders these seven items in the same way. Support is highest for abortions when the mother's health is in danger and lowest for a professional woman who does not want to interrupt her career. There are few state differences in support for abortion when the mother's health is in danger, and there is wide support for legal abortion for all three traumatic circumstances. State differences are far larger on abortion for social reasons. In California, Florida, and Illinois, there are narrow majorities favoring legal abortion in all circumstances except for professional women who would abort to maintain their careers. In Texas, in contrast, majorities oppose legal abortion for all four social reasons, including poverty and unmarried women.

The *CBS News/New York Times* survey did not include any states that passed stringent abortion restrictions in 1989 or 1990.[7] A University of New Orleans survey in 1990 revealed that pro-life and pro-choice forces constituted an identical 21 percent of the Louisiana sample, with 53 percent favoring some restrictions. There had been a slight increase in support for legal abortion since a similar poll in 1988, but these data show that citizens of Louisiana are much less supportive of legal abortion than citizens in the United States in general or in the six states in the *CBS News/New York Times* survey.

Group Differences in Abortion Attitudes

In the rest of this chapter, we examine demographic, or social group, differences in attitudes toward legal abortion. Where we observe differences between social groups, we attempt to explain them. Often this explanation consists of a discussion of the ways that other demographic characteristics or attitudes influence the attitudes of the social groups in question. When we say that, for example, blacks are less supportive of legal abortion than whites because they have lower levels of education, are more likely to hold orthodox religious beliefs, and are more likely to have large families, we suggest that there is nothing inherent in race that influences support for abortion--rather, African-Americans are less supportive because of their other social characteristics and attitudes. This means that if we compare (for example) African-American and white evangelical Christians with high school degrees and five children, we will find no significant differences in abortion attitudes.

In the next two chapters, we more fully examine two other sources of abortion attitudes. In Chapter 3, we examine the effects of attitudes on related issues such as feminism, euthanasia, and ideal family size, while Chapter 4 deals with the effects of religion. Many of the demographic differences in this chapter are ultimately explainable by differences in these related attitudes and behaviors.

Gender and Racial Differences

Spokespersons for both pro-life and pro-choice groups often claim that women should be especially supportive of their cause. Some pro-life groups claim that the special role of women in procreation makes them less likely than men to support legal abortion and that this gender difference should be largest among those with young children. Some pro-choice spokespersons argue that because women bear a disproportionate share of the costs of unwanted pregnancies, they should be more supportive of legal abortion.

In fact, there is practically no relationship between gender and attitudes toward legal abortion. Women are slightly less supportive of legal abortion than men, but the differences are very small. The gender gap is somewhat larger among older Americans, but only among those citizens over 65 are these differences large enough to

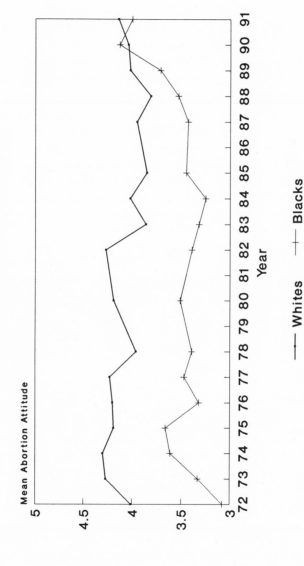

Figure 2.6

Mean on Legal Abortion Scale for Blacks
and Whites 1972–1991

Source: Compiled from the General Social
Survey 1972–1991

be confident that women are significantly less supportive of legal abortion. Men are significantly more supportive of legal abortion than homemakers, but among men and women who work outside the home there is no difference in degree of support for legal abortion. Interestingly, among those respondents with small children, the gender gap entirely disappears.

Racial differences do exist, however. For all but one of the surveys between 1972 and 1991, whites were more supportive of legal abortion than African-Americans. Why do these racial differences occur? Differences between whites and blacks have been the subject of a good deal of academic study.[8] African-American women are twice as likely to have abortions as are white women, although this is primarily because they are more likely to become pregnant.[9] A similar percentage of white and black pregnancies end in abortion. Nonetheless, abortions are more common among African-Americans, yet blacks are less supportive of legal abortion. Between 1987 and 1991, 40 percent of whites supported abortion under all circumstances, compared with only 30 percent of blacks. Racial differences are largest among the oldest Americans, and during much of the 1980s these differences were larger among those who lived in the South.[10]

Why are blacks more likely than whites to oppose abortion? Several factors come into play. First, African-Americans are more likely than whites to have been raised in rural areas or in the South, and to have lower levels of education. These factors all influence abortion attitudes, as we will see below. Second, African-Americans are much more likely to oppose euthanasia (mercy killing), which is shown in Chapter 3 to be a strong predictor of abortion attitudes. Finally, blacks are more likely to hold orthodox religious beliefs, to attend doctrinally conservative churches, to attend church regularly, and to pray frequently. In Chapter 4, we will see that religious attitudes and behaviors are the strongest predictors of abortion attitudes.

Once we have held constant demographic factors, attitudes toward sexual morality, and religious affiliations and behaviors, racial differences in abortion attitudes disappear. This means that blacks are less supportive of legal abortion than whites because of their social characteristics, attitudes toward sexual morality, and religion. Indeed, after we control for attitudes and religion, African-Americans are significantly *more* supportive of legal abortion than whites.

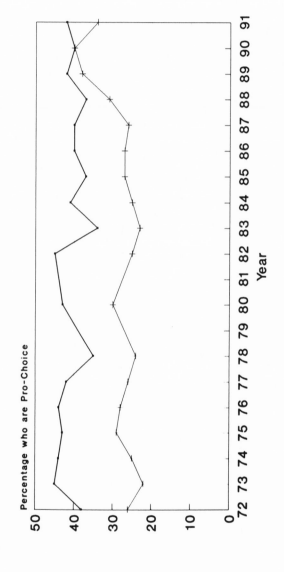

Figure 2.7
Pro-Choice Respondents by Race
1972-1991

Percentage who are Pro-Choice

Year

——— Whites   —+— Blacks

Source: Compiled from the General Social
Survey 1972-1991

Over the past several years, racial differences in abortion attitudes have declined. Figures 2.6 and 2.7 show that between 1985 and 1991, the racial gap in abortion attitudes narrowed, and in the 1990 survey, blacks were actually *more* supportive of legal abortion than whites.[11] Indeed, the increase in support for legal abortion observed above in 1989 and 1990 was largely confined to the African-American community. The African-American respondents to the GSS surveys in 1989, 1990, and 1991 were more supportive of legal abortion than were black respondents in any previous years.

Several factors combined to change black attitudes on legal abortion during this period. First, as the oldest generation of African-Americans has died off, it has been replaced by a younger generation that is far more supportive of legal abortion. This oldest generation of blacks was strongly opposed to legal abortion, but from 1989 to 1991 there were fewer of this generation in the population. In addition, the average education level of blacks has climbed steadily during this period, and education is strongly associated with support for legal abortion. Finally, there has been a decline in the religiosity and religious orthodoxy of blacks (especially outside of the South) during this period, and a subsequent change in certain social issue attitudes.

Education and Social Class Differences

Of all the social characteristics that help us understand abortion attitudes, education is the strongest predictor. Opposition to legal abortion is highest among those who have dropped out of high school and lowest among college graduates. The effects of education are generally strong and exist across the entire range of educational attainment, with each increasing year of education leading to more liberal beliefs about abortion. Between 1987 and 1991, only 21 percent of those who dropped out of school before completing high school supported abortion in all circumstances, but nearly two-thirds of those who had attended graduate school supported unlimited access to abortion. The strength of this relationship is shown graphically in Figure 2.8.

Why is education associated with liberal attitudes on abortion? In part, education is associated with other attitudes and characteristics

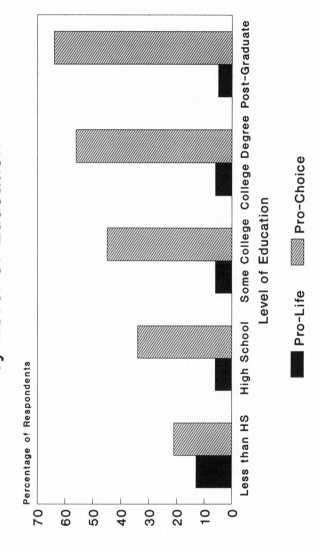

Figure 2.8
Pro-Life and Pro-Choice Attitudes
by Level of Education

Source: Compiled from the General Social
Survey 1987-1991

that predict abortion attitudes. College-educated citizens are more tolerant of sexual behavior outside of marriage and are more likely to support gender equality. They are more likely to favor small families and to value their control over the size and timing of their families. They are also less likely to attend church regularly, or to hold orthodox religious beliefs. Once controls for these religious characteristics and social attitudes are introduced, the effects of education are reduced. Yet even after controls for all types of social characteristics, attitudes, and religious beliefs, education remains a strong predictor of liberal attitudes on abortion.

One reason for the relationship between education and abortion attitudes may lie in the other values and attitudes that education fosters: Education is a strong predictor of tolerance of unpopular opinions, support for civil rights for racial and behavioral minorities, and the rights guaranteed (and implied) in the Bill of Rights. Increases in formal schooling appear to lead to exposure to alternative beliefs and values and to inculcate a general value of respect for such opposing viewpoints. Education may therefore lead citizens to view issues in terms of individual liberties, which is the framework that pro-choice activists use for their arguments.

We also know, however, that those who do go on to college already hold somewhat different attitudes even before their exposure to higher education. M. Kent Jennings and Richard G. Niemi interviewed a set of high school students in 1965, then reinterviewed them in 1973.[12] They found that those who would later go on to college showed higher levels of civic tolerance while they were high-school seniors than those who terminated their education with high school and that this gap widened by 1973, presumably as a result of the continued education of the college students. In other words, some of the relationship between college education and support for legal abortion is possibly due to self-selection--pro-choice high school students may be more likely to continue their education in college than their pro-life counterparts. However, an important part of the relationship between high levels of education and liberal attitudes toward legal abortion is clearly due to the socializing experiences of education.

Other characteristics of socioeconomic status also predict support for legal abortion. Those citizens in high-prestige jobs and who have high family incomes are also more supportive of legal abortion.

TABLE 2.2 Demographic Variables and Abortion Attitudes,
1987-1991 (in percent)

	Pro-life	Situation-alist	Pro-choice	Mean Value
Men	41	53	6	4.08
Women	37	54	9	3.84
Housewives	29	60	11	3.52
Whites	40	52	8	3.99
Blacks	33	58	9	3.71
High school dropout	21	66	13	3.19
High school grad.	34	60	6	3.85
Some college	45	49	6	4.20
College degree	56	38	6	4.45
Post-graduate	63	32	5	4.71
Raised--Live:				
South--South	28	63	9	3.54
South--North	36	52	12	3.66
North--South	47	45	8	4.22
North--North	43	50	7	4.10
Raised:				
On farm or in country	28	61	11	3.47
Small or medium city	39	54	7	3.95
Suburbs or big city	51	44	5	4.45

Final colum is the mean value (on six-point legal abortion scale) for each group.

Source: General Social Survey.

These patterns are partly but not entirely attributable to the relationship between education and social class. High family income often characterizes two-career couples, who generally want to control their fertility, and this accounts for part of the relationship between income and abortion attitudes. For high-income, two-career families, the opportunity costs of an unexpected pregnancy may be very high. Even after controls for education and two-income couples, however, occupation and income are weak but significant predictors of support for legal abortion.

Geographic Differences

Where people live influences their attitudes toward legal abortion. More importantly, where they were raised plays an even greater role. Those Americans raised in the South are less supportive of legal abortion than those raised elsewhere, regardless of where they currently live. Those raised in rural areas are more likely to oppose legal abortion than those raised in a city, regardless of where they currently live. The data in Table 2.2 show the differences in attitudes.

In part, the explanation for these geographic patterns lies with other demographic variables. Southerners and those who live in rural regions have lower levels of education than other Americans, and blacks disproportionately live in the rural South. Even more important are the religious characteristics and social attitudes that are fostered in rural regions and in the South. Rural residents and those in the South are more likely to hold orthodox religious views and be highly involved in their religion, and it appears that those raised in these areas maintain at least some of their religious characteristics when they move. Moreover, southerners and rural residents are less likely to support gender equality and are more likely to be conservative on questions of sexual morality and other issues.

Generational Differences

Abortion is a topic that affects the young somewhat differently than the old. Young men and women are more likely to confront unwanted pregnancies; for people over 50, abortion is unlikely to affect their lives directly. It seems likely, then, that abortion attitudes will differ across age groups. Two different processes could produce differences on abortion attitudes among different age groups. First, attitudes can change over the life cycle. Second, different generations of citizens may hold different sets of beliefs. It is possible that abortion attitudes could change during the life cycle. Life-cycle changes may occur as people age and their lifestyle changes.

TABLE 2.3 Support for Legal Abortion by Cohort, 1987-1991 (in percent)

	Depression	WWII	Mystique	1960s	Women's Lib	Reagan
WHITES ONLY:						
Trauma:						
None	12	10	9	7	5	4
All	74	77	75	79	79	81
Elective:						
None	56	51	49	44	42	44
All	29	30	37	43	46	37
N	389	637	880	814	1045	688
Health of mother	83	88	88	91	93	94
Rape	80	83	81	83	85	89
Fetal defect	78	81	80	83	83	85
Poverty	40	42	44	50	53	49
Single mother	35	40	42	49	50	43
No more children	34	38	42	49	50	44

(continues)

TABLE 2.3 (continued)

	Depression	WWII	Mystique	1960s	Women's Lib.	Reagan
BLACKS ONLY:						
Trauma:						
None	20	16	12	9	5	3
All	41	56	65	75	76	76
Elective:						
None	65	57	56	51	42	43
All	18	24	24	39	34	34
N	47	96	164	138	248	158
Health of mother	82	82	86	90	93	90
Rape	55	65	75	83	83	86
Fetal defect	54	63	69	78	82	80
Poverty	33	35	38	45	47	51
Single mother	22	30	30	42	40	39
No more children	22	34	34	44	49	46

Source: General Social Survey.

At different ages, people have different circumstances and different needs, and these may lead to different attitudes as well. This life-cycle pattern could be linear--as people get older, they may become more conservative on abortion, or life cycle differences could follow a more complex pattern.

Let us consider one hypothetical example of a life-cycle pattern to abortion attitudes. It could be that young, predominantly single people would generally favor legal abortion, but that those in their late twenties and early thirties, many of whom have young children, might be less supportive. Parents of teenaged children (especially daughters) may be more supportive, since they fear the consequences to their children of unwanted pregnancies, while grandparents of young children might be less supportive. In this hypothetical life-cycle pattern, those who face the highest costs of unplanned pregnancies (either for themselves or their offspring) are the most supportive of a legal abortion option, and those with young children or grandchildren are less supportive.

A second process can produce age-related differences in abortion attitudes: Generational differences may persist throughout the life cycle. Karl Mannheim argues that those who came of age during the same time (called cohorts) and who also shared unique political and social experiences could form a political generation.[13] This generation would remain distinctive in its attitudes and orientations as it passed through the life cycle. Generational effects would occur when a particular cohort retains the historical imprint of the social and historical context in which its members grew up and came of age.

A variety of studies has shown that the political circumstances existing when people reach adulthood may continue to influence them throughout their lives. These generational differences have been found in a number of areas. Those people who reached adulthood during the Great Depression have been generally more financially cautious than those who grew up during the booming 1950s. Some scholars have argued that those who grew up during World War II generally view military force as essential to deter aggression, but those who came of age during the Vietnam War are more skeptical of the use of force.[14]

We can test whether a life-cycle or a generational account of abortion attitudes provides a better explanation by comparing the attitudes of various generations over time. Although our data do not allow us to see if specific people change their attitudes, if each successive generation becomes more conservative when it reaches the age at which most women begin their families or becomes more liberal when its children are in their teens, we will have evidence of one type of life-cycle effect. If each generation remains relatively constant in its attitudes, but is notably different in ways that reflect the circumstances that existed when its members became adults, we will have evidence of generational effects.

In order to examine possible generational differences, we must identify cohorts (people who turned age eighteen during a specified time period) who have had distinctly different experiences. We have posited six possible generations that might differ on abortion attitudes. Five of our generations are adapted from the work of Virginia Sapiro.[15] Sapiro defined seven coming-of-age cohorts by historical events affecting women. We define the cohorts according to when respondents reached age eighteen, and these parallel many of Sapiro's cohorts, including those who came of age during or before the Great Depression (prior to or during 1933), those who came of age before or during World War II (1934-1944), a *Feminine Mystique* cohort from the 1950s (who reached eighteen between 1945 and 1960), a sixties cohort (1961-69), and a women's liberation cohort that came of age during the early years of the women's movement in the 1970s (1970-1979). Finally, we add a Reagan cohort (not included in Sapiro's earlier work) that reached age eighteen after 1979.

Kristin Luker characterizes the period prior to 1960 as the "century of silence," during which there was little organized challenge to the status of abortion as regulated primarily by medical doctors. In the 1960s, however, abortion-reform forces began to push for easier access to abortion. The claim that women had a "right to control their bodies" was made during this period, when advocates of legal abortion had the rhetorical field to themselves. The 1960s was also the decade in which the birth control pill became widely available, ensuring women greater control of their fertility. After the *Roe v. Wade* decision in 1973, however, pro-life forces organized and began to publicize their position widely. Thus, those who came of age during the 1970s experienced both the rise of the women's movement and that of the pro-life movement. Sapiro's women's liberation cohort is also the cohort that was first exposed to the arguments and organizing of pro-life activists.

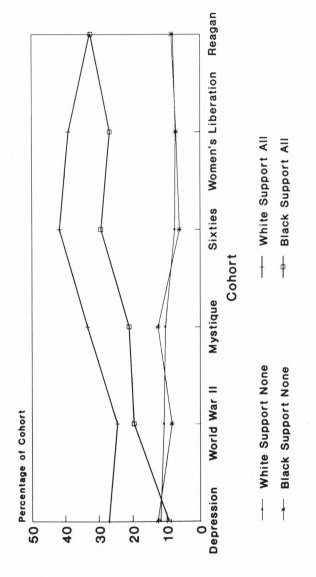

Figure 2.9
Support for Legal Abortion under Six
Circumstances by Cohort

Percentage of Cohort

50
40
30
20
10
0

Depression   World War II   Mystique   Sixties   Women's Liberation   Reagan

Cohort

— White Support None   — White Support All
—*— Black Support None   —□— Black Support All

Source: Compiled from the General Social
Survey 1985-1988

The 1980s saw the increasing politicization of the abortion issue, with the national Republican party officially adopting a pro-life position and most national Democrats publicly endorsing legal abortion. Those who came of age in the 1980s saw a popular conservative president espouse a pro-life position. Thus the 1960s, the women's liberation, and Reagan cohorts were socialized in eras with differing laws regulating abortion and different levels of elite debate on abortion. We expect smaller differences between those cohorts that came of age prior to 1960, for there were no notable changes in legal abortion during this period. Nonetheless, because part of the abortion debate concerns gender roles and these cohorts experienced differences in roles available to women, we do expect some slight cohort differences among these older respondents. In addition, we are unable to predict the direction of the responses of those who came of age during the 1970s. This cohort was exposed to the efforts of the women's movement to build feminist consciousness and also to those of the pro-life forces to regulate abortion access.

Figure 2.9 shows the percentage of whites and blacks in each generation who consistently oppose or support legal abortion. The figure shows that among blacks, support is highest among the youngest citizens, but for whites, support is highest for men and women who came of age during the 1960s and 1970s. This lowered support for legal abortion among the youngest white respondents is not accompanied by an increase in the number who take positions consistently opposing legal abortion. Indeed, the Reagan generation whites are the most supportive of legal abortion under the three traumatic circumstances. Younger whites are not joining the pro-life cause, but they approve abortion in fewer circumstances than those who came of age during the 1960s.

Instead, younger whites are less likely to approve of elective abortion than those who came of age during the 1960s. The data in Table 2.3 show that whites who came of age during the Reagan era are less likely than their somewhat older counterparts to approve of legal abortion when the mother is unmarried or when a married couple wants no more children. In contrast, young blacks are *more* likely than other blacks to approve of abortion in these circumstances.

These generational changes appear to persist through the life cycle. The data in Table 2.4 show that the relative ordering of the different generations has remained nearly constant since 1972. This constancy

TABLE 2.4 Cohort Differences in Abortion Attitudes:
Longitudinal Trends, 1972--1991

	1972-76	1977-80	1981-85	1986-91*
WHITES ONLY:				
Depression	3.99	3.94	3.72	3.57
WWII	4.17	4.18	3.78	3.74
Mystique	4.12	3.97	3.93	3.85
1960s	4.45	4.28	4.19	4.12
Women's liberation	4.30	4.25	4.19	4.24
Reagan			3.79	4.07
BLACKS ONLY:				
Depression	2.53	2.33	2.24	2.73
WWII	2.85	2.86	3.00	3.13
Mystique	3.93	3.73	3.22	3.40
1960s	3.88	4.08	3.99	3.95
Women's liberation	3.78	3.61	3.65	3.99
Reagan			3.61	4.00

Mean values for each cohort on sex-point legal-abortion scale. Higher
scores indicate greater support for legal abortion.
*Data in this column for blacks are for 1987 to 1990.

Source: General Social Survey.

implies that abortion attitudes are generational, and although adults
do change their attitudes, this change is not related to stages of the
life cycle.[16]

As a further test of the life-cycle theory, we compared young women
with children and those who have no children. One version of this
theory would predict that those young women with children would be
less supportive of legal abortion because at that stage of their lives
they are less likely to experience unwanted pregnancies and possibly
make them more likely to believe that the fetus represents human

life.[17] Luker has argues that some housewives were fearful that their status as mothers was devalued by the feminist movement and felt they had a vested interest in preserving the sanctity of motherhood. Restrictive attitudes about abortion were seen as an important component of a "pro-family" ideology.

Predictably, young women with children were less supportive of legal abortion. However, this difference was entirely accounted for by differences in education, occupational status, attitudes, and religion. Young mothers are less supportive of legal abortion than other young women not because their babies make them more likely to believe that an embryo is a human life, but because their religion, education, occupational status, and religion make them both more likely to have children at a young age and less likely to support legal abortion. In contrast, those women who choose to have their children later in life are more likely to value control over their childbearing decisions.

These data suggest that abortion attitudes vary across generations but do not change as individuals move through their life cycle. Why, then, are younger whites less supportive of legal abortion than those who came of age during the 1960s? Several possible explanations exist. First, it is possible that the pro-life movement, which began organizing after the *Roe v. Wade* decision in the early 1970s, has influenced the attitudes of younger whites. The evidence does not support this explanation. First, the youngest whites are actually slightly *less* likely than older whites to take a consistently pro-life position and more likely to support legal abortion under all three traumatic situations. Second, in data from the American National Election Study (ANES) in 1988, the youngest whites were somewhat less favorable toward pro-life activists than older whites.[18] Although this evidence is not conclusive, it seems to us that the explanation of this generational pattern must lie elsewhere.

A second possible explanation is that Ronald Reagan influenced young people (especially young Republicans) by his strong opposition to legal abortion. This explanation fits the racial differences in generational patterns, where the youngest blacks are the most supportive of legal abortion. Young blacks were quite negative toward Reagan, so his persuasive powers are more likely to be effective on young whites than on blacks.[19]

Yet once again the data do not support the hypothesis. Although young whites liked Reagan more than their older counterparts, feelings toward Reagan are not at all related to abortion attitudes among this group. Young whites who were most positive toward Reagan in 1984 were no more likely to favor restrictions on abortion than those who did not like Reagan. Thus, we can reject the opinion leadership of a popular, conservative president as a possible explanation for generational differences in abortion attitudes.

A third potential explanation for the decline of support for legal abortion among younger whites is that they are more conservative in general than those who came of age during the 1960s. Again the data do not support this explanation. Younger whites are slightly less supportive of gender equality than the 1960s and 1970s cohorts, but these differences are small. They are the most permissive generation on issues of sexual morality and the most likely to call themselves liberals. Of course, this generation is also more Republican than the older generations and more likely to have supported Reagan. At most, however, the Reagan generation shows evidence of a confused ideology, not a consistently conservative pattern.

We believe that the Reagan generation came of age during a period in which the media presented a consistent message that abortion was ultimately a woman's choice but one that should not be taken lightly. We are persuaded by Condit's evidence (discussed in Chapter 1) that the media consensus during the 1980s was critical of abortions that were chosen without a compelling justification. Condit's claim fits well with these data, for the Reagan cohort of whites is primarily different from its older counterparts on two abortion items--when a married couple wants no more children and when a pregnant, unmarried woman does not want to marry.

In both cases, the Reagan cohort may feel that the need for abortion under these circumstances is not compelling. Younger respondents may be less likely to feel that there will be a substantial societal stigma for an unmarried mother. Unmarried motherhood has become more widespread since the 1960s, and the popular media (especially television) have treated unmarried mothers in a much more positive light in recent years than previously. During the 1991-1992 television season, popular television charcater Murphy Brown deliberately had a baby out of wedlock, as the fictional charcater desired a child, but did not wish to be married. Vice President Dan Quayle attacked the script as an example of the decline of traditional values.

The Reagan generation may also be more likely to believe that a married couple should have just "been more careful" and not gotten pregnant in the first place. Younger Americans may underestimate the chances of contraceptive failure, for they have had less chance to experience it. We noted in Chapter 1 that a married couple who correctly used the most successful contraception available still bore a sizable risk of an unwanted pregnancy. Young people have had less time to experience this type of contraceptive failure themselves and are less likely to know someone else who has. A woman of twenty-one who has been consistently contracepting for three years using a method 99 percent successful in each year bears only a 3 percent chance of becoming pregnant during this period. A similar woman from the sixties generation who is now 40 would have experienced a 20 percent chance of pregnancy using this same method, as would her friends of the same age. A woman of the sixties generation is therefore more likely to be aware of the probabilistic nature of contraceptive failure than a young woman of the Reagan generation. If the Reagan generation underestimates the chance of contraceptive failure, young whites may believe that such pregnancies should simply have been avoided. Thus the Reagan cohort may disapprove of abortions in these two circumstances because they do not find these situations compelling justifications for abortion.

Demographic Differences in Abortion Attitudes: Multivariate Analyses

How do these demographic variables combine to explain abortion attitudes? In order to determine how useful each demographic variable is in explaining abortion attitudes, we use a statistical procedure called multiple regression. This technique enables us to determine how much effect a variable (say, education) has on abortion attitudes when other variables have been held constant.

The nine demographic variables combined to explain approximately 9 percent of the variation in abortion attitudes. This relatively low figure suggests the need for additional explanations of abortion attitudes. In the next two chapters, we consider the effects of other, related attitudes and of religion on abortion attitudes.

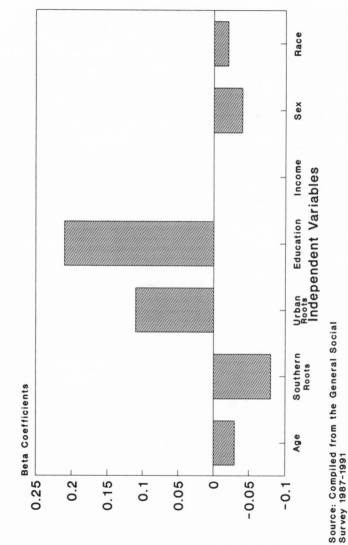

Figure 2.10
Demographic Predictors of
Abortion Attitudes

Source: Compiled from the General Social
Survey 1987–1991

Figure 2.10 presents the results of the analysis. The height of the bar is proportional to the strength of the relationship between the variable and overall abortion attitudes. Those bars that lie below the line suggest that the relationship is negative. For example, the bar representing those raised in the South lies below the line, indicating that those who grew up in the South are less supportive of legal abortion. In contrast, the bar for education is above the line, indicating that those with higher levels of education are more supportive of abortion than those who completed less formal education. A detailed presentation of the results can be found in the Appendix.

Among the social variables that we have considered here, education is by far the most important predictor. Geographic variables are also important, with those who were raised in the South or in rural areas markedly less supportive of legal abortion. Women were significantly less supportive of abortion, and further analysis shows that this relationship is entirely due to less support among housewives. Income and race are not significant predictors of abortion once other variables are controlled. In other words, we cannot dismiss the possibility that the observed relationships are not attributable to sampling error.

Conclusions

Memberships in social groups do help us account for differences in attitudes toward legal abortion to some extent. Differences in education, region, and family structure all help explain some of the variation in abortion attitudes. However, the explanatory power of such demographic variables is rather weak, and much remains to be explained after the effects of these variables have been taken into account. What is needed is a more detailed analysis of the reasons people have for their abortion attitudes, and it is to this task that we now turn.

Notes

1. These data and others in this book are made available by the Inter-University Consortium for Political and Social Research. We are responsible for all interpretations. James Davis and Tom Smith, *General Social Surveys, 1972-1991.* [machine readable data file] Chicago: National Opinion Research Center, (1991).

2. The dimensionality of the abortion items has been widely documented, and we have confirmed this with factor analysis. Moreover, we find that this same factor structure holds for the somewhat different items included in the 1989 *CBS News/New York Times* survey in several different states. In using this terminology, we are mindful that all abortions are traumatic for the women involved, and that all abortions are in some sense elective. Moreover, extreme poverty is a traumatic circumstance. Some other researchers have used the terms "hard" and "soft" reasons for abortion, but we believe that elective and traumatic conveys more of the core of the distinction. Note that the distinction between these two sets of items is not our own categorization, rather it emerged from the pattern of public response to these questions.

3. Aida Torres and Jacqueline Forrest, "Why Do Women Have Abortions?" *Family Planning Perspectives* 20 (1988), pp. 169-176.

4. We refer to only those citizens who oppose abortion in all circumstances as pro-life supporters. Because some pro-life organizations allow for exemptions when the mother's life is in danger, this may seem an arbitrary decision. We make this choice for two reasons. First, political actors call themselves pro-life or pro-choice for political reasons. Although President Bush calls himself pro-life, he has at various points endorsed exemptions for the life and health of the mother, for rape and incest, and for severe fetal defect. This position would be at 3, near the mid-point of our scale. Similarly, some of those who call themselves pro-choice favor restrictions. It is therefore cleaner to limit our pro-life and pro-choice categories to those positions held by most activists on both sides. Second, note that the GSS question refers to the *health*, not life of the mother. Pro-life activists are quite wary of this exception. Prior to the *Roe* decision when states were allowed to regulate abortion, several states with exemptions for the mother's health allowed that clause to become quite elastic--for example, allowing doctors to certify that a live birth would upset the mother and therefore interfere with her *mental* health.

5. Abortion attitudes appear to be remarkably stable at the individual level as well. See Philip E. Converse and Gregory B. Markus, "Plus ca Change.... The New CPS Election Study Panel," *American Political Science Review* 73 (1979), pp. 32-49.

6. Malcolm L. Goggin and Christopher Wlezien, "Interest Groups and the Socialization of Conflict: The Dynamics of Abortion Politics" (paper presented at the annual meeting of the Midwest Political Science Association in Chicago, 1991). Goggin and Wlezien argue that interest group activity in anticipation of *Webster* may have influenced public attitudes.

7. Pennsylvania passed a package of restrictions including parental consent, spousal notification; a twenty-four hour waiting period; requirements that doctors inform patients of the development of their fetuses; health risks from abortion and alternatives to abortion; and a requirement that abortion providers supply the state health department with information about each procedure, including the basis for determining the gestational age of the fetus.

8. For a discussion of racial differences in abortion attitudes, see M. Combs and S. Welch, "Blacks, Whites, and Attitudes Toward Abortion," *Public Opinion Quarterly* 46 (1982), pp. 510-520; E. Hall and M. Ferree, "Race Differences in Abortion Attitudes," *Public Opinion Quarterly* 50 (1986), pp. 193-207; P. Secret, "The Impact of Region on Racial Differences in Attitudes Toward Legal Abortion," *Journal of Black Studies* 17 (1987), pp. 347-369; C. Wilcox, "Race Differences in Abortion Attitudes: Some Additional Evidence," *Public Opinion Quarterly* 54 (1990), pp. 248-255; C. Wilcox, "Race, Religion, Region, and Abortion Attitudes," *Sociological Analysis* (1992), forthcoming.

9. S. Henshaw and J. Silverman, "The Characteristics and Prior Contraceptive Use of U.S. Abortion Patients," *Family Planning Perspectives* 20 (1988), pp. 158-168.

10. P. Secret, "The Impact of Region on Racial Differences in Attitudes Toward Legal Abortion," *Journal of Black Studies* 17 (1989), pp. 347-369. But see also C. Wilcox, "Race, Religion, Region, and Abortion Attitudes," *Sociological Analysis*, forthcoming.

11. In the late 1980s, the GSS began asking many of its questions of two-thirds of all respondents. This allowed NORC to include more questions, but it reduced the already small number of black respondents to the

abortion items. Beginning in 1988, therefore, we have averaged the respondents in each year with those in the previous year for Figure 2.6. This allows us to smooth trends in black attitudes by reducing sampling error.

12. M. Kent Jennings and Richard G. Niemi, *Generations and Politics* (Princeton: Princeton University Press, 1981).

13. Karl Mannheim, "The Problem of Generations." in Philip Altbach and Robert Laufer, eds., *The New Pilgrims* (New York: David McKay, 1972).

14. See Graham Allison, "Cool It: The Foreign Policy Beliefs of Young America," *Foreign Policy* 1 (1971), pp. 150-154; Ole Holsti and James Rosenau, "Does Where You Stand Depend on When You Were Born? The Impact of Generation on Post-Vietnam Foreign Policy Beliefs," *Public Opinion Quarterly* 44 (1980), pp. 1-22; and Michael Roskin, "From Pearl Harbor to Vietnam: Shifting Generational Paradigms," *Political Science Quarterly* 89 (1974), pp. 563-588. Yet other studies show an opposite pattern, with those who came of age during World War II the least supportive of military action in the Persian Gulf; those who grew up during the Vietnam war were the most supportive. See Clyde Wilcox, Joseph Ferrara, and Dee Allsop, "Before the Rally: Public Attitudes on the Iraq Crisis" (paper presented at the annual meeting of the American Political Science Association, Washington, D.C., September 1991).

15. Virginia Sapiro, "News from the Front: Intersex and Intergenerational Conflict over the Status of Women." *Western Political Quarterly* 33 (1980). pp. 260-277.

16. These data show evidence of period effects, with all generations becoming more conservative during the mid-1980s and more liberal at the end of that decade.

17. Alternatively, pro-choice activists would hypothesize that women who have experienced childbirth would be less likely to want other women to go through the experience unless they chose to.

18. For details of this and other tests of explanations for generational differences, see Elizabeth Cook, Ted G. Jelen, and Clyde Wilcox, "Generations and Abortion," *American Politics Quarterly*, forthcoming.

19. A more likely influence on the attitudes of young blacks would be Rev. Jesse Jackson, who took a pro-choice position in his 1984 and 1988 presidential campaigns, despite his earlier pro-life position.

3

The Subjective Bases
of Abortion Attitudes

In Chapter 2, we saw that support for legal abortion is not randomly distributed throughout the American population but that different types of people are more or less likely to favor access to the legal termination of pregnancies. For example, we saw that people with high levels of education are more supportive of legal abortion than their less-educated counterparts, that blacks have historically been less supportive of legal abortion than whites, and that the various generations of Americans differ in their attitudes toward abortion.

Many people object to social scientific analyses because they feel that the statistical treatment of public attitudes is dehumanizing. By placing people in socially constructed categories such as male/female, black/white, southern/northern, we do not mean that such categories *determine* their attitudes on issues of public policy. Social groups differ in their attitudes on abortion because of the values, attitudes, and beliefs they hold that, in turn, influence abortion attitudes.

In this chapter, we examine the *reasons* people might have for holding permissive or restrictive attitudes on questions of legal abortion. Clearly, there is nothing intrinsic to being black, or young, or rich, that affects abortion attitudes. Rather, occupying a particular social location makes various arguments for taking political positions seem more or less compelling.

What is most fascinating about the abortion issue is the variety of reasons people bring to bear on their abortion attitudes. The abortion controversy generates such intense feelings precisely because abortion attitudes seem related to so many other important facets of life. Amy Fried calls the abortion issue a "condensational symbol,"[1] by which she means that abortion attitudes crystallize and represent other attitudes about different values relating to lifestyle, gender roles, human life, and appropriate sexual behavior. In this chapter, we will single out four major reasons for variation in abortion attitudes: general ideology, beliefs about the inviolability of human life, attitudes toward the appropriate role of women in society, and attitudes about sexual morality. The effects of these attitudes will first be considered separately. After these relatively simple analyses, we will examine the joint effects of these attitudes on beliefs about legal abortion in order to assess the relative importance of each set of reasons.

Ideological Self-Identification

The first general attitude to be considered in this chapter is political ideology. Although relatively few Americans take consistently liberal or conservative positions across a range of specific issues,[2] the labels "liberal" and "conservative" are powerful symbols by which people organize and evaluate beliefs about political matters.[3] For example, an important part of George Bush's strategy in the 1988 presidential election was to label Michael Dukakis as a liberal and to then define that term with reference to unpopular groups such as criminals and child pornographers.

Why are those who call themselves conservatives less likely to support legal abortion than self-labeled liberals? In part, the answer may lie in the nostalgic view many conservatives have of the past. Many conservatives wish to return to the "good old days," when traditional values may have been more universally accepted. One meaning of the term "conservative" is that slow, gradual social change is seen to be preferable to rapid or abrupt societal shifts. In this sense, opposition to abortion is almost a classic conservative position. Kristin Luker describes the years prior to the 1973 *Roe* decision as a "Century of Silence."[4] During this period, abortion was not only illegal but was seen to be an unfit topic for polite conversation. "Good people" were simply not involved with such sordid matters.

A feature of some popular fiction in the 1950s was that abortion and even contraception were deeply held, dark secrets, that were literally unspeakable. For example, a recent abortion provides the dramatic backdrop for a complex set of relationships in Tennessee Williams's play *Sweet Bird of Youth*. Similarly, in Edward Albee's *Who's Afraid of Virginia Woolf?*, George characterizes Honey's use of contraception (which she has concealed from her husband) as consisting of "little murders."[5] In these dramatic works, the social and psychological pathology associated with reproductive control is contrasted with normality, in which such issues are not part of everyday discourse. One possible basis for the opposition of self-styled conservatives to legal abortion may be a feeling of nostalgia for a relatively recent period in which people were not required even to think about such uncomfortable issues.

By contrast, self-styled liberals are relatively more supportive of abortion rights. The term "liberal" carries a connotation of receptivity to new ideas and a more limited respect for tradition. Thus, those who consider themselves liberals do not value the nostalgic view of the past typical of conservatives. Moreover, contemporary liberals are more likely to value individual liberty in the area of personal morality. Thus, liberals are more receptive to arguments about abortion being a private matter, with which government should not interfere. Finally, in contemporary political discourse, liberalism has come to connote a high positive value for equality. Thus, liberals are more sympathetic to arguments that reproductive freedom is necessary if women are to be fully equal to men.[6]

In the GSS, self-identification as a liberal or conservative was measured with the following question:

We hear a lot of talk these days about liberals and conservatives. I'm going to show you a seven-point scale on which the political views that people might hold are arranged from extremely liberal--point 1--to extremely conservative--point 7. Where would you place yourself on this scale?

1. Extremely liberal.
2. Liberal.
3. Slightly Liberal.
4. Moderate, middle of the road.
5. Slightly conservative.
6. Conservative.
7. Extremely conservative.

TABLE 3.1 Relationship Between Ideological Self-Identification
and Support for Legal Abortion

| | Attitudes Toward Abortion (in percent) | | | | |
	Pro-life	Situation-alist	Pro-choice	Mean	N
Liberal	5	43	52	4.51	1403
Moderate	7	56	37	3.96	1789
Conservative	10	58	32	3.55	1620

Source: General Social Survey, 1987-1991.

We have classified all respondents selecting codes 1 through 3 as liberals, respondents who select point 4 as moderates, and people who place themselves at 5 through 7 as conservatives.

As Table 3.1 shows, liberal/conservative self-identification is strongly related to abortion attitudes. As might be expected, self-described liberals are much more supportive of legal abortion than are people who call themselves conservatives. Thus, over half of all liberals reject any restrictions whatsoever on access to legal abortion, but approximately a third of conservatives take a consistently pro-choice position. Conservatives are twice as likely to take a consistent pro-life position as are liberals, although only a small minority of either group take that position. Thus, general orientations toward politics are strongly related to attitudes about the abortion controversy. The next several sections of this chapter deal with more specific bases for abortion attitudes.

A Matter of Life and Death?

For some, the abortion controversy is literally "a matter of life and death."[7] Perhaps the most basic issue in the abortion controversy is the status of the embryo. Although we will show that considerations of human life are not the only or necessarily even the primary reasons people oppose legal abortion, the obvious starting point for a discussion of the subjective bases of abortion attitudes is the claim that the human embryo is a person. Such persons are thought to bear rights, including what is considered the most basic right of all: the right to life. Indeed, the fact that those who would restrict access to legal abortion have adopted the label "pro-life" reflects the sanctity human life has in Western culture and the rhetorical power of the life symbolism.

Moreover, even if subsequent examination of abortion attitudes shows that a respect for human life is only one of several anti-abortion rationales, the life connection is of cardinal importance for political discourse. As we noted in the first chapter, many Americans would make a distinction between "self-regarding" and "other-regarding" behavior and would argue that governmental regulation of self-regarding behavior is quite problematic.[8] After all, if a person is not hurting anyone but her/himself, why should the coercive power of government be used to alter such behavior? Indeed, the Supreme Court's ruling in *Roe v. Wade* locates the right to abortion within a more general right to privacy, in which government intervention is thought to be illegitimate. Conversely, opponents of legal abortion argue that abortion is a fit subject for government regulation precisely because the interests of another person--the embryo--are at stake. For people with pro-life views, abortion is an "other-regarding" behavior, in which individuals should not be free to do as they please because abortions directly affect another person.

As we saw in Chapter 1, opponents of legal abortion typically argue that the embryo attains its status as a person at the moment of conception. They regard a fertilized egg (zygote) as the bearer of rights the rest of society is bound to respect. Historically, the human status of the embryo has been quite controversial. Some analysts have argued that the idea that the embryo is a person has roots in ancient times, but the Anglo-American common law has traditionally regarded abortion as a potentially criminal act only after quickening. This common law tradition closely resembles the holding of the Supreme Court in *Roe v. Wade,* which provides that governments may regulate abortion to protect embryonic life only after viability--the point at which the embryo is thought to be capable of sustaining life outside the womb. Implicit in both the common law tradition and in contemporary American jurisprudence is the assumption that "personhood" is attained fairly late in embryonic development, and, therefore, abortions performed early in pregnancy do not involve the taking of human life.

Thus, the idea that abortion is a "matter of life and death" is a very controversial one in the contemporary debate. Does a belief in the inviolability of human life affect attitudes toward legal abortion? This fairly straightforward question is more difficult to answer than one might imagine. Because we are interested in an empirical examination of public attitudes on abortion, we need to measure, with reasonable accuracy and precision, the concepts under consideration. Measurement, in the study of public opinion, typically involves the asking of questions in opinion surveys. It is difficult to formulate a question that might elicit the respondent's beliefs about the inviolability of human life. If, for example, we were simply to ask people "Do you believe in the sanctity of human life?" in a direct, general way, it is hard to imagine that anyone would report *not* respecting life. We assume that a belief in the inviolability of human life varies across individuals, and our measure should reflect such variation.

Alternatively, if it is not possible to formulate a general question about the sanctity of life, we might ask respondents about specific issues in which life and death matters seem to be involved. For example, we might ask people whether they favor or oppose the death penalty or whether they favor U.S. military intervention in a variety of international circumstances. Unfortunately, measures such as these are not strongly related to each other nor are they related to abortion attitudes.[9] A moment's reflection should make this easy to understand. In the case of capital punishment, either favoring or opposing the death penalty *might* be regarded as "pro-life." Opponents of the death penalty might argue that a respect for the sanctity of human life makes it wrong to kill convicted criminals. Conversely, supporters of the death penalty might argue that capital punishment is really a "pro-life" policy because they believe that the threat of the death penalty makes murder less likely.

Another possible item to measure attitudes toward the sanctity of life might focus on opposition to war. But some people have argued that timely military intervention, such as the 1991 war against Iraq, is a life-preserving measure because the loss of life is less than the killing that might occur in the absence of military activity. Many people, in fact, argued that an unchecked Saddam Hussein would likely have killed more people than were lost in Operation Desert Storm. Thus, it seems apparent that questions about military policy, or about domestic crime policy, are poor measures of respect for human life.

Given that the measurement of respect for the sanctity of life is difficult, and must necessarily be indirect, we have chosen the following question as our "pro-life" indicator: "When a person has a disease that cannot be cured, do you think doctors should be allowed by law to end the patient's life by some painless means if the patient and his family request it?" We assume that a response indicating disapproval of active euthanasia (mercy killing) indicates a higher support for the inviolability of human life than a pro-euthanasia response. We recognize that using an item involving active mercy killing as an indicator of "pro-life" sentiments has its limitations, and we would certainly not argue that respondents who favor mercy killing are indifferent to human life. Indeed, many proponents of euthanasia would argue that they are highly concerned about the *quality* of life.

Nevertheless, we believe that this measure has a certain face validity in at least three senses. First, the life of a person or potential "person" is about to be terminated by a medical procedure in both abortion and euthanasia. Second, in both cases, the actual or potential "person" whose right to life is in question is innocent, in the sense of not having done anything to deserve their fate. A human embryo and a candidate for euthanasia have this quality of innocence in common, as opposed to enemy soldiers or persons convicted of capital crimes. Finally, both involve human intervention instead of leaving the fate of the "person" up to nature, fate, or God.[10]

To what extent is a restrictive attitude about mercy killing related to opposition to legal abortion? This question is addressed in Table 3.2, which shows that our measure of the belief in the inviolability of human life is a strong predictor of abortion attitudes. As the table shows, the life measure is strongly related to abortion attitudes. Among the minority of Americans who disapprove of mercy killing, there are more who take a consistently pro-life position on abortion than who consistently approve of legal abortion. Those who approve of euthanasia are three times as likely to take a pro-choice position as those who disapprove.

TABLE 3.2 Relationship Between Respect for Life Measure
and Support for Legal Abortion

	Pro-life	Situation-alist	Pro-choice	Mean	N
	Attitudes Toward Abortion (in percent)				
Euthanasia should be permitted	2	50	48	4.48	1173
Euthanasia should not be permitted	20	64	16	2.56	453

Source: General Social Survey, 1987-1991.

Thus, it seems apparent that beliefs about the inviolability of life, as measured by our euthanasia question, are strongly related to abortion attitudes. For many, there seems to exist a relationship between skepticism about mercy killing and a commitment to an embryonic "right to life." We are confident that attitudes toward mercy killing and abortion are, at least in part, components of a more general respect for the sanctity of human life. However, these data also indicate that the "life connection" is by no means a complete explanation for attitudes toward legal abortion. Table 3.2 shows that many people approve of both legal abortion and euthanasia and that many others disapprove of both. The fact that a consideration for human life is limited as a rationale for abortion attitudes suggests that we need to look at other possible sources of support for or opposition to legal abortion.

Abortion and Gender Role Attitudes

As we saw in the first chapter, other values besides human life are at stake in the abortion controversy. Of particular importance to contemporary abortion discourse is the role of abortion in promoting full equality for women. If women do not have control over their own fertility, it is argued, they can be denied equal access to opportunities in the workplace and elsewhere because employers may fear the loss of the investment made in female employees who quit when they become mothers, and consequently they may discriminate against fertile females on that basis.

Kristin Luker's classic study of abortion activists[11] shows that elite-level disagreement about abortion is centrally concerned with gender-based divisions of labor. Pro-life activists believe strongly that men and women have fundamentally different natures and that there are clearly defined male and female spheres of activity. Women are viewed as emotionally and biologically equipped to become mothers, and women who do not aspire to motherhood are, in an important sense, denying their own nature. One activist went so far as to argue that women who seek to compete in a "man's world" were... "turn(ing) into men...or being de-sexed...."[12] Pro-life activists argued that reducing or eliminating differences in the social roles played by men and women is degrading to the essentially feminine task of nurturing and caring and threatens an important social function played by traditional women.

By contrast, Luker's pro-choice advocates believed that, apart from different biological roles in human reproduction, men and women are essentially similar. The near-universality of traditional gender roles has been rendered obsolete by the biological and economic alternatives available to contemporary women. Motherhood, for these pro-choice advocates, has dignity precisely because it is a demanding role which, given modern reproductive technology, can be freely chosen. For many of these women, fertility has been an excuse designed to keep females in the status of second-class citizens.

To what extent are gender role attitudes related to abortion attitudes among the mass public? Before addressing this question, it is important to note that there are two distinctive types of gender role attitudes. One set of attitudes, which we will call the public face of feminism, relates to the perceived appropriateness of female participation in the public arenas of business or politics. A person taking a traditionalist position on this aspect of gender role attitudes might argue that women should not participate in government or in business because women are not intellectually or emotionally equipped for such activity. Such a person would regard women as inferior to men in important respects. By contrast, the aspect of feminism that we term private relates to the perception on the part of some people that women have special abilities in the areas of caring, nurturing, and child-rearing. Women, it is argued, should retain their traditional roles as wives and mothers precisely because of their superior talents in these areas.[13]

Our measure of the public face of gender role attitudes was formed through an index of the following questions:

> Do you agree or disagree with this statement? Women should take care of their homes, and leave running the country up to men.

> Do you approve or disapprove of a married woman earning money in business or industry if she has a husband capable of supporting her?

> If your party nominated a woman for President, would you vote for her if she were qualified for the job?

> Tell me if you agree with this statement: Most men are better suited for politics than are most women.[14]

Private feminism was measured by combining responses to a different set of questions. In these questions, the response categories are "Strongly agree, agree, disagree, strongly disagree." This method of providing possible answers to respondents is termed "Likert scoring," and questions posed in this format are called "Likert scales." The following questions were used to form the private feminism scale:

> A working mother can establish just as warm and secure a relationship with her child as one who does not work.

> It is more important for a wife to help her husband's career than to have one herself.

> A preschool child is likely to suffer if his or her mother works.

> It is much better for everyone involved if the man is the achiever outside the home and the woman takes care of the home and family.[15]

As Table 3.3 shows, both types of gender role attitudes are related to abortion attitudes. In the case of the public feminism index, the scale is divided into two categories, because more than 50 percent of the sample selected the most feminist or nontraditional set of responses.

TABLE 3.3   Relationships Between Feminism Measures
and Support for Legal Abortion

	Attitudes Toward Abortion (in percent)				
	Pro-life	Situation-alist	Pro-choice	Mean	N
Public feminism:					
Feminist	4	50	46	4.27	975
Traditionalist	12	59	29	3.36	716
Private feminism:					
Feminist	3	49	48	4.39	741
Moderate	7	56	37	3.92	467
Traditionalist	15	60	25	3.23	484

Source: General Social Survey, 1987-1991.

With respect to the private feminism measure, the index is divided into three categories (feminist, moderate, and traditionalist) as the pattern of responses divides fairly neatly into three groups. Only 4 percent of the respondents taking a feminist position on the public feminism index take a consistent pro-life position on legal abortion, while about 12 percent of the traditionalists are pro-life. Nearly half of all public feminists oppose all restrictions on legal abortion, but just over a quarter of traditionalists are consistently pro-choice. There is a clear relationship between feminism and abortion attitudes in this table, with feminists far more supportive of abortion than traditionalists. Note, however, that even among those who take quite traditional views on questions of public roles for women, there are twice as many who take a pro-choice position as who are pro-life.

The relationship between abortion attitudes and private feminism is even stronger. Persons taking a feminist position on this index are much more supportive of legal abortion than any other group, with nearly half taking a consistent pro-choice position, and only 3 percent taking a pro-life stance. By contrast, respondents who take a traditionalist position on the private feminism index are relatively conservative on the abortion issue, with nearly one in six opposing abortion in all circumstances and one in four favoring legal abortion under all conditions.

Thus, it is apparent that the abortion debate is, for the general public, partially about the appropriate roles of women. Beliefs about the special capabilities or deficiencies of women affect the way in which legal abortion is regarded by the American people. People who believe in a sharp distinction between male and female spheres of activity are much less likely to favor legal abortion than those who believe in gender equality.

Attitudes Toward Parenthood and Female Employment

A few questions asked only on the 1988 General Social Survey permit more direct inquiry into the importance of attitudes toward parenthood in explaining abortion attitudes. Luker reports that pro-life and pro-choice activists have very different attitudes toward the role of children. Pro-life activists regard childless couples as less fulfilled than people who have children. By contrast, pro-choice activists believe that the commitment to raise a child is so important that childrearing should only be undertaken by people who are willing to make serious adjustments in their other roles. "Having it all" is a difficult choice that must be made voluntarily. Childrearing has emotional and financial costs, and many people may find these costs prohibitive.

Do these differences hold up at the level of the mass public? Do people who regard having and raising children as an important aspect of life hold different attitudes about abortion than those who regard parenthood as something of a burden? To answer this question, a Desirability of Children index was computed from the following Likert items:

Children are more trouble than they are worth.

Watching children grow up is life's greatest joy.

Having children interferes too much with the freedom of the parents.

A marriage without children is not fully complete.

TABLE 3.4 Relationship Between Desirability of
Children Index and Support for Legal Abortion

	Attitudes Toward Abortion (in percent)				
	Pro-life	Situation-alist	Pro-choice	Mean	N
Children not desirable	6	45	49	4.30	223
Children moderately desirable	7	58	35	3.89	217
Children highly desirable	13	68	19	3.16	208

Source: General Social Survey, 1988.

It is better *not* to have children because they are such a heavy financial burden.

People who have children lead empty lives.[16]

The relationship between the perceived joy associated with parenthood and abortion attitudes is summarized in Table 3.4. As might be expected, respondents who believe children are important and worth the financial and emotional costs to their parents are less supportive of abortion rights than those with a less positive view of parenthood. Those who regard children as having both costs and benefits are unlikely to adopt a pro-life stance, while respondents who value children highly are much more likely to oppose legal abortion in all or most instances. Conversely, a consistently pro-choice stance is most likely to characterize those who are very concerned with the costs of childrearing. Respondents with moderate or high scores on the desirability of children index are about half as likely to take a strong pro-choice position as those who do not regard childrearing as a rewarding activity. It should also be noted that pro-choice respondents outnumber pro-life respondents, even among those who regard children as an unmixed blessing.

A final set of gender role attitudes relates directly to the value attached to female employment. As was shown in the first chapter, pro-choice advocates value fertility control because motherhood is a status to which women can be "banished" in the event of an unplanned pregnancy. Many women's career opportunities may be limited if employers come to regard fertile women as temporary or unreliable employees. Fertility control is thus likely to seem particularly valuable to women who place a high priority on employment outside the home. If support for legal abortion is related to a belief that women should be able to plan their pregnancies very precisely, abortion rights should be more valued among people who value female employment.

A Desirability of Female Employment index was computed from the following Likert items:

A woman and her family will all be happier if she goes out to work.

Having a job is the best way for a woman to be an independent person.

Both the husband and wife should contribute to the household income.[17]

As Table 3.5 shows, respondents who hold favorable beliefs about the effects of female employment and who believe that wives should contribute to the family income are more supportive of legal abortion than those who believe in a more traditional division of labor. Differences between respondents scoring high on the female employment scale and those with a low value are of a similar magnitude as other differences reported in this chapter. Although employed women are more likely to value female employment than either men or homemakers, the pattern reported in Table 3.5 obtains for all three groups.

Thus, attitudes toward legal abortion are significantly related to beliefs about the importance of children and outside employment for women. If abortion is regarded as an ultimate form of reproductive control, it seems apparent that such control is most important for those who place a high value on paid careers for women and least

TABLE 3.5 Relationship Between Desirability of Female
Employment Index and Support for Legal Abortion

	Attitudes Toward Abortion (in percent)				
	Pro-life	Situation- alist	Pro-choice	Mean	N
Female employment highly desirable	6	51	43	4.13	371
Female employment moderately desirable	4	59	37	3.95	130
Female employment not desirable	12	60	28	3.33	299

Source: General Social Survey, 1988.

important for those who regard parenthood as an important
component of the lives of adults.

Attitudes Toward Sexual Morality

A final set of reasons people might have for their abortion attitudes
relates to differences in attitudes toward sexual behavior. People
differ widely in their attitudes toward appropriate sexual behavior,
and these differences are strongly related to attitudes toward legal
abortion.[18] Some people believe that there exist very specific ethical
values with respect to sexual relations, and that sex outside the
bounds of traditional marriage is morally unacceptable. By contrast,
others believe that the morality of sexual relations depends on the
circumstances in which people find themselves and that a variety of
alternative physical relationships might be acceptable. For example,

TABLE 3.6 Relationship Between Sexual Morality Index
and Support for Legal Abortion

| | Attitudes Toward Abortion (in percent) | | | | |
	Pro-life	Situation-alist	Pro-choice	Mean	N
Permissive toward nonmarital sex	3	43	54	4.62	2476
Not permissive toward non-marital sex	13	63	24	3.25	2490

Source: General Social Survey, 1987-1991.

Rosalind Petchesky notes that an increase in the incidence of abortion is largely attributable to "positive changes in young women's lives," including "later age at marriage *(meaning inevitably more premarital sex)*" (our emphasis).[19] Clearly, the assumption that people will inevitably be sexually active within or without marriage is an increasingly common one in the United States, but one which remains quite controversial.

Such differences seem likely to affect attitudes toward abortion. Whatever one might believe about the morality of sex outside of marriage, many people believe that childrearing outside of traditional marriage is quite difficult. Because of the problems sometimes associated with contraception, every act of sexual intercourse carries at least a small probability that conception will occur. The availability of legal abortion is one way to eliminate the risk of an unwanted pregnancy and to make sex outside of marriage safer from the standpoint of pregnancy. To illustrate this point, it may be recalled that, in the period prior to the *Roe* decision, young couples frequently "had to get married" because their premarital sexual activity had resulted in a pregnancy. It has been some time since the phrase "they had to get married" has been in general circulation. The widespread availability of contraception and abortion, coupled with a greater acceptance of out-of-wedlock births has substantially weakened the perceived linkage between nonmarital sex and "shotgun" weddings.

The value that people place on the ability to use abortion as a last resort means of reproductive control is likely to depend on their evaluation of sex outside of marriage. For those who are willing to suspend judgment on sex outside of marriage, the freedom provided by the availability of abortion is likely to seem quite beneficial. By contrast, if people oppose sex outside of marriage on moral or religious grounds, the threat of an unwanted pregnancy is one means by which the potential cost of such illicit sexual activity might be increased. In the eyes of many sexual traditionalists, one of the worst effects of the *Roe* decision was to make promiscuity easier by reducing the risk factor in sexual intercourse.[20]

To determine the effects of attitudes toward sex outside of marriage on abortion attitudes, we computed a sexual morality index from the following items:

There's been a lot of discussion about the way morals and attitudes about sex are changing in this country. If a man and a woman have sex relations before marriage, do you think it is always wrong, almost always wrong, wrong only sometimes, or not wrong at all?

What is your opinion about a married person having sexual relations with someone other than the marriage partner: Is it always wrong, almost always wrong, wrong only sometimes, or not wrong at all?

What about sexual relations between two adults of the same sex--do you think it is always wrong, almost always wrong, wrong only sometimes, or not wrong at all?[21]

Although it must be admitted that homosexuality does not directly bear on the question of abortion, attitudes toward homosexual relations are thought to indicate a general attitude of permissiveness or restrictiveness with respect to sexual matters. Because homosexuality is unpopular as an alternative lifestyle in the United States, people who are willing to forgo judgment of homosexual relations seem likely to be tolerant of sexual activity generally.

The effects of attitudes toward sexual morality on abortion attitudes are summarized in Table 3.6. As these data show, attitudes toward sex are very strongly related to abortion attitudes. Over half of the respondents who take relatively liberal attitudes toward nonmarital sex would allow access to legal abortion in all six circumstances, but less than a quarter of those holding more conventional values toward sexuality take a pro-choice position. These results make clear that there is a substantial connection between beliefs in traditional sexual morality and opposition to legal abortion.

Putting Things Together: Multivariate Analyses

The results reported in this chapter confirm most of our expectations. Support for legal abortion is highest among those who favor legal euthanasia, who hold feminist attitudes, who are less enthusiastic about childrearing, who value the benefits of female employment, and who have relatively liberal sexual attitudes. Opposition to abortion is based on opposition to euthanasia, a belief in a traditional gender-based division of labor, a high value placed on having children, a low value on female employment, and a sense of traditional sexual morality.

We have considered the effects of each of these attitudes on abortion separately. However, there is likely to be considerable overlap between the various attitudes examined in this chapter because each respondent will hold several attitudes simultaneously. Which of the psychological correlates of abortion are the most important?

We can isolate the unique effect of each attitude considered in this chapter on abortion attitudes through the multiple regression technique described in the previous chapter. The unique effects of attitudinal and demographic variables are shown in Figure 3.1. Because the questions on the desirability of children and desirability of women working were asked in only one year, we have not included them in this figure. We have included a question about ideal family size, however, which is similar to the index on the desirability of children. A detailed description of the results can be found in the Appendix. In addition, we include in the Appendix details of an equation for only those respondents to the 1988 survey, in which we include the indices on the desirability of children and on women working. Both attitudes are significant predictors of abortion attitudes in 1988, even after controls for demographic variables and other attitudes were included.

As Figure 3.1 shows, the two attitudes most strongly related to abortion attitudes are the life measure and the sexual morality index. These two attitudes are also far more important than any of the demographic variables in Chapter 2 in predicting abortion attitudes. Both attitudes are related to all three abortion scales, but the *relative* importance of sexual morality and beliefs about the inviolability of human life vary across the type of abortion being considered. Figure 3.1 shows that the relative importance of these two variables is approximately equal with respect to the overall abortion index. Although this is not shown in Figure 3.1, our analysis reveals that sexual conservatism is more strongly related to attitudes toward elective abortion than are life attitudes, and a belief in the sanctity of human life is a better predictor of attitudes toward traumatic abortion.

This finding suggests that, in general, people who regard abortion as primarily a "matter of life and death" are reluctant to allow any but the most extreme exceptions to a ban on abortion. If the embryo is, in fact, a person, its life may not be taken for any but the most serious reasons. Presumably, we would not kill a two-year-old child with a genetic defect, or a child who had been conceived by rape or incest. A test of the "pro-life" rationale that abortion really is murder might be that one cannot do to an embryo what one would not be willing to do to a baby. Thus, people who sincerely believe in the inviolability of human life and who believe the embryo to be actual, not just potential, human life might not even be willing to permit abortion for fairly serious medical or traumatic reasons.

By contrast, the strongest predictor of attitudes toward elective abortion is the sexual morality index. Although the life measure has a significant relationship with the elective abortion scale, the single variable that best accounts for opposition to elective abortion is the belief that nonmarital sexual activity is immoral. These data suggest that one important basis for opposition to abortion for nonmedical reasons is the desire to increase the potential costs of sexual intercourse outside of marriage.

Figure 3.1 also shows that belief about an ideal family size is a strong predictor of attitudes toward elective abortion and that liberal or conservative self-identification is significantly related to attitudes

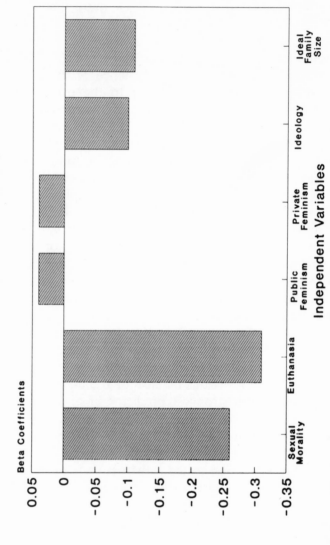

Figure 3.1
Attitudinal Predictors of
Abortion Attitudes

Source: Compiled from the General Social Survey 1989-1991

toward all types of abortion. Conversely, the substantial relationships we observed between gender role attitudes and attitudes toward legal abortion are reduced to insignificance in this multivariate analysis. The unique effects of public feminism and attitudes toward the desirability of female employment are statistically insignificant when controls for other attitudes are imposed.[22]

To make Figure 3.1 more readable, we do not include the demographic variables from Chapter 1, but they are detailed in the Appendix. The effects of most of the demographic variables examined in the previous chapter are substantially reduced by controls for the attitudes examined in this chapter. For example, people raised in the South are less supportive of legal abortion *because* they have a stronger respect for human life and/or more conservative attitudes about appropriate sexual behavior. Once we control for these attitudes, region of birth is no longer a significant predictor. Gender differences are no longer significant once we control for attitudes. The effects of education are also substantially smaller after we hold constant political attitudes, but education remains a significant predictor of abortion attitudes. This suggests that one of the reasons education leads to support for legal abortion is that education is associated with tolerance of extramarital sexual behavior, support for feminism, and greater support for euthanasia. Yet education is significant even after controlling for these attitudes, indicating that education affects abortion attitudes for other reasons as well.

Two demographic variables are even better predictors of abortion attitudes after we control for attitudes. Although in the regression calculated in Chapter 2 the young were significantly more supportive of legal abortion than older citizens, after we control for attitudes older citizens are substantially *more* supportive of legal abortion. This suggests that older citizens oppose legal abortion because of their attitudes toward feminism, sexual morality, and euthanasia, and that if we compare older and younger citizens with the same sets of attitudes on these matters, the older respondents will be more supportive of abortion. In addition, after we control for attitudes, blacks are significantly more supportive of legal abortion. Perhaps surprisingly, the effects of age and race on attitudes toward legal abortion are even stronger, once the effects of attitudinal variables have been taken into account.

Conclusions

A variety of attitudes helps us understand why people differ on the issue of abortion. Although many psychological variables exhibit relationships with abortion attitudes, the two most important sources of opinions about legal abortion seem to be beliefs about human life and attitudes toward sexual morality. The relative importance of these two attitudes depends on the type of abortion being considered.

As might be anticipated with an issue of such profound moral implications as abortion, an important source of differences between people are religious beliefs and practices. Religion can be expected to have a strong impact on attitudes toward legal abortion, and the next chapter examines the effects of religion more directly.

Notes

1. Amy Fried, "Abortion Politics as Symbolic Politics: An Investigation into Belief Systems," *Social Science Quarterly* 69 (1988), pp. 137-154. See also Pamela Johnston Conover and Virginia Gray, *Feminism and the New Right: Conflict over the American Family* (New York: Praeger, 1983); and Suzanne Staggenborg, "Life-Style Preferences and Social Movements Recruitment: Illustrations from the Abortion Conflict," *Social Science Quarterly* 68 (1987), pp. 779-798.

2. See Phillip Converse, "The Nature of Belief Systems in Mass Publics," in David Apter, ed., *Ideology and Discontent* (New York: The Free Press, 1964), pp. 206-261; Norman H. Nie with Kristi Andersen, "Mass Belief Systems Revisited: Political Change and Attitude Structure," *Journal of Politics* 36 (1974), pp. 540-591; Sidney Verba, Norman H. Nie, and John Petrocik, *The Changing American Voter* (Cambridge: Harvard University Press, 1979); and Eric R.A.N. Smith, "The Levels of Conceptualization: False Measures of Ideological Sophistication," *American Political Science Review* 74 (1980), pp. 685-696. For an overview of this extensive literature, see Herbert Asher, *Presidential Elections and American Politics* (Belmont, Calif.: Brooks-Cole, 1991).

3. Pamela Conover and Stanley Feldman, "The Origins and Meanings of Liberal-Conservative Self-Identifications," *American Journal of Political Science* 25 (1981), pp. 617-645.

4. Kristin Luker, *Abortion and the Politics of Motherhood* (Berkeley: University of California Press, 1984).

5. Tennessee Williams, "Sweet Bird of Youth," in Williams, *Eight Plays* (with an introduction by Harold Clurman) (Garden City, N.Y.: Doubleday, 1979). Edward Albee, *Who's Afraid of Virginia Woolf?* (New York: Antheneum, 1963).

6. The relationships between liberal-conservative self-placement and abortion attitudes may be weakened by the imprecision of the terms "liberal" and "conservative." Certain self-identified conservatives have a strong libertarian streak and belief that government, as a matter of principle, ought not interfere in the private affairs of citizens. Conversely, some "liberals" have found the "life connection" very plausible and combine an apparently "conservative" position on abortion with "liberal" positions on other "life" issues, such as military spending, capital punishment, and gun control. See Joseph Bernardin, *A Consistent Ethic of Life* (Chicago: Sheed and Ward, 1988).

7. Ross K. Baker, Laurily K. Epstein, and Rodney D. Forth, "Matters of Life and Death: Social, Political and Religious Correlates of Attitudes Toward Abortion," *American Politics Quarterly* 9 (1981), pp. 89-102.

8. See John Stuart Mill, *On Liberty* (New York: Bobbs-Merrill, 1956) and Brian Barry, "How Not to Defend Liberal Institutions," *British Journal of Political Science* 20 (1989), pp. 1-14.

9. Ted G. Jelen, "Religious Belief and Attitude Constraint," *Journal for the Scientific Study of Religion* 29 (1990), pp. 118-125.

10. Of course, there is one important difference between euthanasia and abortion. In euthanasia in this question, the patient and his or her relatives have *requested* a painless end to a life that will be inevitably short and painful.

11. Luker, *Abortion and the Politics of Motherhood*.

12. Luker, *Abortion and the Politics of Motherhood*, p. 160.

13. See Carol Gilligan, *In a Different Voice* (Cambridge: Harvard University Press, 1982); Emily Stoper and Roberta Ann Johnson, "The Weaker Sex and the Better Half," *Polity* 10 (1977), pp. 192-218; Ted G. Jelen, "The Effects of Gender Role Stereotypes on Political Attitudes," *The Social Science*

Journal 23 (1988), pp. 353-365; Clyde Wilcox and Ted G. Jelen, "The Effects of Employment and Religion on Women's Feminist Attitudes, *International Journal for the Psychology of Religion* 1 (1991), pp. 161-172; and Clyde Wilcox, "Support for Gender Equality in West Europe: A Longitudinal Analysis," *European Journal for Political Research* 20 (1991), pp. 127-147. Stoper and Johnson note that the concept of female superiority in nurturing tasks is a double-edged sword, which has been used by certain feminists to justify enhanced female participation in the public sphere and by certain gender role traditionalists to justify the maintenance of traditional gender-based divisions of labor.

14. To determine whether adding different questions into an index is appropriate, we assess the reliability of the items (the extent to which they measure the same underlying attitude) by computing a statistic called *alpha*. In general, an alpha value of .6 or greater is considered acceptable. The alpha reliability of these particular items is .68.

15. The alpha reliability for these items is .79.

16. The alpha reliability for these items is .70.

17. The alpha reliability for these items is .61.

18. See Ted G. Jelen, "Respect for Life, Sexual Morality, and Opposition to Abortion," *Review of Religious Research* 25 (1984), pp. 220-231; and Ted G. Jelen, "Changes in the Attitudinal Correlates of Opposition to Abortion," *Journal for the Scientific Study of Religion* 27 (1988), pp. 211-228.

19. Rosalind Pollack Petchesky, *Abortion and Women's Choice* (Boston: Northeastern University Press, 1990), p. xvii.

20. It is important to note, however, that 20 percent of abortions are performed on married women. Most married women value control over their fertility. Making abortion illegal would therefore increase the costs of marital sex as well as nonmarital sex.

21. The alpha reliability for these items is .63.

22. These results are substantially unaffected if the model is simplified by excluding the indices for female employment and desirability of children. Most of the covariance between abortion attitudes and attitudes about women's roles is absorbed by the sexual morality index.

4

Religion
and Abortion Attitudes

It will come as no surprise to anyone familiar with the abortion debate that religious beliefs are important determinants of abortion attitudes. When prominent evangelical figures such as the Rev. Jerry Falwell or Marion (Pat) Robertson compare abortion to the Nazi Holocaust, or when Cardinal John O'Connor implies that Roman Catholic Governor Mario Cuomo of New York is risking excommunication because of his failure to seek legal enforcement of the Catholic position on abortion, we know that religion has entered the political arena in a very visible manner. The abortion issue has occasioned a good deal of religiously based political activity.

In this chapter we will address several questions. Do the pronouncements of religious leaders on abortion matter to the lay members of their congregations? If so, how? If not, why not? Are there important differences between religious groups with respect to their support for abortion rights or is the most important distinction the difference between religious and nonreligious people? How effective can religious groups be in convincing their members to take a particular position in the political controversy over abortion rights?

Unlike most European countries, the American religious tradition is quite pluralistic. A variety of religious groups are active in the United States, and each may approach the abortion issue from a different perspective. For this reason, in this chapter we will begin with an examination of four separate Christian groups, then finish the chapter with an examination of the connection between religion and abortion attitudes for American Jews.

Among American Christians, there are several distinctive religious traditions. In this chapter, we distinguish between Catholics and two Protestant groups--those in mainline churches and those in the evangelical tradition. In addition, we will examine separately the connection between religion and abortion attitudes of whites and blacks. Churches remain one of the most segregated institutions in America. Most whites attend churches in which few, if any, blacks are members. Most African-Americans attend predominantly black churches, and more than half attend churches with all-black congregations.[1] Although most African-Americans attend Protestant evangelical churches, these churches often preach a quite different political message from that of white evangelical denominations. Black evangelical pastors frequently oppose legal abortion, but they are far more supportive of public and private feminism than white evangelical churches.[2]

Religion and Abortion Attitudes Among Whites: Theological Traditions

In order to describe the effects of religious belief on abortion attitudes, it is necessary to describe the different theological bases of abortion attitudes. Although these traditions may be strongest among religious elites, we will show later in the chapter that they have important implications for the rank-and-file members of these denominations as well. For purposes of description and explanation, it is convenient to divide white American Christians into three major groups: Roman Catholics, mainline Protestants, and evangelical Protestants. Although this threefold classification does not do justice to the great variety of religious traditions in the United States, and excludes certain groups entirely (for example, Eastern Rite Orthodox), these categories account for a large majority of American Christians.

Roman Catholics

In an important sense, the Roman Catholic Church has been the most visible opponent of legal abortion. Indeed, for many, abortion *is* a Catholic issue.[3] The Catholic Church has opposed both legalized abortion and contraception, and a brief analysis of the Church's position may illuminate the attitudes of lay Catholics in the United States.

The Catholic Church is a hierarchical organization, with the pope at its apex. The pope is regarded as infallible in matters of faith and morals, and derives his authority from the Catholic interpretation of Matthew 16:18-19: "Thou art Peter, and upon this rock I will build my church; and the gates of hell shall not prevail against it. And I will give unto thee the keys of the kingdom of heaven; and whatsoever thou shalt bind on earth shall be bound in heaven; and whatsoever thou shalt loose on earth shall be loosed in heaven." In Catholic theology, the Church and the pope lay claim to this grant of spiritual authority by tracing a direct lineage from Peter to the present day.

Contemporary Catholic teaching on abortion is derived from Pope Paul VI's 1968 encyclical, *Humane Vitae*. In this document, Pope Paul enunciates the Catholic position on abortion and contraception. According to the Catholic concept of natural law, the purpose of human sexuality is procreation. As imperfect creatures because of humankind's sinful nature, we are nonetheless created in God's image, and so are invited, through our sexuality, to participate in the divine act of creation. To interfere with the procreative nature of the sexual union is to misuse the divine gift of human sexuality, and so to pervert the purpose for which we have been endowed with a sexual nature. *Humane Vitae* also reiterates the position of Pius XII, which states that ensoulment occurs at the moment of conception.[4] It is important to note that *Humane Vitae* is a *teaching* document and does not reflect the *ex cathedra* or infallible position of the pope.

The Catholic position on human reproduction is not based primarily on Scripture. Although insights are gleaned from particular biblical passages, Catholic opposition to abortion is based primarily on a tradition of natural law. Briefly, the Catholic position on natural law is that part of God's design is accessible to us through the divine gift of reason. Natural law is the result of a process of uncorrupted reasoning about God's plans and purposes. The pope is seen as Christ's representative on earth, the "Vicar of Christ," and therefore has a unique ability and responsibility to interpret natural law for the faithful.

In this same spirit, the Catholic Church has staked out a nuanced, detailed position on women's rights. In a 1988 draft of a pastoral letter on the status of women, sexism is vigorously condemned as a serious sin, but the American Catholic Bishops' Conference rejected what it called the "false equality" of a "unisex ideal."[5] The Bishops made it clear that discrimination in the workplace is morally unacceptable, but the Church's preference is for traditional gender roles within the family: "The true advancement of women requires that labor should be structured in such a way that women do not have to pay for their advancement by abandoning what is specific to them and at the expense of the family, *in which women as mothers have an irreplaceable role*" (our emphasis).[6] As this passage makes clear, the American bishops accepted the notion of "public" feminism developed in Chapter 3 that women should be treated as equals in politics and in the workplace, but did not endorse the "private" version of feminism previously described, arguing instead that women have special nurturing capabilities as mothers. Although the special role of women as caregivers is not emphasized in *Humane Vitae*, the Church's position on abortion and contraception is consistent with its position on the appropriate roles of women.

Mainline Protestants

Approximately a third of Americans belong to one of the denominations classified "mainline Protestant." The mainline churches would include denominations such as Presbyterians, United Methodists, Episcopalians, and some Lutherans.[7] Protestantism is, literally, based on a "protest" against aspects of the Catholic hierarchy. Rather than placing the power to interpret God's will into the hands of a stratified clergy, Protestantism establishes a "priesthood of all believers." That is, literate people are assumed to be able to read the Bible and understand its meaning for themselves. Understanding God's will and receiving God's grace is a direct, individual process between the believer and God, which is to be accomplished without intermediaries. Moreover, in contrast to the pope's interpretation of natural law, most Protestants regard the Bible as the *sole* source of divine revelation and regard the Scriptures as divinely inspired.[8]

The main difference between mainline and evangelical Protestants concerns the precise nature of the Bible's authority. Contemporary mainline Protestants have historical roots in the "Social Gospel" movement of the early twentieth century. The Social Gospel movement was based on the assumption that God reveals Himself through history and that the events depicted in the Bible are but one set of such revelations. The essential message of the Bible must be adapted to contemporary social and political conditions. Frequently, such adaption of Scripture to contemporary conditions led to a deemphasis on personal piety and a corresponding emphasis on social reform.[9]

The combination of an individualistic theology, in which each person is to work out the meaning of Scripture for her/himself, and a relatively elastic interpretation of the Bible has often left mainline clergy with few leadership resources. Unlike Roman Catholics, mainline clergy cannot point to a theological or authoritative tradition. Unlike evangelical Protestants, mainline clergy cannot point to an inerrant text as the basis for the assertion of religious authority. Thus, many mainline clergy lack a basis for exerting spiritual or theological influence over their congregations.[10] Indeed, several observers have noted a growing disparity between the political and doctrinal positions of mainline clergy and laity.[11] Under such circumstances, many mainline ministers are reluctant to attempt leadership on controversial political issues.

With respect to issues of abortion and reproductive freedom, mainline churches have taken a variety of positions, but most have been relatively supportive of the right to choose.[12] Although abortion is often regarded as a "tragic necessity," or "the lesser of two evils," most mainline clergy seem relatively supportive of abortion rights, although many express reservations that such rights are exercised too casually or easily. The right to an abortion is regarded as an extension of the general social trend toward female equality. However, the views of mainline Protestant clergy may be less relevant to their congregations than those of Catholic priests or evangelical ministers to their congregations because mainline clergy may lack a clear basis for taking positions on controversial issues. Given the lack of a clear source of theological authority, many are uncomfortable "abusing their positions" by "imposing" their own views on their congregation.[13]

In recent years, the national organizations of mainline denominations have attempted to take rather "progressive" positions on issues of gender equality, abortion, and sexual morality. These elite-level pronouncements have been rejected by local congregations or by national assemblies in some denominations, reinforcing the disparity between clergy and laity,[14] although lay members of mainline congregations are typically supportive of gender equality.[15] Thus, mainline Protestant clergy seem most supportive of the right to choose as well as a relatively "accommodating" stance on appropriate gender roles and sexual activities. However, these positions are often not well communicated nor well received at the level of the laity.

Evangelical Protestants

An increasing number of Americans belong to churches generally characterized as "evangelical." The evangelical denominational family would include most Baptists, Assemblies of God, Churches of the Nazarene, Missouri Synod Lutheran, and Apostolic Pentecostals, among others. In contrast to mainline Protestants, evangelical Protestants are distinguished by their view of the Bible as highly authoritative. Most evangelicals view the Bible as the inerrant word of God, and some take the stronger position that all of the Bible is literally true.[16]

When expressing their viewpoints on abortion, evangelical clergy have tended to emphasize the scriptural basis of their pronouncements. Evangelical ministers do not see themselves as imposing their own viewpoints, but simply as revealing the implications of the perfect Word of God.[17] In order to maintain this scriptural "plausibility structure,"[18] evangelical clergy tend to believe that they must provide *specific* biblical passages to support their interpretations.

In general, evangelical clergy take rather restrictive positions on abortion, although some are fairly supportive of abortion under traumatic circumstances.[19] Abortion is never mentioned explicitly in the Bible, but evangelical pastors justify a restrictive position on abortion with a variety of biblical passages. Aside from the Fifth Commandment, which proscribes killing, some ministers cite Luke 1:40-44, to establish the humanity of the embryo: "And it came to pass, that, when Elisabeth heard the salutation of Mary, the babe leaped in her womb, and she spake out with a loud voice. For lo, as soon as the voice of thy salutation sounded in mine ears, the babe leaped in my womb for joy."

Other evangelical spokespersons make a similar point using Psalm 139: 13, 16: "Thou hast covered me in my mother's womb. Thine eyes did see my substance, yet being unperfect, and in thy book all my members were written, when as yet there was none of them."

It should be noted that some biblical scholars take the position that the Bible does not necessarily equate fetal life with life that is fully human. In Exodus 21:12, the Scriptures set forth a justification for capital punishment: "He that smiteth a man, so that he die, shall be surely put to death." However, Verse 22 in the same chapter suggests that the unborn are entitled to *some* protection, but do not receive the same consideration as post-natal humans: "If men strive, and hurt a woman with child, so that her fruit depart from her, and yet no mischief follow; he shall surely be punished, according as the woman's husband will lay upon him, and he shall pay as the judges determine."

The latter passage has caused a large amount of controversy in the abortion debate among evangelicals. Some analysts have emphasized the accidental nature of the miscarriage described in Exodus 21:22 and have considered the termination of pregnancy an ancient version of manslaughter, but others have noted that fetal life is regarded as less valuable than postnatal human life. Unlike murder, the penalty for inducing a miscarriage is a fine determined at the discretion of the judges.[20] Thus, it has been suggested that the Bible is not necessarily a consistent source of antiabortion guidance.

Although the meaning of these passages is open to debate,[21] the rhetorical importance of these scriptural admonitions cannot be overstated. The Bible is regarded by evangelical clergy as the ultimate source of spiritual authority. If legal abortion is to be condemned, the condemnation must be found in the Bible itself. Although some evangelical ministers make use of popular depictions of medical evidence about abortion (for example, photographs of fetuses)[22] these biblical materials provide an important starting point for evangelical involvement in the abortion issue. If evangelical ministers are to take public positions against legal abortion, the position must have an explicit scriptural basis.

Evangelical elites are also likely to speak out against nonmarital sex and against female equality. Once again, evangelical pastors cite specific biblical admonitions to justify their positions. Thus, evangelical spokespersons such as Jerry Falwell cite the scriptural passages noted above as supporting the humanity of the embryo and can cite specific biblical passages proscribing gender equality and nonmarital sex.

It should be noted that within the broad evangelical community there are distinctive theological subgroups that have been mobilized into politics in recent years. Fundamentalist evangelicals believe the Bible is literally true and have generally taken a much more conservative political stance than other evangelicals. Fundamentalists tend to be found in independent Baptist churches and other small denominations. Pentecostal evangelicals believe in the gifts of the Holy Spirit, such as speaking in tongues and healing by faith. Pentecostals are found in the Assemblies of God denomination and in various other pentecostal and holiness churches. These somewhat disparate traditions are united in their understanding that the Bible is the sole source of theological truth, in their belief in the importance of personal salvation, often through a "born-again" experience, and in their emphasis on the value of personal evangelizing, but their doctrinal differences are important. A good deal of scholarly research has shown that fundamentalists and pentecostals are more conservative than other evangelicals,[23] and the GSS shows that this is true on abortion as well. By far the most pro-life denomination is the Assembly of God, whose members are markedly more conservative on abortion than other evangelicals. Both fundamentalist and pentecostal evangelicals are less supportive of legal abortion than other evangelicals.

To summarize, it is useful to divide American Christians into three broad denominational families: Roman Catholic, mainline Protestant, and evangelical Protestant. At the level of religious doctrine, each religious family has a distinctive approach to the abortion controversy, based on its view of religious authority, particular traditions, and view of the Bible. Catholics and evangelical leaders oppose legal abortion, although the religious basis for opposition to abortion is different for each group. By contrast, mainline Protestantism, with its concern for individual autonomy and accommodating view of the authority of Scripture, seems the most likely *religious* source of pro-choice attitudes. We now turn our attention to the attitudes of ordinary citizens who belong to each of these three religious traditions.

Denominational Preference and Abortion Attitudes
Among Whites

We have established that these three religious traditions have different positions, and justifications for those positions, on abortion. Do the members of churches in these three traditions differ in their abortion attitudes? In Table 4.1, we show the abortion attitudes of white Catholics, mainline Protestants, and evangelicals in the GSS data. For comparison, we also include those whites who have no denominational affiliation. As this table shows, Catholics and evangelical Protestants are equally likely to take a restrictive position on legal abortion, although Catholics are more likely than evangelicals to take a pro-choice stance. By contrast, mainline Protestants are more supportive of legal abortion than either evangelicals or Catholics. The main difference among Christian whites is between mainline Protestants and the other two groups. Those who lack a religious attachment are more supportive of legal abortion than members of any of these religious traditions.

Even among evangelicals and Catholics, there are more pro-choice than pro-life citizens. Clearly the strong pro-life stands by evangelical and Catholic leadership has failed to mobilize a majority of the members of these groups to oppose abortion. Moreover, in no religious group does an absolute majority take one extreme position or the other, although in mainline churches the pro-choice contingent approaches 50 percent. Rather, large proportions of all three groups support legal abortion in some but not all possible circumstances.

Denominational differences are relatively constant over time. Figure 4.1 displays the mean score on the abortion rights scale for each denominational group across the 1972-1991 period. For all three groups, support for legal abortion increased slightly during the 1970s, declined during the early and middle 1980s, and (except for Catholics) increased during the late 1980s. Across the entire period in question, Catholics and evangelicals resemble each other rather closely; mainline Protestants are much more supportive of legal abortion. It is perhaps noteworthy that evangelicals were the least supportive of legal abortion during the 1980s, a period in which the New Christian Right was most active, but that Catholics and evangelicals were nearly identical by the end of the decade. Overall, however, the data in Figure 4.1 suggest that abortion attitudes are

TABLE 4.1　Abortion Attitudes by Denominational Preference,
Whites (in percent)

	Catholic	Mainline	Evangelical	No Preference
Pro-choice	34	46	28	74
Situationalist	55	50	62	25
Pro-life	11	4	10	1
Mean	3.70	4.32	3.55	5.26
N	1141	1317	1244	309

Source: General Social Survey, 1987-1991.

quite stable within religious traditions and that the events causing year to year fluctuations affect all three groups in a similar manner.

These three religious groups differ in their religious doctrine and practice.[24] Protestant evangelicals are more likely than mainline Protestants and Catholics to attend church regularly, to pray frequently, to report that religion is very important in their lives, and to believe in the inerrancy of the Bible. It is possible that the differences we observe between denominational groups are, in fact, attributable to differences on these other religious characteristics.

Analysis of intradenominational differences, however, suggests that the distinctions between denominational families are robust and genuine. In Table 4.2, the abortion attitudes of each religious tradition are broken down by levels of religious involvement. Our measure of religious involvement is an index that combines frequency of church attendance, frequency of personal prayer, and subjective religious intensity.[25]

Two aspects of Table 4.2 are of particular interest. First, mainline Protestants are more supportive of abortion rights than other white Christians across levels of religious involvement. For example, only 10 percent of highly religious mainline Protestants[26] take the most restrictive position with respect to abortion rights. The comparable figures for highly involved Catholics and evangelicals are 25 percent

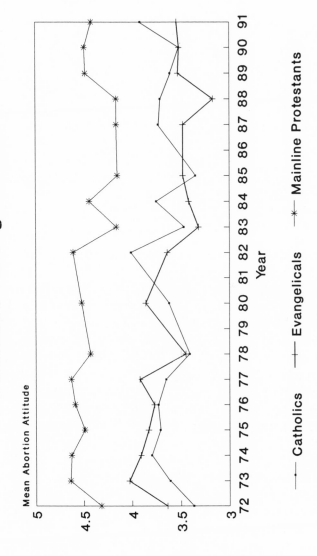

Figure 4.1
Religious Differences in Abortion
Attitudes Among Whites

Mean Abortion Attitude

—— Catholics   —+— Evangelicals   —*— Mainline Protestants

Source: Compiled from the General Social
Survey 1972-1991

Year

TABLE 4.2 Abortion Attitudes by Religious Involvement, by Denomination (White Christians) (in percent)

	Catholic			Mainline Protestant			Evangelical Protestant		
	Low	Med.	High	Low	Med.	High	Low	Med.	High
Pro-choice	48	43	15	55	52	28	41	35	16
Situationalist	49	52	66	43	45	62	55	58	64
Pro-life	3	5	25	2	3	10	4	7	20
Mean value	4.53	4.28	2.52	4.73	4.64	3.46	4.30	3.80	2.46
N	234	501	405	322	610	382	299	514	428

Source: General Social Survey, 1987-1991.

and 20 percent, respectively, and in both groups of highly involved Christians there are more pro-life than pro-choice respondents. Thus, the differences between mainline Protestants and the other denominational families cannot be attributed to differences in religiosity.

Second, it is noteworthy that increased religiosity is associated with restrictive positions on abortion attitudes across all three denominational families. Even among mainline Protestants, highly religious people are less supportive of abortion rights than their less devoted counterparts. This suggests that involvement in a mainline denomination is not a source of pro-choice attitudes but that mainline churches may not be particularly effective sources of socialization on the abortion issue in either direction.[27]

A similar pattern is observed when we examine the impact of different views of the Bible on the abortion attitudes of each group. In Table 4.3, members of each denominational family are divided into those who regard the Bible as an inerrant source of truth and those who view the Bible as less authoritative.[28] Although a "high" view of Scripture is most common within evangelical denominations, all three groups contain substantial numbers of Christians who believe that the Bible is without error.[29] As Table 4.3 shows, the respondent's view of scriptural authority affects members of all three religious traditions in approximately the same manner. Respondents who hold the Bible to be inerrant are much less likely to approve of abortion rights than those who do not, regardless of their religious affiliation. Once again Catholics and evangelical Protestants take similar positions, while mainline Protestants are more supportive of legal abortion regardless of their belief in the authority of the Bible.

For some respondents, of course, the relationship between a "high" view of Scripture and a desire to restrict access to legal abortion means that particular Bible verses have been interpreted to support limits to abortion. As noted above, certain passages have been regarded by evangelical elites as providing guidance on abortion. However, several studies[30] have shown that many people who affirm a literal or inerrant view of the Bible are rather poorly informed about the Bible's content. For these citizens, a belief in a literal or unerring Bible may symbolize the belief in one, unchanging moral code.

TABLE 4.3 Abortion Attitudes by View of the Bible, by Denomination (White Christians) (in percent)

	Catholics		Mainline Protestants		Evangelical Protestants	
	Noninerrant	Inerrant	Noninerrant	Inerrant	Noninerrant	Inerrant
Pro-choice	38	18	51	24	46	14
Situationalist	51	65	46	66	51	69
Pro-life	11	17	3	10	3	17
Mean value	3.86	2.93	4.54	3.39	4.35	2.69
N	659	89	693	267	414	504

Source: General Social Survey, 1987-1991.

TABLE 4.4 Abortion Attitudes by Belief That Sin Must Be Punished,
by Denomination (White Christians) (in percent)

	Catholics		Mainline Protestants		Evangelical Protestants	
	Agree	Disagree	Agree	Disagree	Agree	Disagree
Pro-choice	24	41	35	45	18	23
Situationalist	56	52	62	53	69	67
Pro-life	20	7	3	2	13	10
Mean value	3.37	4.38	4.10	5.16	2.89	3.61
N	34	163	38	161	68	128

Agree = percent strongly agreeing that "those who violate God's rules must be punished." Disagree = percent of other respondents.

Source: General Social Survey, 1988.

As we noted in Chapter 3, much of the opposition to legal abortion seems based on a desire to increase the risks associated with nonmarital sex. An undesired pregnancy might be regarded by some as justified punishment for "illicit" sexual activity. The 1988 General Social Survey contains a Likert item with response categories as follows: strongly agree, agree, disagree, and strongly disagree. The item reads: "Those who violate God's rules must be punished." Agreement with this item indicates both a belief in "God's rules" *and* a punitive orientation toward transgressors. Table 4.4 shows the effects of this item on abortion attitudes across denominational groups of whites. These data show that the desire to punish sinners is strongly related to abortion attitudes for all three groups.

Thus, there are important differences between denominational families with respect to abortion attitudes. Catholics and evangelical Protestants are very similar to each other, but mainline Protestants display more liberal attitudes toward abortion rights. Further, a number of religiously based behaviors and attitudes enhance our understanding of public attitudes toward abortion. These religious variables have a similar effect on the attitudes of white evangelicals, mainline Protestants, and Catholics. However, these three religious groups vary in their *level* of religiosity and orthodoxy. Once we hold constant three attitudes (religiosity, belief in the Bible, and desire to punish sin), the differences we observed in Table 4.1 are substantially reduced. Differences remain, however, with mainline Protestants the most supportive of legal abortion and Catholics the least so.

The Sources of Abortion Attitudes: White Evangelicals, Mainline Protestants, and Roman Catholics

Because the religious leaders in these three different Christian traditions rely on different sources of religious authority, it is possible that the religious sources of the attitudes of the rank-and-file members will differ as well. We have computed separate multiple regression models for each of the three denominational families. Recall from Chapters 2 and 3 that regression is a statistical technique that allows us to see the effects of each variable with all others held constant.

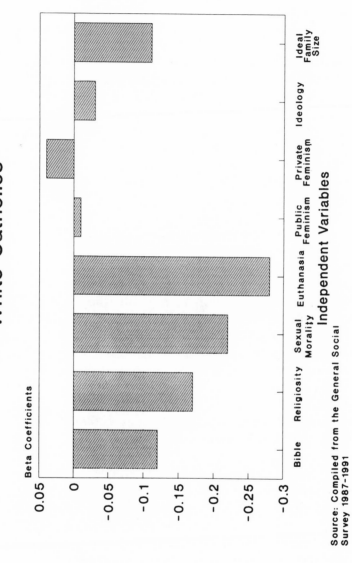

Figure 4.2
Predictors of Abortion Attitudes of
White Catholics

Source: Compiled from the General Social
Survey 1987-1991

In Figures 4.2 to 4.6, we will show the relationships between religion and the overall abortion scale. We will also compare some of the attitudinal sources of abortion attitudes discussed in Chapter 3 across religious traditions. In particular, we will consider the effects of general ideology, feminism, attitudes toward euthanasia, and sexual conservatism on abortion in each of the denominational families under consideration here. In these figures, it is appropriate to compare the height of the bar within each figure, but it is not useful to compare the bars across different figures.[31] As in previous chapters, we present complete results in the Appendix. Because the question on the importance of punishing sin was included only in the 1988 survey, we do not include it in these analyses.

We begin with an analysis of the sources of attitudes of white Catholics. For Catholics, the strongest religious predictor of abortion attitudes is the index of religious involvement. Those Catholics who are involved in organized religious activity are less supportive of legal abortion than their less devout counterparts. The importance of religious involvement suggests that part of Catholic attitudes toward abortion often result from direct religious teaching.[32] Those Catholics who attend church services regularly are much more likely to oppose legal abortion than those who attend less often. This indicates that Catholics are taught about the abortion issue during religious services. Abortion is a sermon topic for Catholic priests-- most Catholic churches hold "Human Life Sundays" at least once a year--and many parishes have organized anti-abortion activity. Of course, those who are most receptive to the Catholic pro-life message are also more likely to frequently attend religious services. Thus, Catholic preachings on abortion may be heard most frequently by those who already hold pro-life views.

Catholic views of the Bible are also related to abortion attitudes, and the relationship between attitudes toward traumatic abortion and the respondent's view of Scripture is even stronger. This is somewhat surprising, for Catholic teachings seldom stress scriptural bases. Recent research has found a type of evangelical religiosity among some Catholics, however, which involves regular Bible reading and is associated with conservative positions on social issues.[33] Our results support this finding. Moreover, we found a rather modest but steady

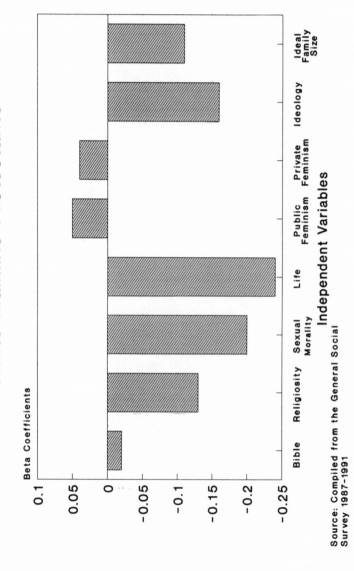

Figure 4.3
Predictors of Abortion Attitudes of
White Mainline Protestants

Source: Compiled from the General Social
Survey 1987–1991

increase in the relationship between Bible beliefs and abortion attitudes among Catholics throughout the 1980s.

Figure 4.2 shows that the euthanasia and sexual morality measures described in Chapter 3 are both strongly related to Catholic abortion attitudes. Our analysis suggests that both of these attitudes are, in turn, related to Catholic religious involvement. Thus, Roman Catholics who are exposed to religious communications learn anti-abortion attitudes directly and learn the religious basis of the values on which the Church's anti-abortion position is based. Feminist attitudes are unrelated to abortion attitudes among Catholics, as is general ideology.[34] Those Catholics who believe that large families are ideal were significantly less supportive of legal abortion. Although once again we do not include the demographic variables in Figure 4.2, none were significant predictors of Catholic attitudes.

Figure 4.3 shows that religious involvement is a weak but significant predictor of the abortion attitudes of mainline Protestants, when the effects of other variables have been controlled. The respondent's view of the Bible is not significantly related to abortion attitudes.[35] Other sources of the abortion attitudes of mainline Protestants are attitudes toward the inviolability of life, attitudes toward sexual morality, attitudes toward ideal family size, and the respondent's general ideology. Once again feminism was not associated with abortion attitudes once we hold constant other variables. Older and better educated mainline Protestants were also significantly more supportive of legal abortion.

Finally, in Figure 4.4 we show the sources of abortion attitudes among evangelical Protestants. Both religious involvement and a high view of Scripture are significant predictors of abortion attitudes among evangelical Protestants. Evangelical pastors discuss abortion from the pulpit at least as often as Catholic priests, and they generally base their discussion on Scripture. Additional analysis (not shown) suggests that those evangelicals who both believe the Bible to be inerrant *and* who are highly involved in religious devotion are by far the least supportive of abortion. This type of result is called an "interaction effect" and it suggests that when frequent attendance and orthodox view of Scripture combine, they are even more predictive of opposition to legal abortion than either is separately. This synergistic interaction between religiosity and Bible views suggests that for most evangelicals, religious learning is rather unlikely to occur unless the

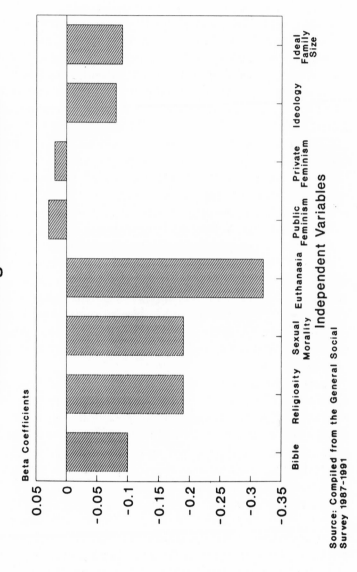

Figure 4.4
Predictors of Abortion Attitudes of
White Evangelical Christians

Source: Compiled from the General Social
Survey 1987-1991

evangelical churchgoer believes in the authority of the Bible *and* is regularly exposed to religious communications on the issue. Thus, evangelical Protestantism, like Roman Catholicism, is an independent source of abortion attitudes.

As was observed for Catholics and mainline Protestants, pro-life attitudes among evangelicals are related to opposition to mercy killing, to conservative positions on issues of sexual morality, and to a preference for large families. General self-classification as liberal or conservative is unrelated to abortion attitudes among evangelicals, and once again neither public nor private feminism is associated with abortion attitudes. As was the case with mainline Protestants, older and better educated evangelicals were more supportive of legal abortion.

We see important similarities and differences in the sources of abortion attitudes among white Catholics and Protestants. For all three groups, the euthanasia item is the strongest single predictor of attitudes. For all three groups, attitudes toward appropriate sexual behavior are also important as determinants of anti-abortion attitudes. Those who found large families desirable were more likely to oppose legal abortion in all three groups.

Those who are more deeply involved in religious activity in all three traditions are more likely to oppose unlimited access to legal abortion, although this connection was much weaker among mainline Protestants. Attitudes toward the authority of Scripture are not associated with abortion attitudes among mainline Protestants, but they are strong predictors of the attitudes of evangelicals, and, surprisingly, of Catholics.

It is also noteworthy that attitudes toward appropriate social roles for women make no independent contribution to abortion attitudes for any of the three groups of white Christians. Whatever connection exists between feminist attitudes and support for legal abortion appears coincidental.

Religion and Abortion Attitudes Among African-Americans

We noted in Chapter 2 that throughout the 1970s and most of the 1980s, African-Americans were less supportive of legal abortion than whites. In all but one of the surveys between 1972 and 1991, blacks were less supportive of abortion than whites. A number of explanations have been offered for black opposition to legal abortion. Some have pointed to the position of certain African-American elites during the 1970s that legal abortion constituted genocide for blacks.[36] Others have noted that the greater religiosity and doctrinal orthodoxy of black Americans is a major source of abortion attitudes.[37]

Blacks are more likely than whites to report the types of religious beliefs and behaviors that decrease support for legal abortion among whites. Blacks are more likely than whites to pray daily (70 percent of blacks compared with 53 percent of whites), to attend church fairly regularly (54 percent to 42 percent), to believe that the Bible is inerrant (57 percent to 32 percent), to attend evangelical churches (69 percent to 29 percent), and to report an intense personal religious experience (30 percent to 18 percent). These religious characteristics lead to consistent conservatism among whites, but in the African-American community, evangelical churches frequently preach a doctrine of Christian liberation. Many black pastors interpret the Scriptures to support racial and gender equality and preach that Christians have the obligation to band together to fight discrimination. Although this message does not generally include an endorsement of legal abortion,[38] it does suggest that religious values and behaviors have different political consequences in the African-American community.

In Table 4.5 we present the relationships between various religious measures and the abortion attitudes of African-Americans. Black Catholics are the most supportive of legal abortion and are even less likely to take a pro-life stance than those with no religious preference. Protestant evangelicals are slightly less supportive of abortion than their mainline brethren. Yet note in this table that the overwhelming majority of blacks are evangelicals, and our estimates of the attitudes of the other groups are based on only a few cases.

We have merged all of the black respondents to all of the GSS surveys from 1972 to 1991, and the results are quite similar to those reported in Table 4.5. Catholics are the most supportive of the three Christian traditions of legal abortion, and there are only modest differences between mainline and evangelical Protestants. In earlier surveys, however, those with no religious attachments are the most supportive of legal abortion.

TABLE 4.5 Religion and Abortion Attitudes Among African-Americans
(in percent)

	Denomination				Involvement			Bible		Punish Sin?*	
	Main.	Evan.	Cath.	None	High	Med.	Low	Inerr.	Noninerr.	Agree	Disagree
Pro-choice	28	28	36	43	21	36	44	24	37	29	42
Situationalist	58	61	62	49	64	57	51	62	55	58	54
Pro-life	14	11	2	8	15	7	5	14	8	13	4
Mean value	3.60	3.48	4.12	3.95	3.14	3.87	4.27	3.24	3.96	3.40	4.39
N	57	622	59	40	344	386	118	381	307	25	36

*Asked only in 1988.

Source: General Social Survey, 1987-1991.

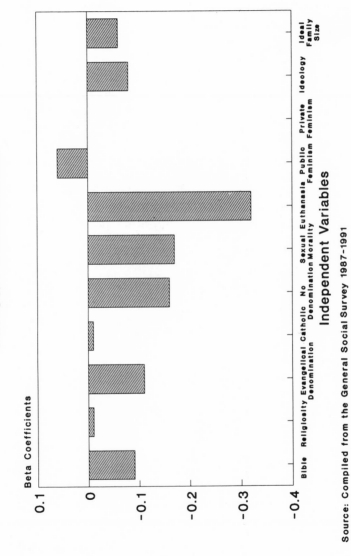

Figure 4.5
Predictors of Abortion Attitudes of
African-Americans

Source: Compiled from the General Social Survey 1987-1991

The same religious variables that influence white attitudes on abortion also are associated with African-American attitudes. Those blacks who take a "high" view of Scripture, who show high levels of religiosity, and who believe that sin must be punished are more likely to oppose legal abortion than other blacks.[39] This finding suggests that although black churches frequently preach a gospel of gender equality and female liberation, that message does not translate into support for legal abortion.

Figure 4.5 shows the results of a separate regression equation to determine the independent effects of religion, attitudes, and demographic variables among African-Americans. Religious variables are generally not significant predictors of black attitudes toward abortion after we control for other attitudes. For African-Americans, religion influences abortion attitudes only by affecting intervening beliefs about the inviolability of human life and appropriate sexual behavior. This does not mean that religion is not an important source of abortion attitudes in the black community, but rather that the effects of religion are indirect. Surprisingly, those with no denominational attachment are significantly *less* supportive of legal abortion after we control for other factors. We will discuss this finding more fully below.

As was the case for white Christians, feminist attitudes make no independent contribution to abortion attitudes. As these data show, the life measure is a stronger predictor of opposition to abortion rights than is the sexual morality index, but both are significant predictors of African-American attitudes. Unlike all three groups of white Christians, attitudes toward ideal family size have no effect on abortion attitudes among blacks.

Religion and Abortion Attitudes Among American Jews

Many of those who identify themselves as Jews in surveys are claiming an ethnic or national, not religious, identification. Among Christian groups, those who are uninterested in religion or who lack a basic faith in God generally claim no religious affiliation, but among Jews, such nonreligious individuals frequently identify themselves as Jews in response to questions of basic religious orientation. Thus, many Jewish respondents to national surveys are not observant Jews.

TABLE 4.6 Religion and Abortion Attitudes Among Jews
(in percent)

| | *Religious Involvement* | | |
	Low	Medium	High
Pro-choice	85	84	68
Situationalist	14	16	26
Pro-life	1	0	6
Mean value	5.66	5.61	4.92
N	298	151	50

Source: General Social Surveys, 1972-1991.

In the GSS surveys between 1972 and 1991, over 60 percent of self-identified Jews had little attachment to organized religion. Only 10 percent meet the criteria for high levels of religiosity that we have used above.[40]

Among religious Jews, there are three distinct theological groups. On the religious "left" are the Reformed synagogues, on the "right" the Orthodox; the Conservative occupy a middle position. Conservatives and Reformed scholars take the position that abortion is *mandatory* when the life and the health of the mother is in danger and that abortion should generally be avoided if possible.[41] Many orthodox leaders take pro-life positions. Unfortunately, the surveys we have used in this book do not include questions to help us distinguish between these three traditions.

We have combined all of the GSS surveys from 1972 through 1991 to get a large enough sample of American Jews. This procedure is quite important when examining the attitudes of American Jews, for they constitute a small proportion of the population. A national sample of 2,000 respondents will typically include only 30 Jews, which poses a serious problem for statistical analysis. By pooling the surveys from 1972 through 1991 together, we get a sample of nearly 500 Jews.

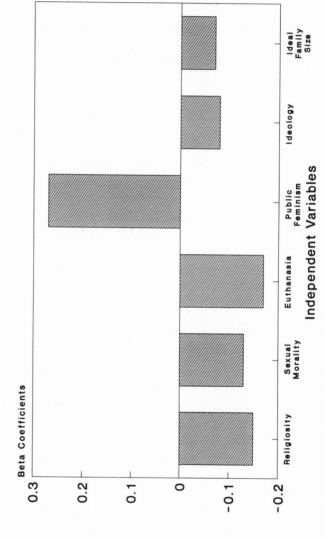

Figure 4.6
Predictors of Abortion Attitudes
of Jews

Beta Coefficients

Religiosity Sexual Morality Euthanasia Public Feminism Ideology Ideal Family Size

Independent Variables

Source: Compiled from the General Social
Survey 1987-1991

Of all the religious groups identified in this chapter, Jews are by far the most supportive of legal abortion. Eighty-two percent took a consistent pro-choice position, with only 2 percent holding consistent pro-life views.[42] Support for abortion under traumatic circumstances is almost universal among Jews: 96 percent supported legal abortion in all three circumstances involving physical trauma. This support is at least partially related to religiosity, as Table 4.6 shows. Yet American Jews with the *highest* levels of religiosity are more supportive of legal abortion than the *least* active Christian groups discussed above. Because the Bible item was only asked in the most recent surveys, there are not enough Jewish respondents to this question to estimate reliably the attitudes of that small minority of Jews who regard the Torah as being without error. The correlation between Bible views and Jewish attitudes on abortion is statistically significant, however, so even with this small sample, we are confident that a relationship exists.[43]

In Figure 4.6 we present the sources of Jewish attitudes on abortion. Once again these results are presented in more detail in the Appendix. Most Jews favor legal abortion, regardless of their levels of education, their religiosity, or their other attitudes. However, four variables significantly influence the attitudes of Jews toward legal abortion: attitudes toward euthanasia, public feminism, religiosity, and education. Religious involvement is also a significant predictor of attitudes toward euthanasia, so religion does have an indirect effect on Jewish abortion attitudes. The effects of the sexual morality measure do not achieve statistical significance for any of the three abortion scales. General ideology and attitudes toward family size are virtually irrelevant in explaining support for legal abortion Among Jews.

Religion and Abortion Attitudes: A Comprehensive Model

We have seen that religion affects the attitudes of white Catholics, evangelicals, mainline Protestants, African-American Christians and American Jews. Religious influences differ from group to group-- among white evangelicals and Catholics, attitudes toward the Bible are important predictors, among white Catholics, evangelicals, and mainline Protestants involvement in religious activity are significant sources of attitudes. Among Jews and African-Americans, the effects of religion are indirect, through the other attitudes religion influences. Yet religion influences the attitudes of each group.

In Table 4.7 we show the effects of religion on abortion attitudes for the entire public, and also show the effects of all attitudes and demographic variables included in earlier equations. Because of the large number of variables in this comprehensive model, we present it as a table instead of a figure. The values for evangelicals, Catholics, and Jews are all assessed relative to mainline Protestants.[44] For example, the table shows negative values beside Catholics and evangelical Protestants. This means that evangelicals and Catholics are substantially less supportive of legal abortion than mainline Protestants. If a number is followed by one star, it means that we are confident that the number is not zero given the size of the sample. If the number is followed by two stars, we are very confident of the significance of this relationship. If no star follows the number, then we are unable to state with any certainty that this relationship is not due to sampling error.

Both evangelicals and Catholics are significantly less supportive of legal abortion than mainline Protestants, even after controls for religious doctrine, religiosity, and other attitudes. Those with no religious affiliation are also significantly *less* supportive of legal abortion, as we saw above in our analysis of the attitudes of African-Americans. Recall from Table 4.1 that before we control for other variables, those with no religious affiliation are among the most supportive of legal abortion. Why, then, are they less supportive in this table? In this analysis we have held constant both religious involvement and religious orthodoxy. This counterintuitive result means that those with no denominational affiliation are less supportive of legal abortion than others who claim a religious affiliation but who share their lack of religious activity and lack of belief in the Bible.

Although Jews are the most supportive group toward legal abortion, after we have controlled for other variables, we cannot be confident that their attitudes are different from those of mainline Protestants. This means that once we have accounted for the generally high level of education of American Jews, their relatively liberal positions on general ideology, private feminism, sexual morality, and lower levels of religious committment, we have entirely explained their greater support for legal abortion.

TABLE 4.7 The Sources of Abortion Attitudes:
A Comprehensive Model

	Beta
Demographics:	
Sex	-.01
Age	.11**
Education	.08**
Income	-.01
Region at age 16	-.02
Urbanization at age 16	.08**
Attitudes:	
Euthanasia	-.27**
Sexual morality	-.20**
Public feminism	-.02
Private feminism	-.04
Ideal family size	-.10**
General ideology	-.10**
Religion:	
Bible attitude	-.10**
Religious involvement	-.15**
Evangelical denomination	-.07*
Catholic	-.13**
No religious preference	-.08**
Jew	-.00
Adjusted R^2	.38
N	1403

Entries are standardized regression coefficients.
*=p<.05; **=p<.01.

Source: General Social Survey, 1987-1991.

Belief in the authority of the Bible and religious involvement are
strong predictors of abortion attitudes. The two strongest predictors
of abortion attitudes, however, are belief in the inviolability of human

life and attitudes toward sexual morality. Other attitudes are significant as well. Conservatives are more likely to oppose legal abortion, as are those who believe a large family to be ideal. Neither type of feminism is a predictor of abortion attitudes after we control for other variables.

Several demographic variables remain significant predictors. Note that after we have held constant religion, social attitudes, and demographic variables, blacks are significantly *more* supportive of legal abortion than whites. Older Americans are also more supportive of legal abortion, as are those who were raised in urban areas and those with higher levels of education.

Clearly, religion is a very important source of abortion attitudes. It is also important to remember that the attitudes that are the strongest predictors of abortion attitudes--attitudes toward the inviolability of life and sexual morality--are themselves strongly influenced by religion. Those who are the most actively involved in religious life and who hold orthodox views of the Bible are the most likely to condemn extramarital sexual activity and to oppose euthanasia. Therefore, religion has both a direct effect on abortion attitudes and an indirect effect through its impact on other attitudes.

Conclusions

Religion has been shown to be an important source of abortion attitudes for many Americans. Across all three white denominational groupings, religious involvement, biblical inerrancy, and punitive attitudes toward sinners are all negatively related to support for abortion rights. However, there are important differences in the manner in which religion and abortion attitudes are related. Among mainline Protestants, religious involvement appears to be part of a more general conservative ideology. Involvement in a mainline denomination is only a weak *direct* source of abortion attitudes. Direct religious socialization about abortion is more evident among Catholics and evangelicals. Among evangelicals and Catholics, abortion attitudes seem at least partially based on the interpretation of biblical passages.

There are certain similarities and differences among religious groups that are of interest. Among all religious groups considered here, abortion is seen as an issue involving human life. The question concerning euthanasia is strongly related to abortion attitudes across all groups. Similarly, for all denominational families, feminism is *not* strongly related to abortion attitudes, once other attitudes have been taken into consideration. This finding might be quite sobering to pro-choice activists, who have made the connection between female equality and the right to choose an integral part of their rhetorical strategy. Pro-life activists who make the case against abortion on grounds of the sanctity of human life may have an easier case to make than pro-choice activists who base their support for legal abortion on the desire for female equality, since many Americans seem to regard feminism and abortion as separate issues.

Yet another important source of opposition to legal abortion is opposition to extramarital sexual behavior. Among all groups except Jews, a major anti-abortion rationale seems to be to regulate sexual behavior. The importance of the view that sin must be punished is relevant in this regard, for it appears that at least some of those who seek to ban abortion want to punish sexual behavior they believe is sinful.

Notes

1. Clyde Wilcox and Leopoldo Gomez, "Religion, Group Identification, and Politics among American Blacks," *Sociological Analysis* 51 (1990), pp. 271-285.

2. For a discussion of politics and religion in the black community, see Kenneth D. Wald, *Religion and Politics in the United States*, 2nd edition (Washington, D.C.: CQ Press, 1991). For an analysis of the impact of religion on black attitudes toward feminism and abortion, see Clyde Wilcox and Sue Thomas, "Religion and Feminist Attitudes Among African-American Women: A View from the Nation's Capital," *Women and Politics*, forthcoming.

3. Kenneth Wald, *Religion and Politics in the United States*; Marian Faux, *Roe v. Wade* (New York: MacMillan, 1988).

4. See John Connery, *Abortion: The Development of the Roman Catholic Perspective* (Chicago: University of Chicago Press, 1977); John T. Noonan, Jr., "An Almost Absolute Value in History," in John T. Noonan, Jr., ed., *The*

Morality of Abortion: Legal and Historical Perspectives (Cambridge: Harvard University Press, 1970).

5. This pastoral letter has been the subject of some debate among the Catholic bishops, and it has not yet been officially released. It nonetheless provides some insight into the current thinking of Catholic leaders on gender issues.

6. U.S. Catholic Conference, "Partners in the Mystery of Redemption: A Pastoral Response to Women's Concerns for Church and Society," *Origins* 17, No. 45 (April 21, 1988).

7. There are many denominations within the broad family traditions such as Presbyterian and Methodist, however, and not all fit into the "mainline" category. The Free Methodists are a small evangelical denomination, for example. Somewhat counterintuitively, the Evangelical Lutherans are a mainline denomination, while the Missouri Synod Lutherans are often classified as evangelicals.

8. The belief in the inspiration of the Bible is not unique to Protestants, although they are more likely than Catholics to believe that the Bible contains no errors.

9. See Wald, *Religion and Politics*.

10. Ted G. Jelen, "Church-State Relations: The View from the Pulpit," (paper presented at the annual meeting of the American Political Science Association, Washington, D.C., 1991).

11. Jeffery K. Hadden, *The Gathering Storm in the Churches* (Garden City, N.Y.: Doubleday, 1969); Harold E. Quinley, *The Prophetic Clergy: Social Activism Among Protestant Ministers* (New York: John Wiley and Sons, 1974).

12. Faux, *Roe v. Wade*.

13. Ted G. Jelen, "The Clergy and Abortion," *Review of Religious Research*, forthcoming.

14. See Richard N. Ostling, "What Does God Really Think About Sex?" *Time* (June 24, 1991), pp. 48-50.

15. Ted G. Jelen, "Helpmeets and Weaker Vessels: Gender Role Stereotypes and Attitudes Toward Female Ordination," *Social Science Quarterly* 70 (1989), pp. 575-585.

16. Those who hold the Bible to be literally true believe that the world was created in six 24-hour days, and those who believe that the Bible is inerrant believe that although there are no errors, some parts are not meant to be interpreted literally.

17. Jelen, "The Clergy and Abortion."

18. Kathleen C. Boone, *The Bible Tells Them So: The Discourse of Protestant Fundamentalism* (Albany, N.Y.: SUNY Press, 1989); Wade Clark Roof, "Traditional Religion in Contemporary Society: A Theory of Local-Cosmopolitan Plausibility,"*American Sociological Review* 41 (1976), pp. 195-208.

19. Jelen, "The Clergy and Abortion"; Lisa Langenbach and Ted G. Jelen, "Ministers, Feminism and Abortion: A Causal Analysis," *Women & Politics* 11 (1991), pp. 33-52.

20. In the next verse, a death penalty is prescribed in this same case if *any mischief follow*, a life for a life, which is the general rule for punishment in this chapter. Although the meaning of the phrase "mischief" has been the occasion for some debate, many biblical scholars argue that this passage means that if the woman should die as a result of the miscarriage, the penalty would be death. If the only loss is that "her fruit depart from her," however, the penalty is less severe. This interpretation would suggest that the "fruit" is not accorded the same protection as a person.

21. See Garry Wills, *Under God: Religion and American Politics* (New York: Simon and Schuster, 1990) for a critique of biblical arguments against abortion.

22. Jelen, "The Clergy and Abortion"; Celeste Michelle Condit, *Decoding Abortion Rhetoric* (Urbana: University of Illinois Press, 1989).

23. See Clyde Wilcox, "The Fundamentalist Voter: Politicized Religious Identity and Political Attitudes and Behavior," *Review of Religious Research* 31 (1980), pp. 54-67; Clyde Wilcox, *God's Warriors: The Christian Right in Twentieth Century America* (Baltimore: The Johns Hopkins University Press, 1991); Clyde Wilcox and Ted G. Jelen, "Evangelicals and Political Tolerance,"*American Politics Quarterly* 18 (1990), pp. 25-46; Ted G. Jelen,

"Politicized Group Identification: The Case of Fundamentalism," *Western Political Quarterly* 44 (1991), pp. 209-219; Corwin Smidt, "Evangelicals vs. Fundamentalists: An Analysis of the Political Characteristics and Importance of Two Major Religious Movements within American Politics," *Western Political Quarterly* 41 (1988), pp. 601-620; Kathleen Beatty and Oliver Walter, "Fundamentalists, Evangelicals and Politics," *American Politics Quarterly* 16 (1988), pp. 43-59; Lyman Kellstedt, "The Falwell Issue Agenda: Sources of Support among White Protestant Evangelicals," in M. Lynn and D. Moberg, eds., *An Annual in the Sociology of Religion* (New York: JAI Press, 1989).

24. Wade Clark Roof and William McKinney, *American Mainline Religion* (New Brunswick: Rutgers University Press, 1987).

25. To determine whether it is appropriate to combine these variables into an index, we compute a statistic called *alpha*. A set of variables has an acceptable reliability if the alpha statistic exceeds .60. For these variables, alpha=.64. The results reported here are similar when the individual components of the index are used as control variables.

26. Those who attend church at least weekly, who pray at least daily, and who are strongly committed to their religion.

27. See Jelen, "The Clergy and Abortion."

28. Here we combine the literal and inerrantist positions. For an account of the interchangeability of these items see Ted G. Jelen, "Biblical Literalism and Inerrancy: Does the Difference Make a Difference?" *Sociological Analysis* 49 (1989), pp. 421-429. For further discussion of this issue, see Ted G. Jelen, Corwin Smidt, and Clyde Wilcox, "Biblical Literalism and Inerrancy: A Methodological Investigation," *Sociological Analysis* 51 (1990), pp. 307-315.

29. In the 1988 GSS data, 56 percent of whites who attended evangelical churches took an inerrant view of Scriptures, compared with 21 percent of Catholics and 24 percent of mainliners.

30. Rodney Stark and Charles Y. Glock, *American Piety: The Nature of Religious Commitment* (Berkeley: University of California Press, 1968); Ted G. Jelen and Marthe A. Chandler, "An Exploratory Study of the Validity of Indicators of Biblical Literalism" (paper presented at the annual meeting of the Western Social Science Association, Ft. Worth, Texas, 1985).

31. For those interested in comparing the effects of a given variable across groups, it is appropriate to compare the magnitude of the b in the regression results in the appendix for each group.

32. Examination of the components of the religious involvement index shows that, among Catholics, church attendance is a stronger predictor of abortion attitudes than are prayer or subjective religious intensity.

33. See Michael Welch and David Leege, "Catholic Evangelicalism and Political Orientations: A Case of Transcended Group Boundaries and Distinctive Political Values," *American Journal of Political Science* 35 (1991), pp. 197-212.

34. We also estimated a model that included items asked only in the 1988 survey. Belief in the need to punish sin was not a significant predictor nor was the desirability of female employment. The desirability-of-children scale had a weak but statistically significant relationship.

35. Religious involvement is an even stronger predictor of attitudes toward abortion for circumstances involving physical trauma.

36. Rosalind Pollack Petchesky, *Abortion and Woman's Choice* (Boston: Northeastern University Press, 1990).

37. Clyde Wilcox, "Race, Religion, Region, and Abortion Attitudes," *Sociological Analysis*, forthcoming.

38. Clyde Wilcox and Sue Thomas, "Religion and Feminist Attitudes."

39. Because the item on punishing sin was only included in the 1988 survey, these results are based on a relatively small number of cases.

40. In contrast, about a third of white Christians fall into the high religiosity category, and more than 40 percent of African-Americans.

41. See Elliot Dorff, "A Statement on the Permissibility of Abortion," *The United Synagogue Review* 42 (1988), pp. 16-17; and Judith Hauptman, "A Matter of Morality," *The United Synagogue Review* 42 (1988), pp. 17-28.

42. Of the 90 Jews in the 1987-1991 surveys, fully 90 percent took a pro-choice position and only 1 percent were consistently pro-life.

43. We experimented with including the Bible item in the regression analysis for Jews. This resulted in an equation with only 45 cases, and Bible was not a significant predictor. Only 6 Jews out of more than 100 who responded to the Bible item since 1985 indicated that the Bible was inerrant.

44. If dummy variables are included to identify all religious groups in the same equation, the value on at least one of these variables will be a linear combination of the others. For example, if we know that someone is *not* a Jew, Catholic, mainline Protestant, or someone with no religious affiliation, we can be reasonably sure that she or he is an evangelical Protestant.

5

Who Is Pro-Life, Pro-Choice, and In Between?

In the preceding chapters, we have examined the social characteristics, attitudes, and religious attributes that influence abortion attitudes. In this chapter, we will focus on a related but different question: What types of people take various positions on the abortion issue? In Chapters 2 through 4, we asked what percentage of people with a given characteristic (say a college degree or Catholic affiliation) took pro-choice or pro-life positions. In this chapter, we ask (for example) what percentage of pro-choice or pro-life citizens have a college degree. In other words, we seek to understand the *composition* of the different groups of citizens who take various positions on abortion.

To see how this question differs from those of the previous chapters, consider one of the relationships discussed in Chapter 2. In that chapter, we noted that pro-life sentiments were highest among those who had not completed high school and lowest among those who had additional education beyond a college degree. This does not mean that all or even most pro-life citizens have little education, however. Although 23 percent of pro-lifers dropped out before *entering* high school, 16 percent had a college or advanced degree. Moreover, not all pro-choice respondents had a college degree--fully 12 percent did not receive a *high-school* diploma, although nearly a third have a college or advanced degree.

Although the differences between the pro-life and pro-choice citizens noted in Chapter 2 are obvious in these data, by looking at the composition of various attitudinal groups we may get a somewhat different perspective on who takes pro-life and pro-choice positions. Citizens with an eighth-grade education are more likely to take a pro-life position than those with a college degree, but among pro-life citizens there are nearly as many with some college training as those who completed only the eighth grade.

Why are we interested in the composition of the pro-choice and pro-life groups and those who fall in neither camp? There are several reasons for examining this question. First, some people have argued that the pro-life and pro-choice activists differ so drastically in their life circumstances and disagree so fundamentally in their world views, that it is impossible for them to exchange ideas. If this is true of the non-elite supporters of these positions as well, then compromise on the abortion issue may be impossible.

Second, the composition of the group that favors abortion in some but not all circumstances may be critical to any understanding of the future of the abortion debate. It may be, for example, that Catholic situationalists will favor legal abortion only when the mother's life is in danger, that African-American situationalists will allow abortion under circumstances of physical trauma and poverty but under no other circumstances, and that West Coast situationalists will favor legal abortion under almost all circumstances. Alternatively, it may be that situationalists will generally view the abortion debate as one of degree and that there will be no readily identifiable demographic or attitudinal groups within their ranks. If the situationalists are composed of readily identifiable and quite different groups of citizens, then compromise may be difficult.

Finally, we will look for distinctive subgroups within the pro-choice and pro-life ranks. If we find sharp conflicts within either or both groups, then this may have important implications for the way the abortion issue is debated and possibly compromised.

In this chapter, we will examine separately three groups of citizens. First, we will consider those who take consistently pro-life views--who oppose abortion in all circumstances. Second, we will focus on those who take consistently pro-choice views--who favor legal abortion under all six circumstances. Finally, we will turn to the narrow majority who favor legal access to abortion under some, but not all, circumstances. We wish to know whether, and to what extent, the distinctions between the three groups are differences of degree or of kind.

Pro-Choice and Pro-Life Supporters: An Overview

Before focusing separately on those who take consistent pro-choice and pro-life positions on abortion, it is instructive to compare these two groups at the level of political activists. The attitudes of the small minority of people who devote substantial time and energy to the issue of abortion will serve as a baseline with which mass abortion attitudes can be compared. Kristin Luker,[1] in an important study of pro-choice and pro-life activists in California, reports that these two groups differed on many characteristics other than abortion attitudes. Her results are confirmed by a survey of activists in Missouri, conducted by Donald Granberg.[2] These activists differ from ordinary citizens in several important ways. Like activists in all types of political organizations, they are better educated, more involved in politics, and more consistent in their attitudes.

Luker and Granberg both reported that the pro-choice activists tended to be women with full-time jobs, college degrees, and high incomes. They were only nominally attached to religious institutions, had married later in life and had, on average, two children. In contrast, the pro-life activists were more likely to be housewives with some college education and lower family incomes. They were disproportionately Catholics with high levels of religiosity, had married early in life, and had three or more children. Luker reports that a surprising number of pro-life activists in California were converts to Catholicism.

More interesting than the simple demographic differences were the differences Luker and Granberg describe in the world views of these activists. Luker found that the pro-choice activists in California generally believed that men and women were essentially equal (and essentially similar in many important respects), and that unplanned pregnancies could be a barrier to a woman's career path and therefore to gender equality. Involuntary motherhood was seen as limiting a woman's human potential.

Most pro-choice activists were parents and believed that motherhood was a satisfying role, but most also believed that women could be happy without children. They saw children as a burden in some circumstances, for they can disrupt families, stress budgets, and interrupt careers. They believed that contraception was important to allow women to experience sex without the fear of pregnancy and that nonmarital sex was not always wrong. They believed that a fetus has some moral rights, though not those of a living human. Their position was therefore nuanced--the rights of the mother need to be balanced against the more limited rights of the fetus, and in this moral calculus each woman must make her own choice.

In contrast, the pro-life women in Luker's study believed that men and women are intrinsically different and have different roles in life. They believed that women are best suited for childrearing, and motherhood was seen as the most fulfilling role for a woman. Children may be unplanned, but all children were viewed as a blessing. The traditional gender-role attitudes of the pro-life activists were one source of their opposition to abortion. Luker argues that although the primary argument pro-life activists made was that abortion was murder, they also believed that abortion was wrong for two other reasons. First, abortion gave women control over their fertility and consequently disrupted the delicate emotional balance between men and women. Second, the pro-life activists believed that the availability of abortion fostered a world view that devalued motherhood.

Granberg reports that both pro-life and pro-choice activists in Missouri generally supported equality for women, although the pro-life contingent was markedly less supportive. Although majorities of pro-life activists thought women and men should have equal roles in society, that women should participate in politics, and would vote for a woman for president, only a small minority favored the Equal Rights Amendment (ERA).

Granberg's survey echoes Luker's findings on religious differences. He reports that 70 percent of pro-life activists rated personal salvation as the most important of eighteen possible values and that 62 percent of pro-choice activists rated salvation as the *least* important value. Granberg also found that the pro-life forces were generally opposed to contraception. Nearly half thought that a sterilization operation for couples not wanting more children (the most common form of contraception in the United States) was *always* wrong.

Granberg notes that pro-life activists were less supportive than pro-choice activists of civil liberties for unpopular minorities. He concludes that the most important differences between the two groups were, in order, gender (the pro-life forces had more men), number of children, Catholicism and religiosity, support for the ERA, political tolerance (pro-choice activists were more tolerant of diverse views), and attitudes toward the inviolability of life.

It must be remembered that Luker and Granberg studied *activists* in the abortion debate. These men and women not only took consistent pro-life or pro-choice positions, but they volunteered their time to support that cause or paid dues to belong to an organization. Activism is rather unusual in American politics. A variety of studies suggest that only a small minority of the American public is as active in politics as those Granberg and Luker studied.[3] Activists are generally better educated than other citizens and more consistent in their attitudes. In part, they are more consistent because their education and political experience make them better able to see the connections between the issues. They are also exposed to political interactions that may influence their views on other issues. For example, a Catholic pro-life activist who initially opposes the death penalty (also a Catholic position related to the sanctity of life) will regularly interact in meetings with Protestant pro-lifers who strongly support capital punishment. As a consequence, they may change their attitudes. Note above that Granberg found that pro-life activists are generally supportive of gender equality, but strongly opposed to the ERA. Pro-life activists would likely have had regular contact with other conservatives who opposed the ERA, and quite possibly this social interaction would affect their attitudes on the amendment.

Our study is of attitudes of the mass public, not of activists. Although citizens may consistently oppose legal abortion, they may not see that issue as related to the ERA, or to capital punishment, or to birth control information for teenagers. It is therefore not clear from Luker's or Granberg's studies that these same differences will appear among nonactivists.

Table 5.1 compares the demographic characteristics and attitudes of those citizens with consistent pro-choice or pro-life attitudes and allows us to see if Luker's or Granberg's insights are applicable to the mass public as well. The data in Table 5.1 show that pro-choice and pro-life citizens differ in ways that are similar to the activists described by Luker and Granberg. When compared with people who take a pro-life position, those who consistently favor legal abortion are less actively religious, better educated, more likely to be in the labor force, and likely to have smaller families.

TABLE 5.1 Pro-Life and Pro-Choice Citizens:
A Compositional Analysis of Demographic and Religious Differences
(in percent)

	Pro-life	Pro-choice
Demographics:		
College degree+	14	31
Less than high school	40	13
Black	14	10
Women	66	55
Housewife	40	21
Live in South	36	27
Raised in South	36	23
Raised in rural area	68	50
Average number of children	2.7	1.5
Religion:		
Evangelical Protestant	42	22
Catholic	34	22
Catholic Converts	3	2
Bible inerrant	63	17
Attend church at least weekly	62	15
Attend church more than weekly	27	2
Never attend church	8	21
Pray several times a day	51	14
Pray less than weekly	7	33
Sin must be punished	92	49

Source: General Social Survey, 1987-1991.

At the same time, it is important to note that these groups are not entirely homogeneous. Although those who consistently oppose abortion are generally religious, nearly 10 percent never attend church services. Similarly, approximately one in six of those who consistently favor legal abortion attend church more than weekly and believe that the Bible is the inerrant word of God. Although this is not shown in Table 5.1, approximately a quarter of pro-life respondents call themselves liberals, and a similar number of pro-choice citizens call themselves conservatives.

Table 5.2 shows the family and gender attitudes of the pro-life and pro-choice respondents. Those who consistently oppose abortion are more likely to believe that large families are desirable, are substantially less likely to believe that children can be a burden, and more likely to believe that children are life's greatest joy. Note, however, that many pro-choice citizens also believe that children are a joy and never a burden, and that most are parents.

Table 5.2 also shows the gender-role attitudes of the pro-life and pro-choice respondents. Included are some of the items that composed the public and private feminism scales in Chapter 3. Although the pro-life contingent is much less egalitarian than those who consistently support legal abortion, majorities take liberal positions on each of the public feminism items, as Granberg reports. On the questions that tap private feminism, however, majorities of those who consistently oppose abortion take conservative positions. Only a third of pro-lifers believe that a preschool child is not harmed when his or her mother works outside the home, and less than a third favor equal roles within families. These results again fit with Luker's descriptions of the attitudes of elites. The differences between those who favor and oppose legal abortion are greatest on attitudes toward family roles.

There are large differences in attitudes on sexual morality as well, with those who oppose legal abortion consistently opposed to nonmarital sexual activity. Pro-life citizens want to regulate adult access to "pornographic" publications, while those who take a pro-choice position are generally willing to allow adults to choose what they want to read. The differences in attitudes toward the inviolability of life are also quite large and consistent with those reported by Luker and Granberg.

Finally, in Table 5.2 we turn to attitudes toward contraception and government help for the children of the poor. One way to reduce the demand for abortions would be to make contraceptive devices and information more widely available, and/or to provide more financial

TABLE 5.2 Pro-Life and Pro-Choice Citizens' Attitudes (in percent)

	Pro-life	*Pro-Choice*
Familes and children:		
Families of four or more		
children are desirable	60	27
Strongly believe:		
Children are *not* more		
trouble than they are worth	46	20
Having children is life's		
greatest joy	63	32
Sexual morality:		
Premarital sex is *always* wrong	73	9
Extramarital sex is *always* wrong	83	32
Pornography for adults should		
be banned	71	25
Life connection:		
Euthanasia wrong	75	14
Suicide OK for terminally ill	9	77
Public feminism:		
Would vote for woman for President	75	93
Women equally suited for politics	51	79
Private feminism:		
Preschool children not hurt by		
employed mothers	33	59
Equal family roles	28	71
Support more spending on:		
Child care	60	62
Food stamps	32	23
Support for unwanted children	77	72
Birth control information should be		
available to adults	75	98
To teenagers	61	95

(continues)

TABLE 5.2 (continued)

	Pro-life	*Pro-choice*
Birth control devices should be available to teenagers even if parents disapprove	27	75
Approve sex education in public schools	61	94
Abortion-related attitudes:		
It is very likely that state will impose more restrictions	41	20
If abortion is illegal, number of abortions will decline	74	36

Sources: American National Election Study, 1988; General Social Survey, 1987-1991; *CBS News/New York Times* Survey, 1989.

assistance to poor pregnant women. Despite this fact, most pro-life organizations take no position on contraception, and many pro-life Senators vote against funding of nutrition programs for pregnant women and young children. Some pro-choice activists charge that these pro-life policymakers who oppose programs that would support children of the poor believe that life begins at conception and ends at birth.

Among the general public, however, support for funding of child care and food stamps is actually slightly higher among pro-life citizens, although support for increased funding for these programs is quite high among both groups. Moreover, a large majority of pro-life citizens believe that state funds should be used to support unwanted children.[4] Among nonactivist pro-lifers, support for contraception is generally strong. Majorities believe that birth control information should be available to adults and teenagers, and favor sex education in the classroom. Pro-choice supporters are predictably more supportive, and it is noteworthy that fully a quarter of pro-life supporters do not favor birth control information for adults. Nonetheless, these results suggest that the pro-life public is much less opposed to contraception than the activists described by Luker and Granberg.

We draw three conclusions from these data. First, the demographic and attitudinal differences between pro-choice and pro-life activists described by Luker and Granberg are generally mirrored in the general public. These two groups differ on far more than abortion attitudes, for their backgrounds and world views are so markedly different as to make communication between them difficult. Second, the pro-life portion of the mass public is far more favorably disposed to contraception and public gender equality than the pro-life activists in Luker's study. Finally, although the differences between these two groups are large, neither group is homogeneous. Not all of those who consistently oppose abortion are highly religious, conservative, or anti-feminist, nor are all pro-choice citizens non-religious, liberal, or feminist.

Pro-Life Citizens

Our data show that only 8 percent of citizens from 1987 through 1991 took a strictly pro-life position. If we relaxed our definition a bit, including those who favor abortion only when the woman's health is in danger, the percentage would increase to 14 percent. As we noted in Chapter 2, however, we do not include this latter group in the pro-life category because pro-life activists are quite wary of an exception based on the health but not on the life of the mother. This concern dates to the days of abortion reform legislation in the 1960s,[5] when pro-choice doctors interpreted the concept of a woman's health to include psychological health. Thus, "health"-related abortions were often performed to avoid psychological discomfort.[6]

Of this 8 percent, not all are strongly committed to their position. The 1989 *CBS News/New York Times* survey asked several versions of abortion questions, and in that survey more than 15 percent of pro-life respondents to our six-point scale later qualified their position and indicated that they would allow abortion in some circumstances. Moreover, one item framed the question in the way the pro-choice partisans most prefer: "Do you agree or disagree with the following statement: Even in cases where I might think abortion is the wrong thing to do, I don't think the government has any business preventing the woman from having an abortion."

TABLE 5.3 Issue Groups Among Pro-life Citizens (in percent)

	White Catholics	White Evangelicals	Blacks
Birth control information should be available to:			
Adults	74	74	67
Teenagers	60	57	56
Birth control devices to young teens without parental approval	24	24	40
Sex education in public schools	70	48	58
Liberal position on:			
Public feminism	36	19	33
Private feminism	11	5	8
Make divorce easier	10	11	33
Ban pornography for adults	68	83	41
Euthanasia legal	20	20	14
Suicide OK for terminally ill	9	6	13
Support death penalty	62	75	43
Full civil rights for homosexuals	41	14	22
Full civil rights for atheists	32	17	12
Conservative	38	54	28
Liberal	21	16	34
Democrat	50	36	80
Republican	36	39	7
Spend more on:			
food stamps	33	24	54
Child care	69	55	75
AIDS	81	66	82
Environment	74	55	56
Unemployed	41	49	64
Help blacks	37	17	65
Inequality not a problem	38	51	12

(continues)

TABLE 5.3 (continued)

	White Catholics	White Evangelicals	Blacks
Group affect:			
Affect, Fundamentalists	-17	14	4
Affect, Catholics	21	-3	-7
Affect, Blacks	1	2	16

Sources: American National Election Study, 1988; General Social Survey, 1987-1991.

More than a quarter of otherwise pro-life citizens agreed that the government should not prevent abortions even when they were wrong, and others were undecided.[7] When these qualifications are combined with the inconsistent responses mentioned above, only about 3 percent of the public took a consistent position that abortion should *always* be illegal.

Pro-life citizens are divided about their movement's strategy. Approximately half of pro-lifers accepted the tactics of Operation Rescue, where pro-life demonstrators placed their bodies in front of abortion clinics and tried to deter women who sought to enter for abortions. This data is from the *CBS News/New York Times* survey in 1989, before the publicity for Operation Rescue in Wichita, Kansas, in 1991. On the other hand, more than one in five of those who consistently opposed legal abortion categorized the pro-life movement as mostly populated with extremists.

Issue Divisions Among Pro-Life Citizens

Although the pro-life contingent in our data is small, there are important issue cleavages that prevent the movement's full political mobilization. The most important cleavage is religious: 75 percent of those who believe abortion should be illegal are either evangelical Protestants or Catholics. As noted in Chapter 4, there is some religious tension between evangelicals and Catholics, which prevents a united pro-life front.

To understand why this presents a political problem for the pro-life community, consider the fate of one evangelical organization of the 1980s, the Moral Majority. Although the Reverend Jerry Falwell claimed that his organization appealed to conservative Catholics and Jews, research showed that state-level organizations did not attract Catholic members.[8] The Moral Majority instead attracted one subgroup of evangelicals called fundamentalists, who believe that the Bible is literally true. Historically, fundamentalists have disliked Catholics, and this lingering religious prejudice prevented the Moral Majority from attracting Catholic members. At one sermon preceding a Moral Majority meeting in Columbus, Ohio, the fundamentalist preacher referred to the Catholic church as "the harlot of Rome."[9] Thus, although the Moral Majority took a pro-life position and its leaders attempted to appeal to Catholics, the anti-Catholicism of the fundamentalist preachers who headed county organizations prevented such a coalition from forming.

In Table 5.3, we present some attitudinal differences between Catholic and evangelical pro-lifers. We have isolated white Catholics, white evangelicals and blacks in this table. We separate African-Americans from whites because there are important racial differences in some of the issue positions we examine here and because black pro-lifers are overwhelmingly evangelical. All of those included in this table oppose abortion in all of the six circumstances discussed in Chapter 2.[10]

The Roman Catholic Church has taken a position in opposition to contraception, a position not shared by evangelical churches. Surprisingly, however, there are no real differences between Catholics and evangelicals in attitudes toward birth control, although African-Americans are substantially more likely to favor providing contraception to teenagers without their parent's consent. Catholics are much more likely than evangelicals to favor sex education in schools.

White Catholics and blacks are much more likely than white evangelicals to take feminist positions on our public and private feminism scale, and to favor general societal equality. White Catholics and evangelicals are equally opposed to euthanasia and suicide (blacks are slightly more supportive), but Catholics are less supportive of the death penalty, and African-Americans are even more strongly opposed.[11]

Many African-American and Catholic pro-lifers call themselves liberals, but white evangelical pro-lifers are quite conservative. They are less supportive of civil rights for unpopular minorities than are Catholics.[12] Catholics and blacks are more supportive of spending on programs to aid the poor than white evangelicals, and Catholics are more likely to favor spending on the environment and other liberal programs.

Finally, in the bottom of Table 5.3 we show the affect of each group toward the other two. The questions that generated these data (in the 1988 ANES) asked respondents to place each group on a feeling thermometer, where 100° is very warm or positive, and 0° is very cold or negative. We have adjusted these numbers so that positive scores indicate that the respondent is warm toward the group, and negative scores indicate coolness.[13] Each group is warm toward members of their own group and cool or indifferent to the others. Note that Catholics are quite cool toward fundamentalists, but evangelicals are only slightly cool toward Catholics. Among fundamentalist evangelicals, however, hostility toward Catholics is much more evident. Those evangelicals belonging to fundamentalist churches were even more negative toward Catholics than Catholics were toward fundamentalists.

The cleavage between at least some groups of white evangelicals and white Catholics is wide, and makes cooperation between the two groups difficult. Blacks who take a pro-life stand are even more liberal on other issues than Catholics, with little in common with white evangelicals except some religious doctrine and their opposition to abortion. This explains the tendency of pro-life groups to take positions on only the abortion issue--their consensus is quite fragile, and any discussion of other political issues is likely to lead to disagreement.

Pro-Choice Citizens

The plurality position on abortion in our GSS data is that abortion should be allowed for any reason. In other words, more people take that position than any other single position on our six-point scale.

Yet this does not mean that most Americans favor unrestricted access to legal abortion. The 1989 *CBS News/New York Times* survey contained a series of questions on restrictions on legal abortion that would not constitute an absolute ban.

These restrictions included parental notification and/or consent for minors, mandatory tests for fetal viability after twenty weeks of pregnancy, making it more difficult for private clinics to perform abortions, and prohibiting public hospitals from performing abortions. Many of those who believed that abortion should be legal under all circumstances supported some of these restrictions on abortion. More than three in four pro-choice citizens supported parental notification (86 percent of all respondents supported this restriction). Slightly more than half took the stronger position that parental consent should be required before abortions are performed on teenaged women. More than two in three pro-choice citizens favored fetal viability tests, and also favored making it more difficult for private clinics to perform abortions. In contrast, only a small minority of pro-choice respondents favored a ban on abortions in public hospitals.[14] Only 7 percent of pro-choice respondents favored no limitations on legal abortion, and these constituted only 3 percent of the sample.

These results suggest that most pro-choice citizens favor at least some restrictions on abortions, especially for minors. It seems likely that some pro-choice citizens believe that there were too many abortions in the 1980s, and perhaps many abortion decisions were made too hastily. Evidence for this point comes from the *CBS News/New York Times* survey, in which 15 percent of otherwise pro-choice respondents agreed with a statement that abortions should be more difficult to obtain. Moreover, pro-choice citizens do not believe that abortion is always the correct choice--only 9 percent favored abortions as a primary means of birth control.[15] Finally, more than 10 percent of the consistent pro-choice respondents believed that abortion is murder, but that it is nonetheless sometimes the best course.

This view of abortion as morally ambiguous leads them neither to favor a ban on abortion, nor to let anyone but the woman make the ultimate decision, however. Although many of the pro-choice respondents support restrictions designed to make abortions more difficult to obtain, they believe that abortions should not be illegal for any reason. Moreover, among those pro-choice citizens who favored one or more restrictions on legal abortion, the overwhelming majority agreed that the government should not prohibit abortions even when such procedures were morally wrong.

Issue Groups Among Pro-Choice Supporters

We saw above that those who take consistent pro-life positions are divided between generally moderate and egalitarian Catholics and more conservative evangelicals who support traditional gender roles. Among pro-choice citizens, the major cleavage is ideological, involving liberals and libertarians. In many ways, this division reflects a split between the two parties, for Republicans who are pro-choice are frequently found in the libertarian camp and pro-choice Democrats are more likely to be liberals.

To understand the difference between pro-choice libertarians and liberals, consider that government can regulate at least two distinct types of individual behavior--economic and social. Libertarians generally hold that government should not regulate much in either sphere; populists favor regulation of both economic and social activity. Contemporary American conservatives usually argue that government regulation of the economy is intrusive, but that the government should regulate the social and moral behavior of its citizens. Contemporary liberals believe that the government should regulate economic activity to protect citizens from the abuses of powerful corporations but leave moral and social behavior to the discretion of individuals.

It is difficult to identify libertarians in the General Social Survey data, because the survey contains few questions on economic regulation. The other major national academic survey on political matters, the American National Election Studies, contain few items on social regulation. By examining the differences between pro-choice Democrats and Republicans on issues of economic regulation in the ANES, and on issues of social regulation from the General Social Survey, however, we can indirectly explore this important cleavage in the pro-choice community. Because Republicans who favor choice are more likely to be libertarians than are pro-choice Democrats, in Table 5.4 we compare the views of Republicans and Democrats. Because

African-Americans who are pro-choice are almost all Democrats, we have isolated blacks in this table as well.[16]

The data in this table show some important differences between these groups. At the top of the table, we present some important demographic variables that should be kept in mind as we examine the attitudes below. Note that white Republicans and Democrats have a very similar demographic profile; African-Americans who are pro-choice are less well educated, more religious, and more likely to be working women.

All three groups are generally supportive of civil liberties for unpopular minorities, and although they differ somewhat on the morality of certain types of sexual behavior, they are generally tolerant in that category as well. Democrats are slightly more tolerant than Republicans (especially of homosexuals), and African-Americans are less tolerant than whites. The racial differences are almost entirely attributable to differences in education--blacks with college degrees are as tolerant as white Democrats, except (predictably) of racists.

Large majorities of each group favor allowing adults to read pornographic materials if they wish.[17] They generally disapproved of efforts to make divorce easier to obtain and favored allowing minors access to birth control devices even if their parents disapproved. Majorities of each group favored allowing doctors to end the lives of terminally ill patients if patients request it, and to allow suicide. There are large differences among pro-choice citizens in the approach to the role of government, however. White Democrats are more likely than Republicans to favor an active government role in helping the disadvantaged, and African-Americans were even more supportive.

Although the divisions among the pro-choice contingent are not as deep as among pro-lifers, there is little consensus among those who favor legal abortion on economic issues. There is agreement, however, that the government should not regulate the private lives of American citizens, and that women deserve equal rights and responsibilities in society.

Situationalists

As we noted in Chapter 2, a narrow majority of Americans favors some restrictions on abortion but does not support an absolute ban.

TABLE 5.4 Issue Groups Among Pro-Choice Citizens (in percent)

	White Democrats	White Republicans	Black Democrats
College education	34	35	16
Evangelical	22	21	65
Catholic	24	21	8
High religiosity	15	18	29
Women	56	51	69
Housewives	23	21	21
Conservative	15	46	15
Liberal	53	19	53
Full civil liberties for:			
Homosexuals	71	67	58
Atheists	60	56	47
Racists	49	45	34
Sexual practics always wrong:			
Homosexual	47	65	72
Premarital	7	12	14
Support pornography ban for adults	6	8	3
Support easier divorce	38	39	25
Favor sex education	97	94	95
Favor birth control to teenagers whose parents disapprove	76	75	71
Disapprove of Supreme Court ruling on school prayer	42	51	68
Euthanasia legal	87	87	79
Liberal position on:			
Public feminism	81	75	67
Private feminism	46	29	30

(continues)

TABLE 5.4 (continued)

	White Democrats	White Republicans	Black Democrats
Government should help (vs. help themselves):			
Poor	32	18	60
Sick	60	54	74
Blacks	22	11	62
Government is doing too much	22	48	11

Sources: American National Election Study, 1988; General Social Survey, 1987-1991.

These citizens support legal abortion in some situations but not in others. Many situationalists attempt to balance the individualist value of choice against the limited rights of the fetus. Others merely distinguish between circumstances under which they approve or disapprove of abortion. None view abortion as representing a case of one absolute right.

We do not refer to the situationalists as moderates, for in America that term carries a strongly positive connotation. Moderates are generally portrayed as being pragmatic and reasoned in contrast to ideologues, who are often portrayed as rigid and unyielding. This view of moderates is not entirely accurate nor does it necessarily fit the situationalists. Moreover, we do not refer to them as conflicted, for although some may perceive the necessity to trade off one value against another, others may feel quite comfortable about their position. In fact, approximately a third of situationalists believe that abortion is murder, but that it is sometimes the best course.

Although the situationalists constitute a narrow majority, there is a wide range of possible attitudes between the pro-life and pro-choice absolutes. Some favor only one exception to a pro-life position, others favor legal abortion in all but one of the six possible circumstances. Nearly half (44 percent) favor legal abortion in exactly three circumstances. Approximately 17 percent favor abortion in either two or four situations, and roughly 11 percent approve of legal abortion in under either one or five conditions.

Traumatic and Elective Circumstances

Although there is much disagreement on abortion, there is a greater consensus on which types of circumstances are more or less compelling. Table 5.5 shows the distribution of responses by situationalists to each of the six abortion items crossed with the values on the abortion scale. Because there are subtle racial differences in these patterns, we present them separately for African-Americans and whites.

Clearly, situationalists see the health of the mother as the most compelling reason for abortion. More than 70 percent of those who would allow abortion in only one circumstance make that exception for the health of the mother. Many religious groups (including most importantly the Catholic church) hold that abortion is allowable to save the life of the mother, but as we noted above pro-life activists are quite skeptical of making an exception for the health of the mother. Yet many would be willing to consider a carefully crafted exception for maternal health.

Although the situationalists are divided as to whether rape or fetal defect is a more important justification for abortion, there is strong consensus that abortions under these two circumstances are more acceptable than abortions for poverty, unmarried mothers, or when a couple wants no more children. Note that for those who approve of only two circumstances, the situationalists are divided on which condition is more important, but for those who would allow abortion under exactly three circumstances, nearly all approve of the three trauma items and oppose the three elective items.[18]

Among the elective items, blacks and whites both find poverty the most compelling justification for abortion. Yet African-Americans find poverty relatively more compelling than do whites. Eight percent of blacks who support abortion in three circumstances approve of abortion for poor women (usually instead of approving of abortion in the case of fetal defect), a figure four times that of whites. Because African-Americans are more likely than whites to experience poverty or to have friends or family who live below the poverty line, they may more fully appreciate the difficulty of supporting an additional child.

TABLE 5.5 Abortion Scale and Approval of Specific Items:
Situationalists (in percent)

No. Items Approved	One	Two	Three	Four	Five
Specific Items:					
Whites:					
Mother's health	71	93	99	99	99
Rape	19	56	98	99	99
Fetal defect	10	51	98	98	99
Poverty	1	0	2	46	73
Single mother	0	0	1	31	66
No more children	0	0	3	27	63
Blacks:					
Mother's health	79	96	98	98	97
Rape	13	58	97	95	100
Fetal defect	5	42	88	95	100
Poverty	3	1	8	57	85
Single mother	0	2	5	21	39
No more children	0	1	5	34	80

Source: General Social Survey, 1987-1991.

TABLE 5.6 The Situationalists: A Compositional Analysis (in percent)

No of items approved:	One	Two	Three	Four	Five
Evangelical Protestant	51	49	42	31	29
Bible inerrant	58	54	43	37	31
Catholic	27	27	24	29	28
Attend church weekly	20	11	5	4	3
Pray daily	42	30	27	21	16
Most conservaive position on:					
Sexual morality	74	66	63	49	43
Women's role in society	9	11	8	11	7
Women in politics	17	14	10	8	7
Euthanasia	71	46	29	20	15
Republican	48	40	40	43	39
Democrat	40	50	49	48	51
Conservative	59	41	35	31	30
Liberal	17	23	24	25	33
College degree+	18	15	12	10	14
Less than high school	28	31	25	28	16

No. of items approved:	One	Two	Three	Four	Five
Black	14	16	12	15	16
Women	55	60	57	58	51
Housewife	34	31	32	34	25
Live in South	40	39	37	36	32
Raised in South	39	38	36	33	27
Raised in rural area	71	69	66	59	60

Source: General Social Survey, 1987-1991.

In contrast, although whites find the case of the unmarried mother somewhat more compelling than that of the couple who wants no more children, blacks order these two cases differently. By a ratio of 2.5 to 1, blacks who approve of abortion in all but one situation make their exception for unmarried women, not for married couples who want no more children. The reason for this racial difference may lie in the higher proportion of births to unwed mothers in the black community. Although the rates of births to white unmarried mothers have risen dramatically in recent years, the figure for blacks is substantially higher. African-American respondents may know several successful, loving single mothers, and therefore may not see an unmarried status as a barrier to motherhood. Whites may perceive that society stigmatizes single mothers and therefore favor abortions under this circumstance.

Distinguishing Among the Situationalists

We find that the situationalists range along a continuum from more supportive to less supportive of legal abortion, and that this same continuum orders them on other dimensions such as religiosity, attitudes toward sexual morality, attitudes toward euthanasia, and general conservatism.[19] The data are presented in Table 5.6. Those who favor abortion in only one circumstance are more conservative on these other attitudes than those who favor it in exactly two circumstances; the latter are, in turn, more conservative than those who favor abortion in only three circumstances.

On some other variables, however, there is little difference among these groups. Although we have seen that education is an important predictor of abortion attitudes, it serves mainly to distinguish between pro-choice and pro-life citizens and is not consistently related to differences in the attitudes of the situationalists. Similarly, the proportion of Catholics does not seem to differ across the groups of situationalists.

Although this finding may not seem surprising, it is possible to imagine a different result. It might have been true that Catholics would be disproportionately found among those who favor a single exception to a pro-life stance (health of the mother), that evangelical Protestants would be more likely to favor abortion under traumatic but not elective circumstances, and that mainline Protestants would be more likely to favor abortion under several circumstances. We can also imagine differences between men and women, blacks and whites, and those raised in the South and elsewhere. In other words, we initially considered it possible that the situationalists would constitute several distinct groups of citizens that would differ from each other on demographic, religious, and attitudinal variables.

That we find instead a continuum on all variables is important, for it indicates that the abortion issue is more amenable to compromise than may be commonly thought. Had the situationalists been composed of distinct attitudinal and demographic groups, compromise would have involved negotiations between (for example) Catholics and evangelicals, African-Americans and whites, Republicans and Democrats. Instead, those who support abortion in three circumstances do not differ markedly from either those who support it in two or four circumstances.

Although the situationalists do not comprise distinct demographic and attitudinal groups, there are some interesting differences among them. First, those who would allow abortion only when the health of the mother is in danger are distinctive in their attitudes toward euthanasia and their personal religiosity. They are much more likely than those who would allow abortion in two circumstances to disapprove of euthanasia, to pray daily, and to attend church more than weekly. Our statistical analysis indicates that attitudes toward euthanasia are important predictors of those who support abortion in one or two circumstances,[20] but attitudes toward sexual morality are more important in distinguishing those who would allow abortion in four or five circumstances.

Conclusions

This chapter has illustrated three important points. First, attitudinal and demographic differences between pro-life and pro-choice citizens at the level of the mass public reflect activist-level patterns to some extent. In general terms, our analyses of ordinary citizens reflect the patterns found in the Luker and Granberg studies of abortion activists. However, a second aspect of our findings qualifies the first point. There is considerable overlap between the characteristics of pro-life and pro-choice citizens. Neither group has a monopoly on education, religiosity, feminism, or concern for children. Indeed, the results presented in this chapter suggest that even people who take pro-life or pro-choice stands share many values with their ostensible opponents. Pro-life respondents *do* value personal freedom and autonomy, and pro-choice citizens *do* have some concern for the fate of the embryo.

Third, our data show that a narrow majority of Americans are situationalists, who favor legal access to abortion in some circumstances, but not others. Although there are certainly different levels of support for legal abortion in this group, our results show that these differences are matters of degree. No variable or set of variables clearly delimits any point on the abortion scale among situationalists. Rather, small changes in attitudes related to abortion opinions are associated with subtle changes in abortion attitudes themselves.

What these results suggest to us is that common ground does exist on abortion attitudes. Differences among and between various abortion positions do matter, but the image of two opposed camps, each questioning the integrity and morality of the other, does not describe the mass public in the United States. Pro-life and pro-choice attitudes arise as the result of the interplay of a number of competing values. Our data suggest that most Americans hold values that pull them in both pro-choice and pro-life directions, which makes the search for a middle ground possible.

Notes

1. Kristin Luker, *Abortion and the Politics of Motherhood* (Berkeley: University of California Press, 1984).

2. See Donald Granberg, "A Comparison of Members of Pro- and Anti-Abortion Organizations in Missouri," *Social Biology* 28 (1982), pp. 239-252; "Family Size Preferences and Sexual Permissiveness as Factors Differentiating Abortion Activists," *Social Psychology Quarterly* 45 (1982), pp. 15-23.

3. For a brief introduction to the literature on political participation, see Margaret Conway, *Political Participation in the United States*, 2nd ed. (Washington, D.C.: CQ Press, 1991). For a more detailed but dated analysis,

see Sidney Verba and Norman Nie, *Participation in America* (New York: Harper and Row, 1972). Verba and Nie's analysis suggests that some estimates of participation rates in the United States may be artificially low, because many Americans specialize in particular styles or "modes" of political activity.

4. The data on spending on food stamps and child care come from the 1988 American National Election Study. The data on support for state spending for the care of unwanted children comes from the 1989 *CBS News/New York Times* survey. It should be noted that these results are *not* an artifact of the slightly larger black contingent among pro-life respondents. These patterns persist after the introduction of controls for race.

5. Raymond Tatolavitch and Byron W. Daynes, *The Politics of Abortion: A Study of Community Conflict in Public Policymaking* (New York: Praeger, 1981).

6. Donald Granberg, personal communication.

7. This item was asked immediately after seven concrete items on whether abortion should be legal or against the law. Five of these seven items mirrored those in the GSS, but instead of the question on married couples who want no more children, the CBS survey included two others--when the pregnancy would force a teenager to drop out of school, and when the pregnancy would force the woman to interrupt her career. We thus suspect that the position of this item within the questionnaire generates an *underestimation* of agreement.

8. See Clyde Wilcox, *God's Warriors: The Christian Right in Twentieth Century America* (Baltimore: Johns Hopkins University Press, 1991); and Sharon Georgianna, *The Moral Majority and Fundamentalism: Plausibility and Dissonance* (Lewiston, N.Y.: Edwin Mellon Press, 1989). For further evidence of the fragmenting effects of religious particularism, see Ted G. Jelen, *The Political Mobilization of Religious Belief* (New York: Praeger, 1991).

9. This anti-Catholicism in the Moral Majority prevented a coalition from forming between pro-life groups, which contain substantial numbers of Catholics, and the Christian Right. For more details, see Clyde Wilcox and Leopoldo Gomez, "The Christian Right and the Pro-Life Movement: An Analysis of Political Support," *Review of Religious Research* 31 (1990), pp. 380-390; and Clyde Wilcox, *God's Warriors*.

10. We also include information from the 1988 American National Election Study. In that survey, a single abortion question was asked, with only three response categories included. We have selected those respondents who believed that abortion should never be allowed, distinguishing these respondents from those who take a pro-choice or situationalist position.

11. Blacks and Catholics may oppose capital punishment for different reasons. The Catholic church has opposed the death penalty as part of its "seamless garment" of pro-life positions. African-Americans often note the fact that blacks are much more likely to be put to death in the United States than whites, even when the severity of their crimes is identical.

12. Blacks are also less tolerant of homosexuals and atheists, but this is mostly explained by their lower levels of education.

13. Specifically, we have adjusted the scores by subtracting the mean feeling thermometer score for each individual across a range of groups from the feeling thermometer for the group in question. This allows us to correct for what are termed "response sets": In other words, we can compensate for individuals who use very warm or very cool scores. See Clyde Wilcox, Lee Sigelman, and Elizabeth Cook, "Some Like it Hot: Individual Differences to Group Feeling Thermometers," _Public Opinion Quarterly_ 53 (1989), pp. 246-257.

14. It should be noted that in national surveys, there is a high level of inconsistency among all respondents. It is also true that not all pro-life respondents in this survey favored a ban on abortion in public hospitals. Such inconsistent answers may be the result of several sources--response error, coding error, data entry error, and non-attitudes. The large majorities of pro-choice citizens who favored some restrictions, however, suggests that error or non-attitudes are inadequate explanations in this case, and that even pro-choice respondents desire some restrictions on access to legal abortion.

15. Four percent of those who consistently opposed legal abortion favored abortion as a primary form of birth control. Three percent of pro-life respondents also favored Medicaid funds for abortions for poor women, although if abortion was entirely illegal as these citizens preferred, this public policy would be relatively inexpensive. These seeming irrational responses are likely due to measurement error, rather than representing an unusual combination of beliefs. Such error can occur in several ways. First, a respondent may misunderstand a question. The interviewer may

misunderstand the response, or may record the response incorrectly. Errors can occur when answers to questions are coded into the computer.

16. We are exploring the differences between libertarians and liberals on attitudes toward economic activity, so it is important to isolate blacks. African-Americans are much more supportive of an active welfare state than white Democrats, and combining black and white Democrats would blur the patterns we report.

17. The question used the term "pornography," instead of the more neutral term "erotic material."

18. There is a small but significant difference between men and women in their ordering of the rape and defect conditions. Women generally find fetal defect slightly more compelling than rape, but men are more likely to favor abortion when rape is involved than fetal defect. Only 36 percent of men found fetal defect the most compelling second circumstance in our data, compared with 44 percent of women. In contrast, 44 percent of men and 36 percent of women found rape more compelling. These differences were larger among blacks, but significant among whites as well.

19. This result stands up to a variety of multivariate tests. First, we selected only those who favored abortion in some but not all circumstances, and we predicted abortion stance through discriminant analysis. Only one function was statistically significant, accounting for more than 75 percent of the common variance. That function represented a simple continuum from more supportive to less supportive of legal abortion. Second, we estimated a series of logistic regression equations and included only those citizens with contiguous positions on the abortion scale. In other words, we estimated one equation to distinguish those who favored abortion in two circumstances from those who favored it in three, one to distinguish between those who favored abortion in three circumstances from those who favored it in four circumstances, and so on. The results were remarkably consistent across equations--the same predictors were significant in nearly all equations.

20. Those who support legal abortion in only two circumstances are almost evenly divided between those who would allow abortion for pregnancies resulting from rape and those who would allow abortion for severely defective fetuses. Those who would allow abortion in the case of fetal defect but not in the case of rape resemble those respondents who favor legal abortion in only one circumstance. In other words, attitudes on the value of life are important predictors of those respondents who would allow abortion

only when the mother's health is in danger, and possibly also if the fetus would be severely defective.

6

The Electoral Politics of Abortion

As the eventual reversal of *Roe v. Wade* becomes increasingly likely, the abortion issue will intrude more frequently and more deeply into electoral politics. Already several U.S. Senate, U.S. House, and gubernatorial elections have focused in part on abortion, at least one lieutenant governor's election has hinged almost entirely on the issue, and the abortion controversy has been central in numerous state legislative elections.[1] The increased salience of the abortion issue is not entirely welcome by politicians, who find themselves facing two opposing sets of motivated activists, each of whom sees the abortion issue as one in which compromise is impossible.[2]

During the 1970s and 1980s, pro-life organizations were quite active in electoral politics.[3] Pro-choice groups also mobilized behind candidates,[4] but at least some analysts suggested that pro-choice citizens were less likely to cast a single-issue vote than those who consistently opposed legal abortion. This imbalance has usually been explained by the Supreme Court's *Roe* decision, which guaranteed a woman's right to abortion and therefore left pro-choice voters free to decide their vote based on other issues because they believed that their vote for a pro-life candidate was unlikely to have policy consequences.[5]

Pro-choice activists claim that the *Webster* decision mobilized pro-choice voters into political action. They argue that once abortion rights became contingent on the decisions of elected officials, pro-choice voters became more likely to cast single-issue votes. The victory of pro-choice governors in Virginia and New Jersey in 1989 seemed to provide evidence for this claim. In the 1990 elections, however, governors who favored restrictions on abortion won in Pennsylvania, Michigan, Ohio, and Kansas; candidates who supported legal abortion won the statehouse in Texas, Florida, California, and Illinois.[6] These mixed results suggest that a pro-choice position is no guarantee of electoral success.

Candidates take positions on issues for several reasons. Some voice their deeply held, personal convictions. Others seek to increase their share of the vote. Those candidates who take positions to help their electoral prospects may seek to maximize their votes in their party's primary election or in the general election. Candidates who position themselves to win a party primary may find themselves poorly positioned to do well in a general election. In 1989, for example, Marshall Coleman, winner of the Republican gubernatorial nomination in Virginia took a strong pro-life position in the primary, opposing abortion even in cases of rape and incest. Because he had earlier supported abortion in such cases, it seems likely that he took this position to gain primary-election votes. Yet, in the general election, a strict pro-life position proved to be a liability.

Prior to the *Webster* decision, candidates of both parties often took positions to appeal to a narrow core of party activists. Strong pro-life or pro-choice positions could win some primary election votes and also enable the candidates to get more resources (money, volunteer time) from pro-life or pro-choice groups. Although primary-election voters are not more likely to take consistent pro-choice or pro-life positions on abortion than general-election voters, a pro-choice or pro-life position in a party primary would help candidates appeal to a certain bloc of primary voters. In the general election, extreme positions on the abortion issue had few electoral costs, since most voters realized that the right to an abortion was guaranteed by the Court. If the Court overturns or strongly restricts *Roe v. Wade*, however, then voters will more likely respond to the abortion positions of candidates.

The *Webster* decision in 1989 created an environment in which some voters became more responsive to the abortion issue, for it signaled an increased willingness by the Court to uphold state restrictions on legal abortion. Before 1989, governors and state legislators could not pass binding limits on abortion, for the Court was certain to overturn those limits. Now, however, state legislatures are free to propose new limits on abortion, which the Court might uphold. As a consequence, abortion has become an important issue in many gubernatorial elections, in some U.S. Senate elections, and in some elections for the U.S. House of Representatives.

Even after a possible reversal of *Roe*, abortion will be only one of several important issues on which elections may hinge. Moreover, policy issues are not the only factor influencing vote choice. Voters respond to the quality of candidates, and many will support a stronger candidate who does not completely share their views over a candidate who seems likely to be a weak leader. For many voters, the candidate's party provides an even more important voting cue. Some citizens vote only for candidates of their party, and others evaluate the quality of the candidates and their issue positions through the perceptual filter of partisanship. When elections focus primarily on abortion, however, candidates who are poorly positioned on the issue will lose votes. Because there are differences across the fifty states in support for legal abortion, a winning position in one state may lose votes in another.

In all states, however, a strict pro-life position will be poorly suited to winning elections that focus on legal abortion. We have seen that in the country at large, fewer than 10 percent of the public takes a strict pro-life stand, and fewer than one in six respondents to the General Social Survey favor abortion only when the woman's health is in danger. Pro-life voters are more likely to cast a single-issue abortion vote, so these figures slightly underestimate the potential vote for a strict pro-life position, but more than three in four citizens favor abortion in cases of rape, incest, or fetal defect. Of course, when other issues or candidate characteristics are highly salient, a strict pro-life candidate can win election. However, in those elections in which abortion becomes a key issue, candidates who oppose abortion in cases of rape or fetal defect are at a strong disadvantage.

In many states, a strong pro-choice position will also not be the best means of maximizing votes. Some states (such as Louisiana and Utah) have relatively small pro-choice constituencies,[7] but in most states between a third and half of voters oppose laws that would make abortion illegal under any circumstance. Yet in few states is there a real pro-choice majority, and even in these states, support for restrictions on abortion such as parental notification and waiting periods are strong. Moreover, in many states an absolute majority of citizens opposes abortion in all circumstances except those we have called physical trauma. A pro-choice position will usually defeat a strict pro-life position in elections that hinge on abortion, but a candidate who favors at least some restrictions on abortion will usually defeat a candidate who favors unlimited abortion rights.

Anthony Downs argues that in a two-party system in which attitudes are normally distributed (that is, where they approximate a bell curve, with most voters taking a moderate position), the parties will gravitate to the center of that distribution.[8] We think it likely that candidates will begin to abandon strict pro-life and pro-choice positions if *Roe* is overturned. This is especially true of pro-life candidates, for there are few votes for a position that forbids all abortions.

Although the abortion debate will vary from state to state, we expect the most conservative position taken by serious candidates in most states will be to allow abortion in all cases of physical trauma. We also expect that the most liberal candidates in most states will allow restrictions on abortion such as parental notification and waiting periods. Of course, candidates who are personally or politically committed to pro-choice or pro-life positions will be reluctant to modify their positions. Yet many candidates will be willing to change their stances, for many have already done so. Moreover, new candidates will be more likely to take moderate positions on the abortion issue. Gradually, the party positions will probably move toward the center.

Abortion and Vote Decisions

How can we determine the importance of the abortion issue in voters' decisions? More than three decades ago, the authors of *The American Voter* suggested three minimum criteria for an issue vote.[9] First, a voter must be aware of the issue. The vast majority of voters in America meet this criterion on abortion. Second, the voter must care at least minimally about the issue. Once again many voters meet this criterion for abortion, although as we shall see below, only a minority feel that abortion is one of the most important issues in deciding their votes. Finally, the voter must perceive that one candidate or party is closer to her or his preferred position on the issue. In their study of the presidential elections of 1952 and 1956, the authors concluded that only a minority of voters could have cast an issue vote on any given issue.

The role of issues in vote decisions is one of the most highly contested debates in all of political science.[10] Although there remains considerable disagreement on the subject, a consensus has emerged that issues matter more today than they did in the 1950s. Yet many political scientists argue that issues are less important in influencing votes than the electorate's evaluation of the personal characteristics of the candidates themselves.[11] Moreover, many and perhaps most political scientists believe that party loyalties are more important than issues in most elections.

If issues are only one factor in vote decisions, abortion is but one issue that voters consider. Whenever the economy is troubled, economic issues dominate national and state elections. In state elections, voters consider candidate stands on education, the environment, health care, and crime. In presidential elections voters are influenced by foreign policy issues and events.[12] Frequently voters find themselves in agreement with one candidate on some issues, but closer to the other candidate on other issues.

All of this suggests that abortion will be only one of many factors that influences vote decisions. Under what conditions will abortion be most influential? First, when both candidates discuss the issue and emphasize it in their campaigns' advertising, more voters will be aware of the issue and care about it. Second, when the candidates take positions consistent with those of their national parties, it will be easier for voters to distinguish between the candidates. Third, when the candidates take clearly divergent positions, it is easier to vote on the basis of the abortion issue.[13] Finally, abortion is most likely to influence vote decisions when both economic and foreign policy concerns seem less pressing.

It is important to note that whether voters consider the abortion issue in their vote calculus, the candidates they elect do affect abortion policy. The predominantly Democratic Congress has repeatedly passed pro-choice legislation in the past few years,[14] and Republican presidents have vetoed that legislation. Presidents Ronald Reagan and George Bush appointed new conservative justices to the U.S. Supreme Court who have already restricted abortion rights and may ultimately provide the votes needed to overturn *Roe*. Elections ultimately affect abortion policy, whether voters consider the issue or not.

The Abortion Issue in Presidential Elections

The presidential platforms increasingly diverged on the abortion issue between 1972 and 1980;[15] during the 1980s, abortion seemed a litmus test issue for presidential candidates. In the 1988 presidential elections, formerly pro-choice Republicans felt compelled to adopt the party pro-life line, and Democrats who once favored restrictions on abortion also changed their positions. George Bush, Richard Gephardt and Jesse Jackson all switched earlier abortion positions in the 1980s to be consistent with the party orthodoxy.

During the 1980s, the Republican party platform called for a Human Life Amendment, which would ban abortions with the *possible* exception of when the woman's life was in danger. The platform declared that the fundamental right to life of "unborn children" cannot be infringed. Most Democratic presidential candidates supported an unlimited right to abortion, and many supported public funding of abortions for poor women. Neither position represented a majority of Americans. It is interesting that the winning candidates in these presidential elections took a position on abortion that reflects the views of fewer than one in ten Americans.

Why did the party platforms diverge so widely in the 1980s? One hypothesis is that the parties were pulled apart by the positions of their voters. Our analysis shows that the party platforms were not drawn apart by issue voting by the American public. In Table 6.1 we show vote choice by abortion attitudes for presidential elections from 1972 through 1988. The data come from the ANES for these years. Abortion attitudes were not significantly associated with vote choice before 1984. In both 1984 and 1988, abortion attitudes seem to have influenced vote decisions: there was little difference between pro-life respondents and the situationalists, but pro-choice respondents were more likely than all others to vote for the Democratic candidate. Thus the divergence of the party positions seems to have led to a mild pattern of voting based on the abortion issue, principally among pro-choice citizens.[16]

TABLE 6.1 Abortion Attitudes and Presidential Vote
(in percent)

Democratic Voting	1972	1976	1980	1984	1988
Pro-life	37	58	45	36	46
Many restrictions	31	49	44	37	39
Few restrictions	38	47	33	38	46
Pro-choice	41	53	49	50	55

Source: American National Election Studies, 1972-1988.

The data in Table 6.1 suggest that the party positions did not diverge because the parties were responding to voter preferences; rather voters responded to the increasingly different party positions on abortion. Thus the wide divergence of the party positions remains to be explained. If voters have not pulled the parties toward more divergent positions, perhaps party elites have influenced party positions. In Table 6.2 we show the attitudes of three sets of party elites--those who voted in presidential primaries, those who gave $200 or more to a presidential candidate in 1988, and delegates to the party conventions in 1988. If Democratic elites take strong pro-choice positions and Republican elites consistently oppose legal abortion, then it may be that the party positions were adopted to satisfy demands of party activists.

There is some debate among political scientists about the ideology of primary election voters. James Lengle argues that the minority of Democratic partisans who vote in presidential primaries are far more liberal than the party rank-and-file and therefore pull party candidates to the left. Barbara Norrander, however, finds no evidence that primary voters are more ideologically extreme.[17] The data in Table 6.2 show that those who voted in presidential primaries in 1988 were not more extreme on the abortion issue than other partisans.

Of course, this does not mean that some presidential candidates have not positioned themselves to win votes in party primaries of pro-choice or pro-life activists. Clearly some candidates in gubernatorial primaries have taken positions to appeal to their party's abortion

TABLE 6.2 Sources of Party Positions, 1988
(percent of voters, delegates, and contributors
taking each position)

	Pro-choice	Situationalist	Pro-life
Democrats:			
Voted in primary	38	50	12
Did not vote	36	49	15
Republicans:			
Voted in primary	31	58	11
Did not vote	35	53	13
Convention delegates:			
All Democrats	78	18	5
Dukakis	81	14	6
Gephardt	67	28	5
Gore	66	31	3
Jackson	85	13	2
Simon	62	31	7
All Republicans	33	55	12
Bush	37	55	8
Dole	33	57	9
Kemp	13	42	46
Robertson	2	54	44

	Government should prohibit abortion		
	Strongly disagree	Intermediate	Strongly agree
Contributors to:			
Babbitt	85	13	2
Dukakis	76	15	9
Gephardt	57	35	8
Gore	74	23	3
Jackson	76	20	4
Simon	78	17	5

(continues)

TABLE 6.2 (continued)

| | Government should prohibit abortion | | |
	Strongly disagree	*Intermediate*	*Strongly agree*
Contributors to:			
Bush	49	41	10
Dole	43	42	15
DuPont	66	24	10
Kemp	32	36	32
Robertson	3	12	85

Source: Compiled from American National Election Study, 1988; *CBS News/New York Times* delegate poll, and data collected by Clifford W. Brown, Jr., Lynda W. Powell, and Clyde Wilcox.

activists. Yet it seems unlikely that abortion could become a litmus test issue because of a small subset of primary voters who take pro-life or pro-choice stands.[18]

Our data on political contributors come from a national mail survey of those who gave at least $200 to a presidential candidate during the primaries of the 1988 election cycle.[19] The results are shown in Table 6.2. The data show that political contributors did not pull the parties toward consistent pro-life or pro-choice positions. The survey asked contributors to agree or disagree with a ban on abortion. Only 10 percent of Bush's contributors strongly agreed, and half strongly disagreed. Similar minorities of contributors to Robert Dole and Pierre (Pete) DuPont took strong pro-life positions. Jack Kemp's contributors split evenly, with a third strongly agreeing with a ban on abortion and a third strongly disagreeing. Only those who gave to Rev. Marion (Pat) Robertson were strongly pro-life, with 85 percent strongly agreeing with an abortion ban. These data suggest that the Republican party position on the abortion issue was not attributable to the efforts of financial elites to influence party policy or of candidates to cater to the policy views of monied interests. Democratic contributors were more unified in their support of abortion rights, but there were sizable minorities of situationalists among the contributors to Gore and Gephardt, and among the black (but not the white) contributors to Jackson.[20]

In addition, there is little evidence that other types of party elites have pulled the Republicans toward a pro-life position. Data from a *CBS News/New York Times* poll of delegates to the Democratic and Republican national conventions in 1988 show that fully a third of Republican delegates took a pro-choice position on abortion, but only 12 percent favored banning abortion.[21] Again the Democratic delegates were more unified, with more than 75 percent supporting a pro-choice position. Yet nearly a third of delegates for Paul Simon, Richard Gephardt, and Albert Gore were situationalists or took a pro-life position.

We conclude from these data that the presidential platforms of the two parties have not become increasingly polarized because the parties' voters or their elites have taken consistent pro-life or pro-choice positions. It seems likely that the party positions have diverged as the parties catered to a subset of political activists organized into interest groups. The parties were able to take these positions because such stances had few costs in the general election, for many voters assumed that abortion rights could not be abridged because of *Roe*. Thus the Republicans could take a position to appeal to an active and dedicated small minority of voters, yet not lose votes among the larger bloc of situationalists and pro-choice citizens. Similarly, the Democrats could position themselves to appeal to a larger minority of pro-choice activists without losing votes among the situationalist majority.

If *Roe* is overturned, the parties can no longer assume that their abortion stances have no electoral costs, for election outcomes will have even more important consequences for abortion policy. We therefore expect party platforms to move away from their strong pro-life and pro-choice positions. Because there are fewer pro-life citizens than those who take a pro-choice position, we expect a greater shift in the Republican party position. Already there is a lively debate among Republicans about the party position on abortion in the 1992 platform.[22] Pro-choice Republicans have organized a Political Action Committee, WISH LIST, to support Republican pro-choice women candidates.

These data also show that as the party platforms diverged on abortion, the issue began to influence voters. In 1988, abortion was a significant predictor of presidential votes, even after controls for social characteristics, partisanship, ideology, and other issues.[23] It seems likely that abortion will be an even more important issue in future presidential elections, especially if the Court overturns or further restricts *Roe*.

Abortion and Congressional Elections

Although we can study the impact of abortion on presidential voting, it is more difficult to determine the impact of the issue on congressional elections. Although the national parties have taken clear and distinct positions in their presidential platforms, this does not bind party members in the House or Senate to support that position. Although in many parliamentary systems legislators would be bound to vote the party line, in the United States we lack the party discipline to enforce such conformity. Indeed, both House Democrats and Senate Republicans have elected members to party office whose views on abortion differ from those of their party platforms. In 1991 the House Democrats elected Michigan Congressman David Bonior, who favored restrictions on abortion, as party Whip. In the U.S. Senate, the Republicans have selected pro-choice Senator Alan Simpson of Wyoming as Whip. Yet, although Simpson can win a party post in the national legislature despite his pro-choice credentials, his abortion stand may have cost him a chance at the Vice Presidency in 1988.[24]

Candidates for each party from each state or district take their own, often nuanced positions on abortion. There are many Democrats in Congress who favor limitations on abortion, and a special political action committee (PAC) that marshals contributions from pro-life citizens to them.[25] There is also a smaller but important pro-choice Republican contingent in Washington. Robert Packwood, Republican senator from Oregon, routinely mentions his pro-choice position in his fundraising, and he mails solicitations to the membership lists of pro-choice groups.[26]

Although Congress does not currently play a major role in abortion policy-making, it does consider abortion-related issues on a regular basis. In every session in the 1980s, Congress considered and ultimately did not pass the Human Life Amendment that would declare that life begins at conception. In 1991, Congress voted to allow the District of Columbia to fund abortions for poor women through Medicaid, to allow U.S. military personnel to obtain abortions in military hospitals if they paid for them from their personal funds,[27] and voted to allow doctors in family planning clinics that receive public funds to discuss abortion with their patients. President Bush vetoed each of these provisions.[28] In response to Bush's State of the Union address in 1992, House Democratic Speaker Thomas Foley promised that congressional Democrats would pass the Freedom of Choice Act that would legal abortion before fetal viability in all states. If Congress begins to regularly debate and consider such sweeping legislation, it seems likely that abortion will become even more important in congressional elections.

We will not detail the impact of abortion in congressional and Senate races, but abortion does matter in many of those contests as well. Abortion was a major factor in Iowa's Senate race in 1990, where Republican Thomas Tauke took a strong pro-life stance and the winner, incumbent Democrat Tom Harkin, was strongly pro-choice.[29] Indeed, our research shows that abortion was an important, statistically significant factor in Senate contests in Iowa, New Hampshire, North Carolina, Oregon, and Texas, and was a source of vote decisions in Colorado, Illinois, and Minnesota as well.[30] Abortion also has been a factor in some House elections. One House race in Northern Virginia in 1990 focused almost entirely on abortion, and the issue has become increasingly important in other districts.[31]

Yet, congressional elections are less likely than either presidential or gubernatorial elections to hinge on the abortion issue. First, many voters look to their House members (and increasingly to their senators) to help provide services and government programs for their district and state. Voters may consider their member's success in providing these benefits as more important than their position on issues. Second, many House incumbents and at least a few incumbent Senators face challengers who are inexperienced, who may have few qualifications for public office, and who may raise insufficient funds to mount a credible campaign.[32] Voters may be reluctant to elect an unknown or inexperienced challenger, even if they share some of her or his positions on issues. Because of these factors favoring incumbents, nearly all House incumbents win reelection, and most win by large margins. This is less true in the Senate, although incumbent Senators frequently win handily. When incumbents win easily, issues are less likely to sway the outcome of the election.

For all of these reasons, congressional elections seldom turn on the abortion issue. Abortion is more likely to matter in Senate elections than House contests, for Senate elections are frequently closer, often have experienced and well-funded challengers, and often focus on values or ideological issues such as abortion. If *Roe* is overturned, abortion is more likely to matter in elections for state governor, since governors will be able to propose, sign, or veto restrictions that will influence the availability of abortion throughout the state.

Abortion and State Electoral Politics After *Webster*

The *Webster* decision indicated that the U.S. Supreme Court was willing to consider new state restrictions on legal abortion. Regardless of the ultimate fate of *Roe*, therefore, abortion is now an important issue in state elections. Abortion has been debated by candidates in gubernatorial elections, in lieutenant governor's elections, and in elections for seats in state legislatures. Yet most political science research on gubernatorial elections has focused only on the role of economic issues in state elections and implied that other types of issues are not generally important.[33]

We will now examine the effect of abortion on governor's elections in several populous states in 1989 and 1990. We focus on ten states in which the abortion issue was discussed by gubernatorial candidates in these years. Virginia and New Jersey elected new pro-choice Democrats in 1989, and Texas and Florida did so in 1990. California, Massachusetts, and Illinois elected new pro-choice Republicans in 1990, although in California the Democratic candidate also endorsed abortion rights. Ohio and Michigan elected new Republican governors who backed restrictions on abortion in 1990, and Pennsylvania elected a Democratic incumbent who favored limitations on abortion over a pro-choice Republican. Analysis of these elections will show considerable interstate variation on the electoral effects of the abortion issue.

TABLE 6.3 Salience and Direction of Abortion Attitudes in Gubernatorial Elections (in percent)

	VA	NJ	FL	TX	CA	MA	IL	MI	OH	PA
Importance of abortion:										
Most important	27	30	10	12	12	7	NA	23	16	16
Second most important	23	3	17	15	17	7	NA	15	13	15
Abortion should be:										
Legal	50	57	47	33	54	47	37	43	36	31
Limited	33	28	41	52	34	40	47	44	49	50
Not legal	18	16	12	16	12	14	16	14	16	20

Source: CBS News/New York Times Surveys.

The Context: The Abortion Debate in State Elections

In the fall of 1989, soon after the *Webster* decision, Virginia and New Jersey elected new governors. In both states the Democrats took pro-choice positions and the Republican candidates favored sharp restrictions on abortion, and in both states the Democratic candidate won. In both elections, the party primaries were held before the *Webster* decision, and the Republican candidates took strong pro-life positions in the primary election in an effort to win votes.

The Florida gubernatorial election in 1990 pitted Robert Martinez, an incumbent Republican governor who had ordered a special legislative session in an unsuccessful attempt to restrict abortion, against Lawton Chiles, a pro-choice Democrat who had once favored restrictions on abortion. In Texas, Democrat Ann Richards took a strong pro-choice position, and Republican Clayton Williams favored restrictions.[34] In both elections, the Democratic candidate won.

In California, both Democratic candidate Diane Feinstein and Republican Pete Wilson were pro-choice, although Feinstein's campaign claimed that she was more committed to this stance because she was a woman.[35] In Massachusetts, Republican candidate William Weld was strongly pro-choice and defeated a pro-life Republican in his party's primary, while Democrat John Silber was less strongly committed to legal abortion. In Illinois, Democrat Neil Hartigan had a record of favoring restrictions on abortion, and Republican Jim Edgar took a pro-choice stance. In each state, the pro-choice Republican won.

In Ohio, Democratic candidate Anthony Celebrezze reversed his earlier pro-life position to support abortion rights, and Republican George Voinovich continued to stake a restrictive position on abortion. In Michigan, incumbent Democrat James Blanchard supported abortion rights; Republican challenger John Engler took a pro-life stance. In both states, the pro-life Republican candidate won, although Engler only very narrowly defeated the incumbent Blanchard, who had been favored. Finally, in Pennsylvania, popular Democratic incumbent Robert Casey had pushed for restrictions on abortion in 1989, and Republican challenger Barbara Hafer took a pro-choice position. Casey won in a landslide.

Of course, these ten states differed on many other dimensions: their economic climate, their basic partisan sympathies, their general ideology, and their demographic makeup. In addition, the candidates in these elections took different positions on other issues in addition to abortion. But the different positions on abortion of the winning candidates in these states tells us something important about the role of abortion in state elections. Pro-choice Democrats and Republicans as well as pro-life Democrats and Republicans all won governorships in 1990, despite numerical advantage for the pro-choice forces in each state.

As the diversity of these outcomes indicates, neither pro-choice nor pro-life candidates are assured of victory in state elections. In part, this is because, to date, abortion has not been the most important issue on voters' minds. In Table 6.3, we present the percentage of voters in each state who selected abortion as the first or second most important issue in their vote. Note that in most states few voters indicated that abortion was the most important issue in deciding their vote. Abortion was generally one of five or six issues that influenced vote decision, with education the most important in most states. Yet, a sizable number of voters in each of these states (except Massachusetts) indicated that abortion was one of the most important issues they considered in deciding their vote. Moreover, in Virginia and New Jersey, abortion was the most frequently mentioned issue by voters.[36]

Also shown in Table 6.3 is the percentage of voters in each state who took pro-choice, pro-life, and situationalist positions. In all states, pro-choice voters outnumbered those who were pro-life. Pro-choice voters constituted a majority in Virginia, New Jersey, and California, and a near majority in Massachusetts and Florida. Each of these states elected pro-choice governors in 1989 or 1990. Voters in Illinois, Ohio, Michigan, Pennsylvania, and Texas were the most supportive of restrictions on abortion.[37] Illinois and Texas voters elected pro-choice governors, while the other states elected candidates who advocated restrictions on legal abortion.

Abortion and Vote Choice

In Table 6.4, we show the percentage of Democratic votes in each state by attitudes on abortion. In the upper part of the table, the figures show the percentage of those with each position on abortion who voted for the Democratic candidate. To see the impact of the abortion issue on vote decisions, compare the percentage of pro-choice and pro-life voters who cast Democratic ballots. In Virginia, for example, 70 percent of pro-choice voters cast Democratic ballots, but only 18 percent of pro-life voters supported the Democratic candidate. In Pennsylvania, where the Democrat took a pro-life position, 45 percent of pro-choice voters and 88 percent of pro-life voters selected the Democratic candidate. Abortion is a predictor of vote choice in each state except Illinois.

Note that in Massachusetts and Pennsylvania (but not in Illinois), where the national party positions on abortion were reversed, voters responded. This suggests that many voters are attentive to the abortion stances of political candidates, even when these are not the ones taken by the national parties. Pro-choice voters in states with pro-choice Republicans were more likely to favor the Republican candidate than pro-life voters. Illinois is an exception, for the Democratic candidate received an equal proportion of pro-choice and pro-life votes. The Democratic candidate in Illinois had supported restrictions on legal abortion, but when a recently drafted state law limiting abortion rights was declared unconstitutional by the lower court, he had declined to appeal the case to the U.S. Supreme Court. Thus voters could understandably be confused about the abortion views of the Democratic candidate.

Although the exit polls did not ask voters to identify the positions of the candidates on abortion, a survey conducted by the Ohio State University Polimetrics Laboratory in 1990 showed that many Ohio voters were aware of the positions of the two gubernatorial candidates in that state. Although a quarter of voters were unable to identify the candidates' positions on abortion, nearly half of voters with a position on abortion correctly identified the position of the Democrat Celebrezze (who had switched his abortion stance) and more than half knew the position of Republican Voinovich.

To put the effects of abortion on vote in perspective, Table 6.4 also shows the relationship between partisanship and vote choice. In most states, partisanship is a stronger predictor of votes, but in Virginia and Pennsylvania, abortion is nearly as strongly related to vote choice as partisanship. In Virginia, for example, 85 percent of Democrats and 18 percent of Republicans voted for the Democratic candidate Douglas Wilder, and 70 percent of pro-choice voters and 18 percent of pro-life voters supported him.

TABLE 6.4 Abortion Attitudes and Vote Choice in Gubernatorial Elections,
by State, 1989 and 1990 (in percent)

| | | | | | Percentage Voting for Democratic Candidate | | | | | |
	VA	NJ	FL	TX	CA	MA	IL	MI	OH	PA
Abortion should be:										
Legal	70	70	69	67	58	44	53	56	58	45
Limited	37	56	46	48	40	50	42	58	40	73
Not legal	18	48	43	36	37	59	53	50	29	88
Democrats	85	88	87	84	83	67	76	79	76	80
Independents	50	69	59	49	51	44	46	43	38	66
Republicans	18	27	26	19	13	24	16	22	15	20
Democrats:										
Legal	92	90	95	91	87	60	78	80	84	62
Limited	81	87	79	82	78	71	71	79	70	85
Not legal	51	84	79	73	74	78	85	76	74	92
Independents:										
Legal	68	76	67	68	62	39	51	42	53	41
Limited	38	63	52	40	40	48	41	45	33	75
Not legal	21	48	40	23	29	48	45	37	17	97

| | | | | | Percentage Voting for Democratic Candidate | | | | | |
	VA	NJ	FL	TX	CA	MA	IL	MI	OH	PA
Republicans:										
Legal	35	35	40	31	17	21	29	17	20	27
Limited	13	22	18	15	11	21	14	27	15	51
Not legal	2	13	16	12	4	42	16	23	5	77

Percent of voters who mention abortion as key issue and wish to see abortion:

	VA	NJ	FL	TX	CA	MA	IL	MI	OH	PA
Legal	21	23	5	8	13	7	NA	15	9	9
Not legal	12	15	1	5	4	2	NA	4	6	7

Note: In Virginia, New Jersey, Florida, Texas, California, Michigan, and Ohio, the Democratic candidates took pro-choice stands. In California, Massachusetts, Illinois, and Pennsylvania, the Republican candidates took pro-choice stands.

Source: CBS/New York Times Surveys.

We also show in this table the proportion of Democrats, independents, and Republicans who voted for the Democratic candidate, by abortion attitudes. It is useful to look separately at Democrats, independents, and Republicans to see the effect of the abortion issue after controlling for partisanship. The abortion question has a generally stronger influence on the vote decisions of independents than on those who identify with a party. In California, for example, abortion produces a 13 percent drop in Democratic voting among Democrats (from 87 percent of pro-choice Democrats to 74 percent of pro-life Democrats) and a drop of 13 percent among Republicans, but abortion is associated with a shift of 33 percent among independents. It is interesting, however, that abortion also influences the vote choice of partisans. This is most evident when we consider the defection rate of those who identify with a particular party. In Virginia, for example, 49 percent of pro-life Democrats voted for the Republican candidate, compared with only 8 percent of pro-choice Democrats. In addition, 35 percent of pro-choice Republicans in Virginia defected to Democratic candidate Douglas Wilder, compared with only 2 percent of pro-life Republicans. A similar pattern is evident in most states.

Finally, we show in the bottom of Table 6.4 the size of the pro-life and pro-choice voting blocs in each state. This figure is a function of two factors: the percentage of voters taking pro-choice or pro-life positions and the intensity of their position. In most states, pro-life voters are slightly more likely to mention abortion as an important factor in their votes.[38] Nonetheless, the larger numbers of pro-choice voters results in a larger voting bloc. Within these blocs, the pro-life voters are again slightly more likely to support a pro-life candidate than are the pro-choice voters to vote for the pro-choice candidate, but in each state, there appear to be more pro-choice issue voters than pro-life ones.

Of course, other factors influence vote choice. Partisanship and general ideology influence vote decisions, Catholics vote differently from Protestants, and a number of demographic variables such as race, gender, and income are strong predictors of vote choice. To determine if abortion really influences vote decisions, it is necessary to hold constant these other factors. We have used logistic regression to examine the effects of abortion attitudes on vote choice. This technique allows us to determine whether abortion has an independent impact on vote choice in each state, after holding constant social characteristics, partisanship, and ideology. Our analysis shows that abortion is an important predictor of vote choice in each of these states except Illinois and Michigan. In Pennsylvania, abortion is a stronger predictor of vote choice than even partisanship.[39] The details of this analysis are in the Appendix. These results show that after *Webster*, voters took into account the public stances of the gubernatorial candidates on abortion.

Research suggests that abortion is important in state elections below the top of the ticket, too. In Virginia, voters in 1989 chose a Lieutenant Governor in part based on their stands on abortion. Several factors converged to make abortion an important part of vote decisions for this office. First, the candidates took quite different positions on the issue. Second, their positions echoed those of the gubernatorial candidates and the national parties. Finally, the abortion issue was hotly debated by the candidates for governor as well.[40] Debra Dodson and Lauren Burnbauer have shown that in Virginia and New Jersey in 1989, abortion was a factor in voting in elections for state legislator as well.[41] In Maryland, several veteran state legislators who filibustered an abortion rights bill in the State Senate were defeated in 1990.

If abortion is an important predictor of vote choice, and if there are more pro-choice voters than pro-life voters, how can candidates who favor restrictions on abortion win? In Ohio, Michigan, and Pennsylvania, candidates who favored restrictions on legal abortion defeated pro-choice candidates. Our analysis shows that abortion was not a factor in the Michigan election, but that it was important in both Pennsylvania and Ohio.

In Pennsylvania, a popular governor stood for reelection when the state's economy was prospering and defeated a relatively inexperienced challenger. In Ohio, voters chose a Republican candidate after eight years of Democratic rule. The Ohio economy was stagnant, and ethical issues had been raised about the outgoing Democratic administration. It appears to us that in both Pennsylvania and Ohio, the abortion issue helped the pro-choice candidate, but the abortion issue was insufficient to overcome the other influences on vote choice. In both states, the pro-choice side had only a very narrow numerical advantage.

The Ohio gubernatorial race raises another issue, for the Democratic candidate had originally opposed legal abortion, then changed his position prior to the election. Pro-life activists argued that this flip-flopping on the abortion issue was a factor in his defeat. Voters may be more likely to vote for candidates with whom they disagree than for those who do not have the courage of their convictions. Such an argument is an important political point, for as we have argued above, those Republicans who have previously taken strong pro-life positions are not ideally positioned for a post-*Roe* politics. If a change in position on abortion has political costs, they may outweigh the costs of being poorly positioned on the issue, and it may be better for pro-life Republicans to maintain their position than to switch and appear indecisive.

There is some evidence that Celebrezze's switch on the abortion issue may have hurt him. In a survey of likely Ohio voters in February 1990, more than two-thirds of respondents knew that the Democratic candidate had switched his position on abortion. In another survey, in late October 1990, respondents were asked which they would find more troubling--that a candidate was anti-abortion or that he had changed his position to become more pro-choice. By a margin of 54 percent to 32 percent, Ohio citizens indicated that they would find a switch more troubling. Yet in a June poll, only 6 percent of likely voters mentioned Celebrezze's switch as a reason to vote against him.[42] And a survey by the Ohio State University found a similarly small number of voters who cited the abortion switch as a reason to oppose Celebrezze. A somewhat larger number mentioned his pro-choice stand as a reason to vote *for* him.

Pro-life candidates who abandon their positions immediately prior to an election may face the charge of political opportunism. Such a charge will be damaging if it fits with a general image of the candidate, but in most cases it alone will not guarantee defeat. In Ohio, we calculate that Celebrezze gained a few more votes than he lost by his political conversion, and his loss can be attributed to other factors. Other observers have suggested that Celebrezze's pro-choice stance kept the contest closer than it otherwise might have been.[43] Moreover, Democratic candidate Lawton Chiles of Florida abandoned his earlier support of restrictions on abortion in favor of an abortion rights platform, and his position on abortion contributed to his ultimate victory.

Conclusions

Voters do appear to consider candidate's positions on abortion in their votes for president, Congress, governor, and even state legislator. Most voters are aware of the abortion issue, many care about the issue, and a substantial number are aware of the positions of the candidates. Even when the candidate's positions reverse those of the national parties, many voters are able to distinguish between the positions of the candidates and to cast issue votes on abortion.

During the 1970s and early 1980s, many political commentators decried the rise of single-issue voting. The most frequent example was pro-life voters, whose intense preference on the issue overrode all other considerations. We find that after *Webster*, there are now more motivated pro-choice voters in all of the states we studied than pro-life voters. Yet a pro-choice position does not guarantee victory, for most voters, regardless of their position on abortion, consider the character and personality of the candidates and other issues in deciding their vote.

If abortion continues to matter in state and national elections, we expect that candidates of both parties will begin to moderate strong pro-choice or pro-life positions in favor of more centrist positions. In none of the states we examined is there majority support for restrictions on abortion under circumstances of physical trauma. If abortion becomes even more salient for vote choice, candidates who endorse an outright ban on abortions will be disadvantaged. In most states, the position that will attract the greatest number of votes will be to support legal abortion in most cases but to ban abortion in at least a few symbolic situations such as abortions for birth control or for sex selection. Moreover, many restrictions such as parental notification and parental consent are overwhelmingly popular, and candidates who oppose them may lose votes.

It thus seems likely that a reversal or modification of *Roe v. Wade* is likely to return the abortion issue to the electoral arena. Because candidates are strategic actors, who act upon a variety of motives, abortion politics after *Roe* will be substantially different from those of the recent past. In the final chapter, we turn our attention to the future of the abortion issue.

Notes

1. Debra Dodson and Lauren Burnbauer with Katherine Kleeman, *Election 1989: The Abortion Issue in New Jersey and Virginia* (Rutgers, N.J.: Eagleton Institute of Politic, 1990). Beth Donovan, "Open 2nd District Contests Tests Partisan Trends," *Congressional Quarterly Weekly Report* April 7, 1990, pp. 1090-1091; Elizabeth Adell Cook, Ted G. Jelen, and Clyde Wilcox, "The Electoral Politics of Abortion" (paper presented at the annual meeting of the American Political Science Association, Washington, D.C., 1991); Elizabeth Adell Cook, Frederick Hartwig, and Clyde Wilcox, "The Abortion Issue Down-Ticket: The Virginia Lieutenant Governor's Race of 1989," *Women & Politics*, forthcoming.

2. Glen Halva-Neubauer, "Abortion Policymaking in the Post-*Webster* Age: The Case of Minnesota" (paper presented at the annual meeting of the Midwest Political Science Association, Chicago, 1991); Patricia Bayer Richard, "They'd Rather It Would Go Away: Ohio Legislators and Abortion Policy" (paper presented at the annual meeting of the Midwest Political Science Association, Chicago, 1991).

3. For an excellent description of grass-roots activity, see Marjorie Randon Hershey, *Running for Office: The Political Education of Campaigners* (Chatham, N.J.: Chatham House, 1984).

4. For a discussion of campaign finance activity by pro-choice and pro-life groups, see Clyde Wilcox, "Political Action Committees and Abortion: A Longitudinal Analysis," *Women & Politics* 9 (1988), pp. 1-20.

5. Although elsewhere in the book we use the term "pro-life" to refer to those citizens who oppose abortion under all circumstances, in this chapter we will use the term to refer to those candidates who endorse sharp restrictions on abortion. Few serious candidates oppose abortion under all circumstances, including danger to a woman's health, rape, incest, or severe fetal defect. Pro-life groups endorse candidates who support strong restrictions, even though these candidates might not take a position that totally opposes abortion.

6. The California governor's race pitted two pro-choice candidates against one another, while the Pennsylvania and Illinois contests involved pro-life Democrats against pro-choice Republicans.

7. Polling data suggest that the pro-choice segment of the Louisiana public is as large as the pro-life segment, however, with a majority favoring abortion in some but not all circumstances.

8. Anthony Downs, *An Economic Theory of Democracy* (New York: Harper and Row, 1957).

9. Angus Campbell, Philip Converse, Warren Miller, and Donald Stokes, *The American Voter* (New York: John Wiley & Sons, 1960).

10. For a review of the literature for presidential elections, see Herbert B. Asher, *Presidential Elections and American Politics* (Belmont, Calif.: Brooks/Cole, 1991).

11. See Frederick Hartwig, William Jenkins, and Earl Temchin, "Variability in Electoral Behavior: The 1960, 1968, and 1976 Elections," *American Journal of Political Science* 24 (1980), pp. 553-558.

12. John Aldrich, John Sullivan, and Eugene Borgida, "Foreign Affairs and Issue Voting: Do Presidential Candidates 'Waltz Before a Blind Audience?'" *American Political Science Review* 83 (1989), pp. 123-142.

13. Benjamin Page, *Choices and Echoes in Presidential Elections* (Chicago: The University of Chicago Press, 1978).

14. For example, Congress in 1991 voted to allow abortions for military personnel in military hospitals, to permit the District of Columbia to use its own funds to pay for abortions, and to provide a new interpretation for their earlier legislation on family planning clinics designed to reverse the *Rust* decision. In each case, President Bush vetoed the legislation.

15. For a discussion of the abortion issue in elections, see Elizabeth Adell Cook, "Feminist Consciousness and Candidate Preference Among American Women 1972-1988," (paper presented at the annual meeting of the Southern Political Science Association, Atlanta).

16. The bivariate correlation between abortion attitude and vote decisions was significant in 1984 and 1988, but only in 1988 does this relationship remain after controls for partisanship, ideology, and demographic variables. See Elizabeth Adell Cook, Ted G. Jelen, and Clyde Wilcox, "The Electoral Politics of Abortion." For other evidence of divergence among party voters, see Louis Bolce, "Abortion and Presidential Elections: The Impact of Public

Perceptions of Party and Candidate Positions," *Presidential Studies Quarterly* 18 (1986), pp. 815-829.

17. James Lengle, *Representativeness and Presidential Primaries: The Democratic Party in the Post Reform Era* (Westport, Conn: Greenwood, 1981). Barbara Norrander, "Ideological Representativeness of Presidential Primary Voters," *American Journal of Political Science* 33 (1989) pp. 570-587.

18. Of course, prior to *Webster*, a strong pro-life position in a Republican primary would attract the votes and money of pro-life activists without costing many votes from situationalists or pro-choice Republicans. Yet these data show that only 11% of Republican party primary voters took a pro-life position. These numbers hardly seem adequate to explain a party platform that endorses a Human Life Amendment.

19. These data are from a study by Clifford Brown, Jr., Lynda Powell, and Clyde Wilcox. For details, see "Serious Money: Presidential Campaign Contributors and Patterns of Contributions in 1988," in Stephen Wayne and Clyde Wilcox, eds., *The Quest for National Office* (New York: St. Martin's, 1991).

20. Jackson's contributors included many highly religious blacks who took moderate to conservative positions on moral issues, and many non-religious whites who took extremely liberal positions on these issues. There was a large difference between black and white contributors to Jackson on the abortion issue.

21. The most pro-choice delegation were those pledged to Bush, the most pro-life delegates were those for Robertson. Fully 46 percent of Kemp's delegates took the extreme pro-life position, however.

22. Fred Barnes, "Pregnant Silence," *The New Republic*, August 19 & 26, 1991, pp. 11-12; Eleanor Clift, "The GOP's Civil War Over Abortion," *Newsweek* August 5, 1991, p. 31; Cal Thomas, "Is the Pro-Life Position Proving Harmful to Republicans?" *The Washington Times*, July 29, 1991, p. D3.

23. For details, see Cook, Jelen, and Wilcox, "The Electoral Politics of Abortion."

24. Michael Barone and Grant Ujifusa, *The Almanac of American Politics* (Washington, D.C.: The National Journal,1990).

25. Clyde Wilcox, "Political Action Committees and Abortion: A Longitudinal Analysis," *Women & Politics* 9 (1988), pp. 1-20.

26. Packwood has been criticized for giving some of his surplus campaign funds to other Republican candidates, some of whom take pro-life positions.

27. Other types of medical procedures for military personnel would continue to be funded by the government.

28. For a more detailed discussion of Congressional action on abortion in 1990 and 1991, see Julie Rovner, "Hill Faces Trench Warfare Over Abortion Rights," *Congressional Quarterly Weekly Report*, August 25, 1990, pp. 2713-2720.

29. Richard Cohen, "Clashing on Abortion in Iowa Contest," *National Journal*, September 1, 1990, pp. 2077-2078.

30. Elizabeth Adell Cook, Ted G. Jelen, and Clyde Wilcox, "The Abortion Issue in U.S. Senate Elections in 1990" (Unpublished manuscript, 1992).

31. Beth Donovan with Charles Mathesian, "Early Campaigning Tests Abortion Foes' Muscle," *Congressional Quarterly Weekly Reports*, March 10, 1990, pp. 765-775.

32. Experienced politicians may be reluctant to challenge incumbent members of the House or Senate because the odds against their success are so long. More than 90 percent of House incumbents who have sought reelection in the past two decades have won, as have nearly 80 percent of Senate incumbents.

33. John Chubb, "Institutions, the Economy, and the Dynamics of State Elections," *American Political Science Review* 82 (1988), pp. 133-154.

34. For discussions of the Texas race, see Sue Tolleson Rinehart and Jeanie Stanley, "Claytie and the Lady I: Gender, Political Psychology and Political Culture in the 1990 Texas Gubernatorial Race" (paper presented at the annual meeting of the International Society of Political Psychology, Helsinki, Finland, July 1991); Tolleson Rinehart and Stanley, "Claytie and the Lady II: The 1990 Texas Gubernatorial Race from the Perspectives of

the Campaign and the Citizens" (paper presented at the annual meeting of the American Political Science Association, Washington, D.C., September, 1991); Kent Tedin, Richard Matland, and Richard Murray, "The Acid Test of Gender Voting: The 1990 Election for Governor of Texas" (paper presented at the annual meeting of the Southern Political Science Association, Tampa Bay, 1991).

35. Holly Idelson, "Governors Find Re-election a Trickier Proposition," *Congressional Quarterly Weekly Reports,* November 10, 1990, pp. 3838-3842.

36. It should be noted that not all voters listed a second choice, so it is inappropriate to simply sum the percentage who mentioned abortion as their first and second issue. For example, although 27 percent of Virginia voters mentioned abortion as their most important issue, and 23 percent mentioned it as their second issue, only 40 percent of voters who listed at least one issue selected abortion.

37. The ordering of these data generally follow those reported in Chapter 2, although here we show California more pro-choice than Florida. The questions used in the *CBS News/New York Times* surveys reported in Chapter 2 are better measures of attitudes than those used in the exit polls reported in this chapter.

38. It is interesting to note, however, that the intensity advantage of the pro-life forces in the 1990 exit polls was much smaller than in pre-election surveys in the same states in 1989. For example, in 1990 in Pennsylvania, 27 percent of pro-life voters and 20 percent of pro-choice voters indicated that abortion was the single most important issue in their vote decision. Yet in the 1989 *CBS News/New York Times* abortion survey in Pennsylvania, 31 percent of pro-life respondents and only 7% of pro-choice respondents indicated that abortion would be the most important issue for them in the 1990 governors election. Several factors are at work here. First, the pre-election survey asked questions of a random sample of all citizens, while the exit polls only tapped actual voters. Second, the wording of the question in the pre-election poll asked respondents whether abortion would be the most important, an important, or an unimportant issue in deciding their vote, while the 1990 exit polls listed a series of issues and asked voters to chose the issue that was most important, and second most important.

It is also likely, however, that pro-life citizens believe in the abstract that abortion *should* be the most important issue in determining their vote, but in a real election with real candidates, they also consider education, the environment, the state economy, and other issues, as do other voters. Often these other issues will not conflict with abortion, for pro-life voters may prefer the conservative candidate on abortion, education, and the state economy. Yet like pro-choice citizens, pro-life citizens sometimes must choose between the abortion issue and bread-and-butter issues. These data suggest that the pro-life voters are somewhat more likely than pro-choice voters to decide their vote based primarily on the abortion issue, but only a minority of each group assigns abortion the highest priority.

39. Of course, in Pennsylvania, the most common party positions on abortion were reversed.

40. Cook, Jelen, and Wilcox, "The Electoral Politics of Abortion"; Cook, Hartwig, and Wilcox, "The Abortion Issue Down-Ticket."

41. Dodson and Burnbauer with Kleeman, *Election, 1989.*

42. These results are from polls conducted by Peter Hart and Associates for the Celebrezze campaign.

43. Holly Idelson, "Governors Find Re-election a Trickier Proposition."

7

From Rights to Policy:
The Future of the
Abortion Debate

The preceding chapters have focused on the sources of public attitudes toward legal abortion and on the consequences of these attitudes for electoral behavior. This chapter will first provide a summary of our empirical results, and then offer some thoughts on the future of abortion politics in the United States.

First, it is clear that abortion is an important issue to many members of the mass public. This result is more noteworthy than it might appear at first glance. Many studies have shown that large percentages of the American people are inattentive to political issues and that many people are largely unaware of or unconcerned about matters that are the focus of heated political debate and are widely reported in the news media.[1] Americans are aware of and concerned about the legality of abortion. Many people believe the issue to be an important one. Moreover, the abortion issue is sometimes a significant influence on the outcomes of elections.

Second, the abortion issue invokes a number of different values for many people. A narrow majority of people are situationalists, in that they approve of legal abortion in some circumstances but not others. This ambivalence about abortion does not seem to reflect inconsistency or inattention but rather suggests that many people hold competing values. Americans value both human life and personal freedom, autonomy as well as traditional morality. Thus, Chapter 5 revealed that even people who consistently oppose or support legal abortion in response to the six GSS questions will later qualify their support for or opposition to legal abortion in response to questions about limitations on abortion or on the role of government in regulating individual behavior.[2] Very few people are willing to accord the ability to control one's own fertility or the embryo's survival the status of an unrestricted right.

Third, some of the variables that are related to abortion attitudes show some unexpected patterns. In many ways, mass attitudes about abortion do not reflect the debate as conducted at the activist level. For example, attitudes toward feminism and gender roles are not strongly related to abortion attitudes, once other factors are taken into account. Although pro-life citizens are more likely to oppose gender equality than those who take consistent pro-choice positions, in fact more citizens who oppose gender equality favor legal abortion than oppose it. Members of the mass public do not seem to regard the abortion issue as a women's issue, except to the extent that feminism is part of a set of nontraditional beliefs and lifestyles. Thus mass-level public opinion is relatively unresponsive to the terms of some of the elite-level debate.

For all religious groups, religiosity and doctrinal orthodoxy were correlated with opposition to legal abortion. But the patterns are different for different religious groups. For example, a strong belief in the authority of the Bible is directly related to abortion attitudes for white evangelical Protestants and Catholics, but not for other religious groups. Among white Catholics, evangelical Protestants, and mainline Protestants, frequent church attendance is associated with opposition to legal abortion, but this relationship is weak for mainline Protestants. For African-Americans and Jews, religion only indirectly influences abortion attitudes through its influence on attitudes toward sexual morality and the inviolability of life. As the abortion issue reenters the arena of electoral and legislative politics, these differences may make it difficult for members of different religious groups to work together. Religious particularism--the belief that only one's own religious tradition has a claim on ultimate truth--has been shown to be a powerful inhibitor of political cooperation.[3]

A person who had followed the debate between activists on the abortion issue in the United States might, after reading this book, wonder if this book and other accounts of the abortion issue were describing the same country. Our results show that the American public is concerned, yet divided and ambivalent, about the abortion issue. A minority of Americans take consistently pro-choice or pro-life positions; most seem willing to consider a variety of restrictions that would still make access to legal abortions available under many circumstances. This characterization of public opinion in the United States stands in stark contrast to elite-level debate about abortion, which has been cast in uncompromising terms. Although the contrast between elite-level discourse and public opinion on the abortion issue is not exactly novel,[4] the strong disparity between activist rhetoric and mass attitudes toward abortion requires some explanation.

Abortion and the Anti-Politics of Rights

Perhaps the simplest explanation for the fact that activist-level debate on abortion does not reflect public opinion is that, since *Roe v. Wade*, most abortion politics have been conducted in federal courts. The role of courts in our constitutional system is not disparaged by suggesting that federal courts are perhaps the least representative institutions in American politics and constitute the arena in which public opinion is least influential. In the period between *Roe* and *Webster*, at least part of the audience for activist rhetoric on abortion has been the Supreme Court rather than the mass public or elected officials. The main effect of *Roe* was to deny state and national governments jurisdiction over most aspects of abortion decisions, so both pro-life and pro-choice activists have focused much of their attention on the courts. At a minimum, people wishing to restrict access to abortion must persuade the Supreme Court to return jurisdiction to the elected branches of government, but those who regard abortion as a nonnegotiable right have a clear stake in preventing the return of the abortion issue to state legislatures.

As Mary Ann Glendon notes,[5] courtroom rhetoric is typically exaggerated and partisan. Each side in a *legal* controversy acts as an advocate for its own interests, relying on impartial judges or juries to discern the merits of the opposing sides. Thus, the strident, heated discussion of abortion in the United States may be in large part the result of the arena in which the debate is conducted. Extreme positions, usually considered fatal in the electoral arena,[6] provide an important tactical advantage in legal discourse. However, it is possible that the strong rhetoric characterizing the abortion debate as well as the fact that courts are the principal arena in which abortion politics are conducted, is due in part to the embedding of the contemporary abortion debate in the context of *rights*.[7]

Glendon[8] argues that the United States is unique among Western industrialized nations in that abortion and divorce laws are couched in the language of individual rights. In her recent book, *Rights Talk*, Glendon observes that the American preoccupation with individual rights has distorted political discourse to the point that politics as normally construed has been seriously impoverished: "How often, in daily speech, do all of us make and hear claims that whatever right is under discussion at the moment trumps every other consideration?... In its simple American form, the language of rights is the language of no compromise. The winner takes all, and the loser has to get out of town. The conversation is over."[9]

The reason that the assertion of rights inhibits political compromise is that, in contemporary discourse, a right is taken to mean an unrestrictable prerogative. The assertion of a right entails a claim that competing considerations are secondary or even irrelevant in determining a course of action. In the language of the Declaration of Independence, certain rights are "inalienable," which means they cannot be given or taken away. The successful assertion of a right means that the political system cannot consider the merits of opposing points of view.

An example of the nonnegotiability of rights can be drawn from the case law relating to free speech and a free press. The fact that the First Amendment guarantees a right to free speech and free press has been interpreted by some to mean that government may not base the regulation of expression on the content of the ideas expressed. Thus when a pornographer claims a legal "right" to publish sexually explicit and/or violent materials, that person is not arguing that the materials in question are of high quality or have important social value. Indeed, quite the opposite is the case: the pornographer is claiming an exemption from a discussion of the merits of the publications in question. So strong is the prohibition on content-based regulation of free expression that much First Amendment law is devoted to making subtle distinctions between protected "speech" and unprotected "conduct."[10]

The relevance of this brief analysis of the nature of rights is clear to anyone who has followed the debate concerning abortion over the last two decades. The abortion debate is framed in terms of the competing "right to choose" and "right to life." Indeed, the force of the assertion of rights is to claim the primacy of the consideration in question.

Thus, activists who believe that abortion is murder claim that the embryo's right to exist is more important than any reason a woman might have for not carrying the pregnancy to term, except when doing so might kill her. As Kristin Luker notes, other considerations are dismissed as involving convenience, or the motivations of such women are attacked as selfish. Indeed, the activities of many pro-life as well as pro-choice activists do not seem calculated to find common ground from which the abortion issue can be discussed and negotiated, but rather seem intended to disparage the motivations and character of those who disagree. Comparing doctors who perform abortions to murderers, or the practice of abortion to the Nazi Holocaust, is designed to raise the emotional level, rather than the intellectual quality, of the abortion debate. A few anti-abortion activists have taken to destroying the property of abortion clinics or physically blocking access to abortion clinics. These disruptive and sometimes illegal tactics are again not intended as reasoned, persuasive speech, but appear to entail the assumption that people who seek or perform abortions are beyond saving through the normal processes of civil political discourse. Pro-choice activists often display similarly uncivil discourse, suggesting that those who oppose legal abortion do so out of a wish to oppress women and are indifferent to whether women die in illegal abortions.

Thus, it may be the case that the assertion of unqualified rights inhibits the discourse of democratic civility. By civility, we mean a set of norms involving at a minimum, tolerance of opposing viewpoints, respect for the integrity of people with whom one may disagree, and a willingness to abide by the rules of democratic competition, even when the rules result in unfavorable outcomes. In other words, civility refers to a willingness to compromise and to accept the workings of the political process. In the case of the abortion issue, the respective "rights" of choice and life seem to have eroded the basis for democratic civility at the activist level.

Of course, none of this is meant to suggest the correctness of one position or the other or even to suggest that the assertion of rights in the context of abortion is in any way inappropriate. One concept of rights is that government authority over individuals is limited. Rights are designed to delimit the private, self-regarding space from government jurisdiction or from interference from other people. The assertion of political rights is basic to the American political experience, and most Americans believe that they have certain inalienable rights. Whether there exists a normative right to choose or a right to life is beyond the scope of this book. Our discussion of rights is not about the existence of rights in some absolute sense but rather the empirical question of whether one group or another has asserted a right, whether that claim has been legitimated in the court or legislature, and whether the assertion of rights in the debate about abortion influences the nature of the political discourse.

Precisely because rights mark off the area of individual sovereignty within which government cannot legitimately intrude, when rights are claimed civil democratic discourse is limited. Indeed, the notion of a right suggests that the preferences of others are irrelevant to personal decisions in areas covered by rights. There is thus a trade-off between the general proscription of public discourse with respect to certain subjects and political conversation about those subjects.[11]

The importance of this discussion of the nature of rights is that the incivility of abortion rhetoric and politics may not be intrinsic to the abortion debate itself. It is occasionally asserted that abortion is not easily compromised because abortion either involves the taking of a human life or it does not.[12] However, the data presented in this book suggest that any number of different compromises on access to legal abortion are possible, in the sense of being acceptable to a large percentage of the American public. Of course, these outcomes will seem unacceptable to those on both sides of the issue who view abortion in terms of rights. It is to the prospect of such political discourse to which we now turn our attention.

Abortion Policy in the Post-*Webster* Era

In our view, the abortion right asserted by the Supreme Court in *Roe v. Wade* is likely to be overturned or substantially modified in the near future.[13] With the retirement of Thurgood Marshall in 1991, only one of the seven members of the original *Roe* majority is still on the Court at this writing. Most of the justices who asserted the abortion right in *Roe* have been replaced by more conservative jurists nominated by Presidents Reagan and Bush. Both of these Republican presidents have affirmed their opposition to legal abortion, and it seems likely that their nominees to the high court will follow suit.

In the past two years, the Supreme Court has sent important signals to state governments in *Webster v. Missouri Reproductive Health Services* and in *Rust v. Sullivan*. As noted in Chapter 1, the *Webster* decision upheld several state-imposed restrictions on access to legal abortion. Although *Webster* does not explicitly overrule *Roe*, it does represent a break in a long string of decisions overturning restrictions on abortion. In the *Rust* decision, the Court ruled that the executive branch could interpret a law forbidding family planning clinics that accept federal funds from performing abortions to also forbid doctors at those clinics from discussing abortion with their patients. The Court rejected arguments that these executive interpretations violated the constitutional freedom of speech of health care providers in these clinics. These two decisions suggest a court that is willing at least to erode seriously the *Roe* decision and possibly to overturn it outright. These rulings point to the possibility of a majority on the Court that is willing to restrict or overturn Roe.

What are the likely consequences of an overturning of *Roe v. Wade*? At the simplest level, the reversal of *Roe* would return jurisdiction over the abortion issue to state governments. In a few states, the issue will once again be decided by courts--in this case state supreme courts. Some state constitutions contain an explicit guarantee to privacy, and some state courts will interpret that guarantee as implying a right to choose an abortion. In most states, however, the issue will be debated and decided in the legislatures with the consent of governors. In a legal sense, abortion will no longer be an issue in which inalienable rights are involved, but one in which governments at various levels are permitted to make *policy*. Policy-making involves the creation of solutions to problems that give weight to competing values and considerations. In the absence of a successful assertion of either a "right to life" or a "right to choose," legislators in the post-*Webster* era would be free to attempt compromises partially embodying the different values involved in the abortion issue. We will consider three scenarios that seem possible after the reversal of *Roe*.

Scenario 1: Normal Politics

It is possible that the overturning of *Roe* will result in a compromise of the abortion issue in the same way that most political questions are resolved in the American polity. If a majority of members of the American public are situationalists with respect to abortion, and if abortion is sometimes an important issue in elections, then it is possible that the campaign rhetoric of political candidates will downplay the "rights" aspect of abortion in favor of the language of compromise. This will occur not because activists will stop believing in the right to life or the right to choose, but because policymakers will avoid extreme positions on the issue to maximize their share of the vote.

In two-party systems such as that found in the United States, candidates who take extreme positions are generally at a strong disadvantage in elections. Many political scientists have argued that in such a system the two parties tend to move toward the mid-point in the distribution of public attitudes. As we have seen in the preceding chapters, throughout the 1980s that midpoint was one in which abortion was largely legal but where there were a few restrictions. Thus, candidates who take strong pro-life or pro-choice positions can be expected, other things being equal, to lose to candidates who take more centrist positions on the issue. If most candidates for public office are more interested in electoral success than in enunciating the "correct" position on abortion, it may be that pro-life or pro-choice rhetoric will be become less heated in the political debate.[14]

There are several important consequences that would follow from a post-*Roe* transition from abortion *rights* to abortion *policy*. First, a political debate over abortion that is conducted over the details of particular restrictions would not satisfy activists in either camp. The loss of "rights" in the context of the abortion issue means that pro-life or pro-choice advocates will have to accept compromises that they will find unacceptable. If most states adopt a set of policies that make abortions more difficult to obtain, pro-choice activists will believe that their right to choose has been abridged. Similarly, since these policies would continue to allow some and perhaps most women to obtain abortions, pro-life activists will not be satisfied, for the right to life that they believe exists for the unborn will not be institutionalized.

As noted above, a "normal politics" of abortion would require political candidates to reflect the competing values involved in the abortion controversy. This, in turn, would imply that most political debate about abortion policies would involve discussions of the merits of particular restrictions on access to legal abortion while perhaps deemphasizing the morality of the practice itself.

It is possible that moving the politically acceptable abortion alternatives toward the center would result in a greater willingness to entertain opposing viewpoints and to consider compromises. In other words, shifting the abortion issue from the courts to legislatures may result in greater civility in abortion discourse. Of course, abortion will continue to be a highly emotional issue. Because the abortion debate crystallizes a number of essential values, the issue is likely to receive prominent attention for many years to come. Nevertheless, it is possible that abortion legislation in a post-*Roe* polity would result in greater adherence to the norms of democratic discourse, if for no other reason than the fact that civility is highly valued in national and state legislatures. Ideologues, who are often plaintiffs in court proceedings, are typically shunted to the margins of influence in legislative settings. To the extent that state or federal legislatures are called upon to make abortion policies which are not symbolic, but enforceable, they are likely to conduct the debate in terms of normal politics, which at the elite level includes a willingness to compromise and to consider alternative viewpoints.

Scenario 2: Dysfunctional Politics

Alternatively, the overturning of *Roe* may spark an even more heated political controversy, in which interest groups representing the pro-choice and pro-life viewpoints pressure state legislatures. Although a few state legislative contests have hinged on abortion, most Americans know little about the policy positions or votes of their state representatives or senators, including those on the abortion issue.[15] State legislators may survey their field of forces, and see two active sets of interest groups and an inattentive, more moderate general public. Under such circumstances, the policies that emerge may not necessarily reflect public opinion, but instead the intensity and size of each interest group. Powerful interest groups can prevail over popular majorities in state legislatures. For example, although a majority of citizens in most states favored the proposed Equal Rights Amendment in the 1970s, pressure from dedicated activists led legislators in several of those states to defeat the amendment.

Why would an intense state-level fight lead to dysfunctional politics? It need not, but we think it a distinct possibility. Interest groups could mobilize to put enormous pressure on state legislators, and could enter the electoral arena to organize single-issue voting to defeat members who oppose their positions. In Maryland, for example, a number of experienced state legislators were defeated by pro-choice activists because they filibustered a bill that would have guaranteed a woman's right to choose. In Florida, concerted efforts by pro-life activists to defeat legislators who opposed the pro-life bill introduced by the governor in a special session were less successful. Such single-issue voting is viewed by some as harmful to the political system. However, most state legislators win reelection by substantial margins, so the ultimate impact of electoral mobilization may not be great.

More importantly, emotional debates over abortion policy may disrupt the normal patterns of compromise and accommodation in the legislature and may divert these bodies from considering other pressing policy concerns. Some state legislatures may be consumed by divisive debates over abortion policy. Legislators firmly committed to the pro-life and pro-choice positions may use dilatory tactics and parliamentary procedures in an attempt to defeat legislation they oppose.

If legislative debates on abortion become too heated, this may interfere with the ability of the legislature to function effectively. An unwillingness to compromise can harm the relationships legislators develop that enable them to work together on policy even when they disagree. This may make it difficult for legislators to reach agreement on issues other than abortion. It is difficult to work with people if it is believed they have turned the legislative process into a quagmire. This is particularly a problem for nonprofessional state legislatures that are populated by relatively inexperienced part-time politicians. But our political system depends on legislators with different points of view being able to work together on a broad range of issues. For this reason, many state legislators prefer to avoid the issue altogether, and do not welcome the opportunity to debate abortion restrictions.[16]

Scenario 3: Empowerment Politics

Finally, it is possible that when the abortion issue moves to state government, it will lead to even greater empowerment of previously apolitical citizens. Clearly, one of the types of empowerment politics discussed in Chapter 1 will be lost--for women will no longer have absolute control of their fertility. It is possible to imagine, however, that state-level fights over abortion may energize citizen participation.

Perhaps the best analogy is the state-by-state fights over the ERA. In those battles, the anti-ERA forces mobilized previously apolitical conservative Christians into political action. A number of studies showed that the anti-ERA forces were composed primarily of unlikely activists: Women who were not previously active in politics lobbied state legislators, organized electoral campaigns, and otherwise became more involved in the political process.

The empowerment effects of the ERA fight were largely one-sided, and large numbers of anti-ERA activists convinced many state legislatures to defeat an amendment that had the support of the majority of state citizens. A similar battle over legal abortion might mobilize citizens on both sides of the issue. Young pro-choice women and men might be mobilized into political action to protect or assert abortion rights, and the pro-life forces may energize the same groups who rose to defeat the ERA.

Abortion Policy After a Reversal of Roe

Whichever model proves the most accurate, it is almost certain that a reversal of *Roe* will lead to more restrictions on abortion in many states. Only passage of the Freedom of Choice Act by the U.S. Congress would prevent states from imposing restrictions on abortions, and President Bush has promised to veto any such legislation. It is possible that a newly elected Democratic president (or President Ross Perot) would sign into law a national guarantee of legal abortion, but this seems unlikely in the near future. Instead, abortion regulation will most likely be left to the states.

A few states will guarantee access to abortion during the first trimester to all women. Those restrictions that attract widespread public support, however--waiting periods, parental consent laws, etc.-- will be adopted by many or even most state legislatures. Other states will adopt more stringent limits on legal abortion. Some states may allow local governments to impose their own restrictions. Abortion will still be legal under many circumstances in most states, but will be more difficult to obtain. Our analyses of public opinion suggest that such restrictions would be well received by large proportions of the public.

It is important to note that the effects of some abortion restrictions would be primarily symbolic. For example, *Roe* permits states to impose some limited restrictions on abortion based on *when* the abortion takes place. States cannot regulate abortion in the first trimester, but they can regulate to protect the health of the woman in the second trimester, and can regulate in the interests of fetal life in the third trimester. However, our analyses of public opinion suggest that differences in abortion attitudes are more likely to be based on the reasons a woman might have for seeking an abortion, rather than on the abortion's timing.[17] It is likely that restrictions based on the *why* of abortion decisions (as opposed to *when* the abortion takes place) may be circumvented rather easily.

To illustrate this last point, consider the fact that, at this writing, the state of Pennsylvania prohibits abortions for the purpose of sex selection. It seems unlikely that many prospective parents seek to terminate pregnancies because tests show that they are about to have a girl when they wanted a boy: An ABC poll in 1990 showed that only 3 percent of the public would be willing to abort for the purposes of sex selection. Even if the practice is more common than this poll revealed, however, a prohibition on abortion for sex selection purposes can be evaded by simply offering another reason for the abortion. Such narrow restrictions have little practical impact on the availability or practice of abortion.

Does this mean that Pennsylvania's law is pointless? Not necessarily, since the law has at least two important purposes. The law sets forth proscribed behavior and penalties and also embodies the moral sentiments of the community. Our data suggest that even people who oppose restrictions on legal abortion disapprove of abortions that they believe to be casual or frivolous; laws prohibiting abortion for these reasons send the message that the pro-life or anti-promiscuity values held by many people are accorded some weight in government policy-making. In other words, many abortion regulations that focus on the reasons women offer for seeking abortions may have largely symbolic value.[18]

Some states may adopt restrictions aimed at limiting what we have termed "elective" abortions. Public opinion is generally supportive of at least some restrictions on abortion for social reasons, for example, when a married couple wants no more children. Yet these types of distinctions may also be difficult to embody into law. Allowing legal abortions for unmarried but not for married women may well violate equal protection statutes, and distinctions based on the poverty of the mother might also fail such a test. In the event that these types of restrictions were upheld, however, they would be very difficult to enforce. Imagine a married woman seeking an abortion in a state in which only single women were allowed to abort. If she claimed to be single when applying for the procedure, it would be difficult for the state to prove otherwise. Even a law that would allow abortions in cases of fetal defect may be difficult to enforce, in part because the notion of fetal defect would be difficult to define legally.

Other states will adopt far more sweeping restrictions that will have a major impact on the ability of pregnant women to obtain abortions. By 1991, Louisiana and Utah, along with Guam, had adopted strict laws that prohibited abortion except for the three traumatic circumstances. These laws also proscribed strict tests for when the traumatic circumstances were met. In Louisiana's law, any woman seeking an abortion because the pregnancy was due to rape must have filed a report on the rape to police within two weeks of the incident--before she could be certain that she was pregnant. Such strong restrictions may be adopted in several more states.[19]

Ostensibly, a reversal of *Roe* would increase the powers of state governments, by returning jurisdiction over the abortion issue to state legislatures. However, it is likely that there will be a continual struggle between state and federal levels of government over different components of the jurisdictional issue. It seems that the federal government is likely to retain authority over technological issues related to control over fertility. There will soon be a vigorous controversy over the licensing of the French "abortion drug," RU-486, which can terminate very early pregnancies without surgery. The federal agency that regulates medicinal drugs in the United States-- the Food and Drug Administration--is a federal agency, accountable to the United States Congress. It seems unlikely that the federal government would surrender the decision to permit or proscribe RU-486 to state governments, although already some states have volunteered to test the drug. Under the commerce clause of the Constitution, the federal government has sole jurisdiction in this area. Therefore, whatever decision is made about RU-486 seems likely to be a national policy, applied uniformly throughout the United States.

Thus, abortion policy, like other public issues, will be settled at multiple levels of government, with federal, state, and perhaps even local governments each claiming partial jurisdiction. The details of abortion policies will vary from state to state, according to each state's respective political culture. Because the variables affecting abortion attitudes are not evenly distributed throughout the states, we can anticipate that, to the extent that the policies of state governments are representative of public opinion, different states will adopt different sets of restrictions on abortions. In some states, abortions will be very difficult to obtain; other states will, for practical purposes, permit abortion on demand. Such state differences in abortion policy will have at least two consequences. First, some citizens of various states will see their particular values enacted in public policy. For example, to the extent that Catholics or Mormons have distinctive approaches to the abortion issue, these attitudes are likely to be reflected in public policy in Rhode Island, the state with the highest percentage of Roman Catholics,[20] and Utah, the state with the highest percentage of Mormons. Diverse cultural and religious values will be represented more directly as states make abortion policies.

Second, the impact of these state differences will be greatest on women seeking abortions who are in some ways disadvantaged. The poor, the young, and the unsophisticated who live in states with more restrictive abortion laws will see their access to abortion diminished substantially. For example, a female attorney living in Missouri might find it possible to visit New York for a few days to obtain an abortion in a state with more permissive laws. She is likely to be able to arrange the time off from work (even if a brief waiting period is required), afford the transportation, the lodging, and the procedure, and is also likely to know that New York has a relatively permissive abortion law.[21] A discreet trip to New York may be much more difficult for a high school senior who may lack the money to make the trip, may lack a plausible reason to be absent from her home for a few days, and may not even be aware that there are states with more permissive abortion laws.

This hypothetical example may illustrate the general point that state differences in abortion laws deny abortions to those who have the fewest resources to raise a child. The ability to choose among various state policies is not randomly distributed among people, but tends to characterize those citizens who are already advantaged. Access to legal abortion is already unequal, due to restrictions on abortion funding in many states, and it is likely to become even more non-egalitarian as states assume jurisdiction over the issue. This characteristic of federalism, of course, is not unique to the abortion issue, but applies with equal force to tax policies, welfare benefits, and the like.

Conclusions

This last point brings us full circle. Our analysis of abortion attitudes suggests that abortion will be a highly visible political issue for some time to come. The abortion issue exists at the intersection of a number of central values, including religion and sexual morality. It is difficult to imagine that abortion will be removed from the political agenda in the foreseeable future.

However, the form the abortion debate takes may change if *Roe v. Wade* is reversed. There is a *public* space between the absolutes of the "right to life" and the "right to choose." Whether future debate on abortion will be conducted within this space remains to be seen.

Notes

1. Philip E. Converse and and Gregory Marcus, "Plus ca Change...The New CPS Election Study Panel,"*American Political Science Review* 73 (1979), pp. 32-49; Angus Campbell, Philip Converse, Warren Miller, and Donald Stokes, *The American Voter* (New York: John Wiley and Sons, 1960).

2. See James L. Guth, "Evangelical Activists and Abortion: Factors Influencing Conservative Protestant Attitudes" (paper presented at the annual meeting of the American Political Science Association, Washington, D.C., 1991).

3. Clyde Wilcox, "Political Action Committees and Abortion: A Longitudinal Analysis," *Women and Politics* 9 (1988), pp. 1-20; Ted G. Jelen, *The Political Mobilization of Religious Belief* (New York: Praeger, 1991); Rodney Stark and Charles Y. Glock, *American Piety: The Nature of Religious Commitment* (Berkeley: University of California Press, 1968).

4. Kristin Luker, *Abortion and the Politics of Motherhood* (Berkely: University of California Press, 1984), pp. 224-226.

5. Mary Ann Glendon, *Rights Talk* (New York: The Free Press, 1991).

6. See Anthony Downs, *An Economic Theory of Democracy* (New York: Harper and Row, 1957).

7. Of course, abortion has been vigorously debated in Congress as well, where pro-life forces have pushed for a Human Life Amendment to the Constitution for many years. Moreover, heated abortion rhetoric has been evident in many Congressional elections, even before *Webster*. Yet, as we argued in Chapter 6, if a reversal of *Roe* makes actual legislative policy-making on abortion possible, it is likely that many candidates will take somewhat more centrist positions on the abortion issue.

8. Mary Ann Glendon, *Abortion and Divorce in Western Law* (Cambridge: Harvard University Press, 1987).

9. Mary Ann Glendon, *Rights Talk*, pp. 8-9.

10. L. Kent Sezer and Ted G. Jelen, "Pornography, Feminism, and the First Amendment," (paper presented at the annual meeting of the Northeastern Political Science Association, Philadelphia, 1985).

11. This may seem paradoxical, in that pro-life activists seek to invoke the coercive power of government for their position. However, Luker and others show that this is a unique case of rights, in which the persons (fetuses) who are entitled to rights cannot claim them--"Who speaks for the unborn?" Nevertheless, the "right to life" is at least as non-negotiable as the "right to choose."

12. See especially Laurence Tribe, *Abortion: The Clash of Absolutes* (New York: Norton, 1989).

13. Although we agree that at least some erosion of *Roe* is likely, we disagree on the speed with which the decision will be reversed. We completed this book in early 1992. At the time, Cook and Jelen both predicted a gradual erosion of *Roe* over several years, while Wilcox predicted that *Roe* would be reversed by 1993.

14. Kristin Luker, *Abortion and the Politics of Motherhood.*

15. Debra L. Dodson and Lauren D. Burnbauer, with Katherine Kleeman, *Election 1989: The Abortion Issue in New Jersey and Virginia* (New Brusnwick, N.J.: Eagleton Institute of Politics, 1990). See also Patricia Bayer Richard, "Abortion Policy in a Changing Political Environment: The Case of Ohio" (paper presented at the annual meeting of the American Political Science Association, Washington, D.C., 1991).

16. Glen Halva-Neubauer, "Abortion Policymaking in the Post-*Webster* Age: The Case of Minnesota," and Patricia Bayer Richard, "They'd Rather It Would Go Away: Ohio Legislators and Abortion Policy," (both papers presented at the annual meeting of the Midwest Political Science Association, Chicago, 1990).

17. An anonymous paper reviewed by one of us for a professional journal reported that the public structured its attitudes primarily around reasons for abortion, as do the GSS items we have analyzed in this book. The authors also reported, however, that the timing of abortion, and the nature of the person seeking an abortion also mattered to people. That is, the public was more supportive of early abortions for teenagers, regardless of the reason, than they were of second trimester abortions for affluent, married women.

18. Other restrictions might be unconstitutional. Even if the Court allows states to regulate abortion, a law that allowed abortions for married women but not for unmarried ones would likely violate the Equal Protection clause.

19. In January 1991, the National Abortion Rights Action League (NARAL) reported that Alabama, Louisiana, Michigan, Mississippi, Missouri, Nebraska, Ohio, Pennsylvania, South Carolina, South Dakota, Utah, West Virginia, and Wisconsin all had anti-abortion governors and legislatures. The report listed California, Connecticut, Hawaii, North Carolina, Oregon, Vermont, and Washington state as the least likely to restrict abortion. The National Right-to-Life Committee (NRLC) suggested that NARAL classified as anti-abortion at least some governors who had

vetoed restrictions on abortion. See Maralee Schwartz, "Abortion Rights Group Lists 13 States Likely to Impose Bans," *The Washington Post*, January 8, 1992, p. A2.

20. Interestingly, some Catholic states have moved to implement a state policy of unrestricted access to legal abortion. By the fall of 1991, Maryland had passed such a bill, and the Republican governor of Massachusetts, William Weld, had proposed a legislative package that included state funding of Medicaid abortions.

21. We choose New York as an example, since this state had the most liberal abortion law in the country prior to *Roe*. See Raymond Tatalovich and Byron W. Daynes, *The Politics of Abortion: A Study of Community Conflict in Public Policymaking* (New York: Praeger, 1981).

Appendix: Detailed Results of Multivariate Analyses

TABLE A.1   Predictors of Abortion Attitudes:
All respondents, 1987-1991.

| | Chapter 2: | | | Chapter 3: | | |
| | Demographics | | | Attitudes | | |
	b	t	beta	b	t	beta
Demographics:						
Sex	-.16	-3.05**	-.04	-.11	-1.29	-.03
Age	-.00	-2.05*	-.03	.01	5.09**	.12
Race	-.10	-1.14	-.02	.33	2.39*	.05
Education	.13	13.86**	.21	.06	3.62**	.09
Income	.00	.10	.00	-.00	-1.06	-.02
Region at 16	-.33	-5.18**	-.08	-.14	-1.42	-.03
Urbanization at 16	.15	7.85**	.11	.09	3.16**	.07
Attitudes:						
Euthanasia				-1.35	-13.58**	-.31
Sexual morality				-.67	-10.30**	-.26
Public feminism				-.33	-1.85	-.04
Private feminism				-.15	-1.80	-.04
Ideal family size				-.25	-5.07**	-.11
General ideology				-.15	-4.53**	-.10
Constant	2.36	10.69**		4.68	9.64**	
R^2	.09			.34		
N	4783			1429		

(continues)

TABLE A.1 (continued)

Chapter 4: Religion

	White Catholics			White Mainline Prots.		
	b	t	beta	b	t	beta
Demographics:						
Sex	-.29	-1.60	-.07	.11	.64	.03
Age	.01	1.06	.05	.02	4.05**	.20
Education	.01	.21	.01	.09	2.70*	.13
Income	-.00	-.52	-.04	.01	1.06	.04
Region at 16	-.24	-.94	-.04	-.02	-.09	-.00
Urbanization at 16	.12	2.07	.09	.08	1.45	.06
Attitudes:						
Euthanasia	-1.31	-6.11**	-.28	-1.02	-5.31**	-.24
Sexual morality	-.61	-4.01**	-.22	-.49	-3.82**	-.20
Public feminism	.06	.16	.01	-.38	-1.08	-.05
Private feminism	-.13	-.77	-.04	-.10	-.66	-.04
Ideal family size	-.25	-2.41*	-.11	-.23	-2.52*	-.11
General ideology	-.05	-.73	-.03	-.22	-3.54**	-.16
Religion:						
Bible attitude	-.40	-2.75**	-.12	-.07	-.47	-.02
Religiosity	-.18	-3.45**	-.17	-.12	-2.65**	-.13
Constant	5.00	4.85**		4.55	5.10**	
Adjusted R^2	.35			.28		
N	361			391		

(continues)

TABLE A.1 (continued)

	Chapter 4: Religion (continued)					
	White Evangelicals			Jews		
	b	t	beta	b	t	beta

Demographics:						
Sex	-.03	-.19	-.01	.13	.84	.06
Age	.02	3.50**	.16	.01	1.86	.15
Education	.08	2.38*	.11	.10	3.76**	.29
Income	-.01	-1.38	-.06	.00	.86	.06
Region at 16	-.09	-.53	-.02	.01	.04	.00
Urbanization at 16	.08	1.30	.06	.04	.64	.04
Attitudes:						
Euthanasia	-1.35	-7.22**	-.32	-.52	-2.48*	-.17
Sexual morality	-.58	-3.76**	-.19	-.16	-1.65	-.13
Public feminism	-.19	-.57	-.03	-1.59	-3.61**	-.27
Private feminism	-.07	-.42	-.02	NA		
Ideal family size	-.19	-2.00*	-.09	-.09	-.93	-.07
General ideology	-.12	-1.88	-.08	-.07	-1.16	-.08
Religion:						
Bible attitude	-.31	-2.02*	-.10	NA		
Religiosity	-.16	-3.80**	-.19	-.16	-2.10*	-.15
Constant	4.06	4.50**		5.44	5.58**	
Adjusted R^2	.42			.33		
N	352			162		

(continues)

TABLE A.1 (continued)

	Blacks			All Respondents		
	b	*t*	*beta*	*b*	*t*	*beta*
Demographics:						
Sex	.01	.06	.00	-.03	-.36	-.01
Age	-.00	-.21	-.01	.01	4.58**	.11
Education	.07	1.83	.12	.05	3.23**	.08
Income	-.00	-.38	-.02	-.00	-.51	-.01
Region at 16	-.02	-.09	-.00	-.09	-.96	-.02
Urbanization at 16	.10	1.45	.09	.10	3.47**	.08
Attitudes:						
Euthanasia	-1.24	-5.60**	-.32	-1.17	-11.87**	-.27
Sexual morality	-.46	-2.82**	-.17	-.51	-7.40**	-.20
Public feminism	.39	.86	.06	-.18	-.98	-.02
Private feminism	-.01	-.05	-.00	-.12	-1.51	-.04
Ideal family size	-.12	-1.12	-.06	-.22	-4.51**	-.10
General ideology	-.10	-1.47	-.08	-.15	-4.66**	-.10
Religion:						
Bible attitude	-.27	-1.55	-.09	-.30	-4.08**	-.10
Religiosity	-.01	-.16	-.01	-.13	-5.82**	-.15
Evangelical	-.49	-1.65	-.11	-.30	-2.67*	-.07
Catholic	-.11	-.23	-.01	-.55	-5.07**	-.13
No denomination	-1.63	-2.57*	-.16	-.61	-3.18**	-.08
Jew				-.07	-.23	0.00
Constant	4.83	2.91**		4.60	9.28**	
Adjusted R^2	.25			.38		
N	264			1403		

*significant at .05
**significant at .01

TABLE A.2 Logistic Regression:
Abortion and Vote Choice in Gubernatorial Elections

	VIRGINIA		*NEW JERSEY*	
	MLE	-2 Log LR	MLE	-2 Log LR
Partisanship	1.02**	43.75	1.44**	193.24
Party vote history	1.06**	35.21	.75**	20.86
Ideology	.60**	12.65	.73**	36.37
Approval of incumbent				
Governor	.72**	8.30	-1.32**	50.72
Race	2.79**	42.83	.38	1.41
Sex	.27	1.63	.03	.05
Age	.22*	3.37	-.05	.34
Education	-.19	2.96	-.02	.08
Income	-.01	.00	.05	.54
Raised in South	1.01**	16.67		
Union household			-.02	.06
Catholic	.15	.26	.07	.15
Abortion position	1.06**	49.27	.62**	30.94
Pseudo R^2	.59		.42	
Percentage predicted				
correctly:				
Democrat	84		86	
Republican	87		72	
Overall	85		81	
Unweighted N	823		1130	

(continues)

TABLE A.2 (continued)

	FLORIDA		TEXAS	
	MLE	-2 Log LR	MLE	-2 Log LR
Partisanship	1.25**	202.36	1.46**	301.40
Ideology	.48**	15.90	.68**	38.86
Race	1.19**	11.07	1.59**	35.30
Sex	-.04	.06	.55**	14.24
Age	-.06	1.60	.08*	3.51
Education	.11	2.23	.23**	10.40
Income	-.09	1.41	-.09	1.36
Union household	.39	1.85	.68*	3.95
Urban	.11*	5.98	.14*	4.74
Catholic	-.08	.22	.33*	3.73
No denomination	1.24*	4.32	.04	.01
Church attendance	-.33*	4.41	-.38*	6.50
State economy good	-.45**	13.86	.08	.63 (-)
Personal finances better today	-.07	.38	-.24*	5.88(+)
Abortion position	.57**	22.72	.60**	27.46 (+)
Pseudo R²	.39		.48	
Percentage predicted correctly:				
Democrat	79		83	
Republican	77		79	
Overall	78		81	
Unweighted N	1172		1772	

(continues)

TABLE A.2 (continued)

	ILLINOIS		*MASSACHUSETTS*	
	MLE	-2 Log LR	MLE	-2 Log LR
Partisanship	1.02**	237.52	.95	111.91
Ideology	1.06**	.93	.13	1.98
Race	.51*	5.71	.38	1.09
Sex	-.24*	-3.66	.03	.07
Age	-.10**	8.73	.08*	5.67
Education	-.11*	-3.34	-.00	.01
Income	.24*	4.26	.12*	3.57
Union household	-.04	-.05	.70**	16.52
Urban	-.03	.57	.08*	4.02
Catholic	.04	.08	.37**	8.82
No denomination	-.06	-.02	-.32	.75
Church attendance	-.09	-.48	.02	.04
State economy good	-.29**	-11.04	.13	1.51
Personal finances better today	-.24**	6.55	.11	1.86
Abortion position	-.15*	-2.32	-.23*	5.88
Pseudo R^2	.32		.17	
Percentage predicted correctly:				
Democrat	75		59	
Republican	72		70	
Overall	73		65	
Unweighted N	1811		1454	

(continues)

TABLE A.2 (continued)

	CALIFORNIA		MICHIGAN	
	MLE	-1 Log LR	MLE	-2 log LR
Partisanship	1.55**	514.95	1.37**	273.19
Ideology	.60**	35.83	.10	.96
Race	1.23**	23.73	.28	.19
Sex	.44	11.02	.10	.60
Age	.02	.36	.02	.22
Education	.19**	8.78	-.19**	9.36
Income	-.19**	8.73	-.02	.07
Union household	.60**	8.68	.64**	12.99
Urban	.27**	29.24	.02	.42
Catholic	-.09	.38	-.18	-1.53
No denomination	.39	2.27	-.13	.27
Church attendance	.06	.19	-.13	-.79
State economy good	-.26**	7.18	.33**	13.88
Personal finances better today	-.18*	3.89	.03	.12
Abortion position	.40**	14.37	.04	.18
Pseudo R^2	.52		.30	
Percentage predicted correctly:				
Democrat	83		80	
Republican	82		64	
Overall	82		73	
Unweighted N	2128		1238	

(continues)

TABLE A.2 (continued)

	OHIO		PENNSYLVANIA	
	MLE	-2 Log LR	MLE	-2 Log LR
Partisanship	1.30**	251.95	.72	52.86
Ideology	.26*	6.45	-.22	3.18
Race	1.01**	15.56	1.03*	5.79
Sex	.25	2.95	.17	.98
Age	-.02	.23	.03	.38
Education	-.11	2.30	-.06	.62
Income	-.24**	10.63	-.20*	5.15
Union household	.57**	8.91	-.03	.01
Urban	.03	.31	-.05	.92
Catholic	-.04	.06	.44**	6.34
No denomination	.51	1.58	-.57	.48
Church attendance	-.42**	8.29	-.03	.03
State economy good	.15	1.89	.62**	29.85
Personal finances better today	-.13	1.65	-.01	.01
Abortion position	.54**	22.27	-1.16	76.00
Pseudo R^2	.38		.28	
Percentage predicted correctly:				
Democrats	75		89	
Republican	78		49	
Overall	77		76	
Unweighted N	1278		1092	

*significant at .05.
**significant at .01.

Bibliography

Adamany, David. "The Supreme Court's Role in Critical Elections," in *Realignment in American Politics: Toward a Theory*. edited by Bruce A. Campbell and Richard J. Trilling. Austin: University of Texas Press, 1980.

"Advocating a 'Mommy Track.'" *Newsweek* (March 13, 1989): 45.

Albee, Edward. *Who's Afraid of Virginia Woolf?* New York: Antheneum, 1963.

Aldrich, John, John Sullivan, and Eugene Borgida. "Foreign Affairs and Issue Voting: Do Presidential Candidates 'Waltz Before a Blind Audience?'" *American Political Science Review* 83 (1989): 123-142.

Allison, Graham. "Cool It: The Foreign Policy Beliefs of Young America." *Foreign Policy* 1 (1971): 150-154.

Asher, Herbert. *Presidential Elections and American Politics*. 5th ed. Belmont, Calif.: Brooks-Cole, 1991.

Baker, Ross K., Laurily K. Epstein, and Rodney D. Forth. "Matters of Life and Death: Social, Political and Religious Correlates of Attitudes Toward Abortion." *American Politics Quarterly* 9 (1981): 89-102.

Barnes, Fred. "Pregnant Silence." *The New Republic* (August 19 & 26, 1991): 11-12.

Barone, Michael, and Grant Ujifusa. *The Almanac of American Politics 1990*. Washington, D.C.: National Journal, 1990.

Barry, Brian. "How Not to Defend Liberal Institutions." *British Journal of Political Science* 20 (1990): 1-14.

Beatty, Kathleen, and Oliver Walter. "Fundamentalists, Evangelicals and Politics." *American Politics Quarterly* 16 (1988): 43-59.

Bernardin, Joseph. *A Consistent Ethic of Life*. Chicago: Sheed and Ward, 1988.

Bettelheim, Bruno. *The Uses of Enchantment: The Meaning and Importance of Fairy Tales*. New York: Knopf, 1976.

Bolce, Louis. "Abortion and Presidential Elections: The Impact of Public Perceptions of Party and Candidate Positions." *Presidential Studies Quarterly* 18 (1986): 815-829.

Boone, Kathleen C. *The Bible Tells Them So: The Discourse of Protestant Fundamentalism.* Albany, N.Y.: SUNY Press, 1989.

Bork, Robert H. *The Tempting of America: The Political Seduction of the Law* New York: Simon and Schuster, 1990.

Brown, Clifford, Jr., Lynda Powell, and Clyde Wilcox. "Serious Money: Presidential Campaign Contributors and Patterns of Contributions in 1988." *The Quest for National Office.* edited by Stephen Wayne and Clyde Wilcox. New York: St. Martin's, 1991.

Campbell, Angus, Philip Converse, Warren Miller, and Donald Stokes. *The American Voter.* New York: John Wiley & Sons. 1960.

Chubb, John. "Institutions, the Economy, and the Dynamics of State Elections." *American Politcal Science Review* 82 (1988): 133-154.

Clift, Eleanor. "The GOP's Civil War Over Abortion." *Newsweek* (August 5, 1991): 31.

Cohen, Richard. "Clashing on Abortion in Iowa Contest." *National Journal* (September 1, 1990): 2077-2078.

Combs, M., and Susan Welch. "Blacks, Whites, and Attitudes Toward Abortion." *Public Opinion Quarterly* 46 (1982): 510-520.

Condit, Celeste Michelle. *Decoding Abortion Rhetoric.* Urbana: University of Illinois Press, 1989.

Connery, John. *Abortion: The Development of the Roman Catholic Perspective.* Chicago: Loyola University Press, 1977.

Conover, Pamela Johnston, and Virginia Gray. *Feminism and the New Right: Conflict Over the American Family.* New York: Praeger, 1983.

Converse, Philip E. "The Nature of Belief Systems in Mass Publics." In *Ideology and Discontent.* edited by David Apter. New York: The Free Press, 1964.

Converse, Philip E., and Gregory Markus. "'Plus ca Change...' The New CPS Election Study Panel." *American Political Science Review* 73 (1979): 32-49.

Conway, Margaret. *Political Participation in the United States.* 2nd ed. Washington, D.C.: Congressional Quarterly Press, 1991.

Cook, Elizabeth Adell. "Feminist Consciousness and Candidate Preference Among American Women 1972-1988." Paper presented at the Southern Political Science Association annual meeting, Atlanta, 1990.

------. Frederik Hartwig, and Clyde Wilcox. "The Abortion Issue Down-Ticket: The Virginia Lieutenant Governor's Race of 1989." *Women and Politics*, forthcoming.

------. Ted G. Jelen, and Clyde Wilcox. "The Electoral Politics of Abortion." Paper presented at the American Political Science Association annual meeting, Washington, D.C., 1991.

------. "The Abortion Issue in U.S. Senate Elections in 1990." Unpublished paper, 1992.

------. "Generations and Abortion." *American Politics Quarterly*. Forthcoming.

Dahl, Robert. *A Preface to Democratic Theory*. Chicago: University of Chicago Press, 1956.

Devine, Donald J. *The Political Culture of the United States*. Boston: Little, Brown, 1972.

Dodson, Debra L., and Lauren D. Burnbauer with Katherine Kleeman. *Election 1989: The Abortion Issue In New Jersey and Virginia*. New Brunswick, N.J.: Eagleton Institute of Politics, 1990.

Donovan, Beth. "Open 2nd District Contests Tests Partisan Trends." *Congressional Quarterly Weekly Report* (April 7, 1990): 1090-1091.

Donovan, Beth, with Charles Mathesian. "Early Campaigning Tests Abortion Foes' Muscle." *Congressional Quarterly Weekly Reports* (March 10, 1990): 765-775.

Dorff, Elliot. "A Statement on the Permissibility of Abortion." *The United Synagogue Review* 42(2) (1988): 16-17.

Downs, Anthony. *An Economic Theory of Democracy*. New York: Harper, 1957.

Faux, Marian. *Roe v. Wade*. New York: Macmillan, 1988.

Franklin, Charles H., and Liane C. Kosaki. "Republican Schoolmaster: The U.S. Supreme Court, Public Opinion, and Abortion." *American Political Science Review* 83 (1989): 751-771.

Fried, Amy. "Abortion Politics as Symbolic Politics: An Investigation Into Belief Systems." *Social Science Quarterly* 69 (1988): 137-154.

Friedman, Lawrence M. "The Conflict Over Constitutional Legitimacy." In *The Abortion Dispute and the American System*. edited by Gilbert Y. Steiner. Washington, D.C.: Brookings Institution, 1983.

Furstenberg, Frank, Richard Lincoln, and Jane Meuken, eds. *Teenage Sexuality, Pregnancy, and Childbearing*. Philadelphia: University of Pennsylvania Press, 1981.

Georgianna, Sharon. *The Moral Majority and Fundamentalism: Plausibility and Dissonance*. Lewiston, New York: Edwin Mellon Press, 1989.

Gilligan, Carol. *In A Different Voice*. Cambridge: Harvard University Press, 1982.

Glendon, Mary Ann. *Abortion and Divorce in Western Law*. Cambridge: Harvard University Press, 1987.

------. *Rights Talk*. New York: The Free Press, 1991.

Goggin, Malcolm L., and Christopher Wlezien. "Interest Groups and the Socialization of Conflict: The Dynamics of Abortion Politics." Paper presented at the Midwest Political Science Association annual meeting, Chicago, 1991.

Goldstein, Robert D. *Mother-Love and Abortion: A Legal Interpretation.* Berkeley: University of California Press, 1988.

Granberg, Donald. "A Comparison of Members of Pro- and Anti-Abortion Organizations in Missouri." *Social Biology* 28 (1982): 239-252.

------. "Family Size Preferences and Sexual Permissiveness as Factors Differentiating Abortion Activists." *Social Psychology Quarterly* 45 (1982): 15-23.

------. Personal communication, April, 1990.

Greenawalt, Kent. *Religious Convictions and Political Choice.* New York: Oxford University Press, 1988.

Guth, James L.. "Evangelical Activists and Abortion: Factors Influencing Conservative Protestant Attitudes." Paper presented at the American Political Science Association annual meeting, Washington, D.C., September 1991.

Hadden, Jeffrey K. *The Gathering Storm in the Churches.* Garden City, N.Y.: Doubleday, 1969.

Hall, E., and M. Ferree. "Race Differences in Abortion Attitudes." *Public Opinion Quarterly* 50 (1986): 193-207.

Halva-Neubauer, Glen. "Abortion Policymaking in the Post-Webster Age: The Case of Minnesota." Paper presented at the Midwest Political Science Association annual meeting, Chicago, 1991.

Hartwig, Frederick, William Jenkins, and Earl Temchin. "Variability in Electoral Behavior: The 1960, 1968, and 1976 Elections." *American Journal of Political Science* 24 (1980): 553-558.

Hartz, Louis. *The Liberal Tradition in America.* New York: Harcourt, Brace and World, 1955.

Hauptman, Judith. "A Matter of Morality." *The United Synagogue Review* 42(2) (1988): 17-18.

Henshaw, S., and J. Silverman. "The Characteristics and Prior Contraceptive Use of U.S. Abortion Patients." *Family Planning Perspectives* 20 (1988): 158-168.

Hershey, Marjorie Randon. *Running for Office: The Political Education of Campaigners.* Chatham, N.J.: Chatham House, 1984.

Holsti, Ole R., and James N. Rosenau. "Does Where You Stand Depend on When You Were Born? The Impact of Generation on Post-Vietnam Foreign Policy Beliefs." *Public Opinion Quarterly* 44 (1980): 1-22.

Idelson, Holly. "Governors Find Re-election a Trickier Proposition." *Congressional Quarterly Weekly Reports* (November 10, 1990): 3838-3842.
"Is the Mommy Track a Blessing--Or a Betrayal?" *Business Week* (May 15, 1989): 98-99.
Jackson, John E., and Maris A. Vinovskis. "Public Opinion, Elections, and the 'Single-Issue' Issue" In *The Abortion Dispute and the American System*, edited by Gilbert Y. Steiner. Washington, D.C.: Brookings, 1983.
Jelen, Ted G. "Respect for Life, Sexual Morality, and Opposition to Abortion." *Review of Religious Research* 25 (1984): 220-231.
------."Changes in the Attitudinal Correlates of Opposition to Abortion." *Journal for the Scientific Study of Religion* 27 (1988): 211-228.
------."The Effects of Gender Role Stereotypes on Political Attitudes." *The Social Science Journal* 25 (1988): 353-365.
------."Biblical Literalism and Inerrancy: Does the Difference Make a Difference? *Sociological Analysis* 49 (1989): 421-429.
------."Helpmeets and Weaker Vessels: Gender Role Stereotypes and Attitudes Toward Female Ordination." *Social Science Quarterly* 70 (1989): 579-585.
------."Religious Belief and Attitude Constraint." *Journal for the Scientific Study of Religion* 29 (1990): 118-125.
------."Church-State Relations: The View from the Pulpit." Paper presented at the American Political Science Association annual meeting, Washington, D.C., 1991.
------."Politicized Group Identification: The Case of Fundamentalism." *Western Political Quarterly* 44 (1991): 209-219.
------.*The Political Mobilization of Religious Belief.* New York: Praeger, 1991.
------."The Clergy and Abortion." *Review of Religious Research* Forthcoming.
------., Corwin Smidt, and Clyde Wilcox. "Biblical Literalism and Inerrancy: A Reconsideration." *Sociological Analysis* 51 (1990): 307-315.
------., and Marthe A. Chandler. "An Exploratory Study of the Validity of Indicators of Biblical Literalism." Paper presented at the Western Social Science Association annual meeting, Ft. Worth, Texas, 1985.
Jennings, M. Kent, and Richard G. Neimi. *Generations and Politics.* Princeton, NJ: Princeton University Press, 1981.
Kellstedt, Lyman A. "The Falwell Issue Agenda: Sources of Support Among White Protestant Evangelicals." In *An Annual in the Sociology of Religion*, edited by M. Lynn and D. Moberg. New York: JAI Press, 1989.

Ladd, Everett Carl. "Abortion: The Nation Responds." *The Ladd Report #8.*
    New York: W.W. Norton, 1990.
Langenbach, Lisa, and Ted G. Jelen. "Ministers, Feminism and Abortion: A
    Causal Analysis." *Women and Politics* 11 (1991): 33-52.
Lengle, James. *Representation and Presidential Primaries: The Democratic
    Party in the Post-Reform Era.* Westport, Conn: Greenwood Press,
    1981.
Luker, Kristin. *Abortion and the Politics of Motherhood.* Berkeley: University
    of California Press, 1984.
Mannheim, Karl. "The Problem of Generations." In *The New Pilgrims*, edited
    by Philip Altbach and Robert Laufer. New York: David McKay, 1972.
Mill, John Stuart. *On Liberty.* New York: Bobbs-Merrill, 1956.
Mohr, James C. *Abortion in America: The Origins and Evolution of National
    Policy, 1800-1900.* New York: Oxford University Press, 1978.
"The Mommy Track." *Business Week* (March 20, 1989): 126-134.
MS (June 1989): 67 (Planned Parenthood Advertisement).
Newsweek (May 24, 1982): 24-26.
Nie, Norman H., with Kristi Andersen. "Mass Belief Systems Revisited:
    Political Change and Attitude Structure." *Journal of Politics* 36 (1974):
    540-591.
Nixon, Richard M. *In the Arena.* New York: Simon and Schuster, 1990.
Noonan, John T., Jr., "An Almost Absolute Value in History." In *The
    Morality of Abortion: Legal and Historical Perspectives*, edited by John
    T. Noonan, Jr. Cambridge: Harvard University Press, 1970.
------. *A Private Choice: Abortion in America in the Seventies.* New York: The
    Free Press, 1979.
------. *The Morality of Abortion: Legal and Historical Perspectives*, edited by
    John T. Noonan, Jr. Cambridge: Harvard University Press, 1970.
Norrander, Barbara. "Ideological Representativeness of Presidential Primary
    Voters." *American Journal of Political Science* 33 (1989): 570-587.
Ostling, Richard N. "What Does God Really Think About Sex?" *Time* (June
    24, 1991): 48-50.
Page, Benjamin. *Choices and Echoes in Presidential Elections.* Chicago: The
    University of Chicago Press, 1978.
Petchesky, Rosalind Pollack. *Abortion and Woman's Choice.* Boston:
    Northeastern University Press, 1990.
Poloma, Margaret. *The Charismatic Movement.* Boston: G.K. Hall, 1982.
Quinley, Harold E. *The Prophetic Clergy: Social Activism Among Protestant
    Ministers.* New York: John Wiley and Sons, 1974.
Richard, Patricia Bayer. "Abortion Policy in a Changing Political
    Environment: The Case of Ohio." Paper presented at the American
    Political Science Association annual meeting, Washington, D.C., 1991.

------."They'd Rather It Would Go Away: Ohio Legislators and Abortion Policy." Paper presented at the Midwest Political Science Association annual meeting, Chicago, 1991.

Roof, Wade Clark. "Traditional Religion in Contemporary Society: A Theory of Local-Cosmopolitan Plausibility."*American Sociological Review* 41 (1976): 195-208.

------. and William McKinney. *American Mainline Religion*. New Brunswick, N.J.: Rutgers University Press, 1987.

Roskin, Michael. "From Pearl Harbor to Vietnam: Shifting Generational Paradigms." *Political Science Quarterly* 89 (1974): 563-588.

Ross, John. "Contraception: Short-term vs. Long-term Failure Rates."*Family Planning Perspectives* 21(1989): 275-277.

Rovner, Julie. "Hill Faces Trench Warfare Over Abortion Rights." *Congressional Quarterly Weekly Report* (August 25, 1991): 2713-2720.

Rubin, Eva R. *Abortion, Politics, and the Courts*. New York: Greenwood, 1987.

Sapiro, Virginia. "News from the Front: Intersex and Intergenerational Conflict over the Status of Women." *Western Political Quarterly* 33 (1980): 260-277.

Scott, Jacqueline, and Howard Schuman. "Attitudes Strength and Social Action in the Abortion Dispute." *American Sociological Review* 53 (1988):785-793.

Secret, P. "The Impact of Region on Racial Differences in Attitudes Toward Legal Abortion." *Journal of Black Studies* 17 (1989): 347-369.

Sezer, L. Kent, and Ted G. Jelen. "Pornography, Feminism, and the First Amendment." Paper presented at the Northeastern Political Science Association annual meeting, Philadelphia, 1985.

Simon, Roger. *Road Show: In America, Anyone Can Become President, It's One of the Risks We Take*. New York: Farrar Straus Giroux, 1990.

Smidt, Corwin E. "Evangelicals vs. Fundamentalists: An Analysis of the Political Characteristics and Political Views of American Evangelical and Charismatic Christians."*Western Political Quarterly* 41 (1988): 601-620.

------. "Praise the Lord Politics: A Comparative Analysis of the Social Characteristics and Political Views of American Evangelical and Charismatic Christians." *Sociological Analysis* 50 (1989): 53-72.

Smith, Eric R.A.N. "The Levels of Conceptualization: False Measures of Ideological Sophistication." *American Political Science Review* 74 (1980): 685-696.

Spitzer, Robert J. *The Right to Life Movement and Third Party Politics in America*. Westport, Conn.: Greenwood, 1987.

Spolar, Christine, and Karlyn Barker. "386 Arrested in D.C. Clinic Blockades." *The Washington Post* (January 22, 1992): D1.

Staggenborg, Suzanne. "Life-Style Preferences and Social Movements Recruitment: Illustrations from the Abortion Conflict." *Social Science Quarterly* 68 (1987): 779-798.

Stark, Rodney, and Carles Y. Glock. *American Piety: The Nature of Religious Commitment*. Berkeley, Calif.: University of California Press, 1968.

Stoper, Emily, and Roberta Ann Johnson. "The Weaker Sex and the Better Half." *Polity* 10 (1977): 192-218.

Tatalovich, Raymond, and Byron W. Daynes. *The Politics of Abortion: A Study of Community Conflict in Public Policymaking*. New York: Praeger, 1981.

Tedin, Kent, Richard Matland, and Richard Murray. "The Acid Test of Gender Voting: The 1990 Election for Governor of Texas." Paper presented at the annual meeting of the Southern Political Science Association, Tampa Bay, Florida, 1991.

Thomas, Cal. "Is the Pro-Life Position Proving Harmful to Republicans?" *The Washington Times* (July 29, 1991): D3.

Thompson, Judith Jarvis. "A Defense of Abortion." *Journal of Philosophy and Public Affairs* 1 (1971).

Tolleson-Rinehart, Sue, and Jeanie Stanley. "Claytie and the Lady I: Gender, Political Psychology, and Political Culture in the 1990 Texas Gubernatorial Race." Paper presented at the annual meeting of the International Society of Political Psychology, Helsinki, Finland, 1991.

Tolleson-Rinehart, Sue, and Jeanie Stanley. "Claytie and the Lady II: The 1990 Texas Gubernatorial Race from the Perspectives of the Campaign and the Citizens." Paper presented at the annual meeting of the American Political Science Assocation, Washington, D.C. 1991.

Torres, Aida, and Jacqeline Forrest. "Why Do Women Have Abortions?" *Family Planning Perspectives* 20 (1988): 169-176.

Tribe, Laurence H. *Abortion: The Clash of Absolutes*. New York: Norton, 1989.

Tribe, Laurence, and Michael C. Dorf. *On Reading the Constitution*. Cambridge: Harvard University Press, 1991.

Trussell, James, and Barbara Vaughn. "Aggregate and Lifetime Contraceptive Failure in the United States." *Family Planning Perspectives* 21 (1989): 224-226.

U.S. Catholic Conference. "Partners in the Mystery of Redemption: A Pastoral Response to Women's Concerns for Church and Society." *Origins* (April 21, 1988).

Verba, Sidney, and Norman H. Nie. *Participation in America*. New York: Harper and Row, 1972.

Verba, Sidney, Norman H. Nie, and Jogn Petrocik. *The Changing American Voter*. Cambridge: Harvard University Press, 1979.

Wald, Kenneth D. *Religion and Politics in the United States*. 2d ed., Washington, D.C.: CQ Press, 1991.

Welch, Michael, and David Leege. " Dual Reference Groups and Political Orientations: An Examination of Evangelically-Oriented Catholics." *American Journal of Political Science* 35 (1991): 28-56.

White, John Kenneth. *The New Politics of Old Values*. Hanover, N.H.: University Press of New England, 1988.

Wilcox, Clyde. "Political Action Committees and Abortion: A Longitudinal Analysis." *Women & Politics* 9 (1988): 1-20.

------. "The Fundamentalist Voter: Politicized Religious Identity and Political Attitudes and Behavior." *Review of Religious Research* 31 (1989): 54-67.

------. "Race Differences in Abortion Attitudes: Some Additional Evidence." *Public Opinion Quarterly* 54 (1990): 248-255.

------. "Support for Gender Equality in West Europe: A Longitudinal Analysis." *European Journal of Political Research* 20 (1991): 127-147.

------. *God's Warriors: The Christian Right in Twentieth-Century America* Baltimore: Johns Hopkins University Press, 1991.

------. "Race, Religion, Region, and Abortion Attitudes." *Sociological Analysis* Forthcoming.

------., Joseph Ferrara, and Dee Allsop. "Before the Rally: Public Attitudes on the Iraq Crisis." Paper presented at the American Political Science Association annual meeting, Washington, D.C., 1991.

------., and Leopoldo Gomez. "Religion, Group Identification, and Politics among American Blacks." *Sociological Analysis* 51 (1990): 271-285.

------., and Leopoldo Gomez. "The Christian Right and the Pro-Life Movement: An Analysis of Political Support." *Review of Religious Research* 31 (1990): 380-390.

------., and Ted G. Jelen. "Evangelicals and Political Tolerance." *American Politics Quarterly* 18 (1990): 25-46.

------., and Ted G. Jelen. "The Effects of Employment and Religion on Women's Feminist Attitudes." *International Journal for the Psychology of Religion* 1 (1991): 161-172.

------., and Sue Thomas. "Religion and Feminist Attitudes Among African-American Women: A View from the Nation's Capitol." *Women and Politics*, Forthcoming.

------., Lee Sigelman, and Elizabeth Cook. "Some Like It Hot: Individual Differences in Response to Group Feeling Thermometers." *Public Opinion Quarterly* 53 (1989): 246-257.

Williams, Tennessee. "Sweet Bird of Youth." *Eight Plays*. Garden City, N. Y.: Doubleday, 1979.

Wills, Garry. *Under God: Religion and American Politics*. New York: Simon and Schuster, 1990.

Zelnik, Melvin, John F. Kantner, and Kathleen Ford. *Sex and Pregnancy in Adolescence*. Beverly Hills, Calif.: Sage Publications, 1981.

About the Book and Authors

In the years since the historic *Roe v. Wade* decision that made abortion legal in the United States, pro-life and pro-choice forces have organized, demonstrated, and participated in electoral politics—both sides claiming that the general public supports their position. Now it appears likely that *Roe* will be overturned or limited by the Supreme Court. If abortion politics is returned to national and state legislators, a clear reading of public opinion on abortion will become even more important.

Using extensive analysis of survey data, Cook, Jelen, and Wilcox show that the American public values both individual freedom and fetal life, and that a majority of Americans favors keeping abortion legal in some but not all circumstances. Although most Americans are wary of allowing the government to ban abortion, they are also supportive of restrictions that would make abortions more difficult to obtain. The authors show important differences in the attitudes of Americans based on age, education, religion, and race, and explain who supports and opposes legal abortion and why. The authors also illustrate the increasingly important role abortion plays in national and state elections, arguing that voters will become even more focused on abortion as an issue if *Roe* is overturned.

Elizabeth Adell Cook is a visiting professor at The American University. Her research interests include public opinion, women and politics, and feminist consciousness in America, the subject of a work in progress. **Ted G. Jelen** is professor of political science at Illinois Benedictine College and is author of numerous publications, including *The Political Mobilization of Religious Belief.* **Clyde Wilcox** is associate professor of government at Georgetown University and has authored numerous works, including *God's Warriors: The Christian Right in 20th Century America.*

Index